THE DEVELOPMENT OF CORPORATE
GOVERNANCE IN JAPAN AND BRITAIN

The Development of Corporate Governance in Japan and Britain

Edited by

ROBERT FITZGERALD
Royal Holloway, University of London

and

ETSUO ABE
Meiji University, Japan

ASHGATE

Published by
Ashgate Publishing Limited
Gower House
Croft Road
Aldershot
Hants GU11 3HR
England

Ashgate Publishing Company
Suite 420
101 Cherry Street
Burlington, VT 05401-4405
USA

Ashgate website: http://www.ashgate.com

British Library Cataloguing in Publication Data
The development of corporate governance in Japan and
    Britain. - (Explorations in Asia Pacific business
    economics)
    1.Corporate governance - Japan 2.Corporate governance -
    Great Britain
    I.Fitzgerald, Robert, 1959- II.Abe, Etsuo, 1949-
    658.4'00941

Library of Congress Cataloging-in-Publication Data
The development of corporate governance in Japan and Britain / edited by Robert
    Fitzgerald and Etsuo Abe.
        p. cm. -- (Explorations in Asia Pacific business economics)
    Includes bibliographical references and index.
    ISBN 0-7546-3369-1
        1. Corporate governance--Japan. 2. Corporate governance--Great Britain. I. Fitzgerald,
    Robert, 1959- II. Abe, Etsuo, 1949- III. Series.

HD2741D447 2003
338.6'0941--dc21

2003052109

ISBN 0 7546 3369 1

Printed and bound in Great Britain by MPG Books Ltd, Bodmin, Cornwall

Contents

List of Contributors

Etsuo Abe, Meiji University

Takeshi Abe, Osaka University

Richard Coopey, Business History Unit, London School of Economics, and University of Aberystwyth

Robert Fitzgerald, Royal Holloway, University of London

Terry Gourvish, Business History Unit, London School of Economics

Chikage Hidaka, Tokyo Metropolitan University

Takeo Kikkawa, Tokyo University

Matao Miyamoto, Osaka University

Masahiro Shimotani, Kyoto University

Haruhito Takeda, Tokyo University

Nick Tiratsoo, Business History Unit, London School of Economics

Clive Trebilcock, University of Cambridge

Takau Yoneyama, Kyoto Sangyo University

Chapter 1

What is Corporate Governance?
The Historical Implications

Etsuo Abe

Introduction

Just when the dissolution of the USSR seemed to indicate the triumph of western economic systems, the phrase 'capitalism versus capitalism' was coined by Michel Albert to reflect a continuing conflict. One form of capitalism he labelled Anglo-Saxon, the other Rhineland.[1] Anglo-Saxon capitalism was depicted as quite different to Rhineland capitalism, which is in turn seen as closer to that of Japan. The character of each capitalism is mainly decided by the nature of corporate governance, defined as the relationship between ownership and management. It is fair to say that corporate governance constitutes the pillar of the economic institutions in both systems.

As Berle and Means point out, the separation of ownership and management has become a fundamental base of economic institutions in all advanced capitalist societies, as have the managerial firms defined by Alfred Chandler.[2] However, the relationship between ownership and management varies across countries. In addition, it is not enough to consider only the relation between shareholders and management, for the role of employees, suppliers, customers, banks, or, in other words, stakeholders is also important.[3] By extension, state policy, laws, economic environment, culture and historical background affect the character of corporate governance as specified by the relationship between numerous stakeholders.

The hierarchy from top managers to rank-and-file workers is material in deciding the character of corporate structure. The organizational hierarchy can influence corporate governance, just as corporate governance can affect the organizational hierarchy. Besides this, inter-firm relationships with suppliers and customers are significant. In Japan, these relationships frequently form what are called vertical *keiretsu*, which are particularly conspicuous in the automobile and electronics industries. Moreover, financial institutions such as banks and insurance companies are important sources of investment funds in both Japan and Germany. These financial institutions, especially banks, can exercise monitoring functions, and they can influence and sometimes control the behaviour of firms. They are sometimes called 'relational stakeholders', because they maintain long-term relationships with firms.

With respect to relational stakeholders, the following three questions arise. Who owns the firm? Who governs the firm? Who can determine decisions within the firm? Shareholders legally own the firm, but managers can govern, and banks, labour unions and the state can exert a strong influence. In Japan, employees including top managers govern the firm rather than shareholders. By contrast, in the USA, it is said that shareholders govern the firm, though some scholars insist that strong top managers facing weak owners are dominant, and that, in Japan, shareholder power might in reality be stronger than the USA.[4] Under German law, trade unions can appoint half the members of the supervisory board. Accordingly, they are supposed to exert substantive pressure on decision-making.[5] It is obvious, therefore, that the second and the third questions are more important than the simple ownership structure.

If we think along these lines, it is clear that Anglo-Saxon and Rhineland-style capitalism are appreciably distinct. One might be termed the A-B (American-British) model, the other the G-J (German-Japanese) model, and it is worth considering how this perspective affects our interpretation of the development of business in major countries.

Models of Capitalism

Each country has its own style of corporate governance within the two general models, whether the A-B version controlled by the market, or the G-J type controlled by organizations. How can these models seriously affect economic performance or the competitiveness of nations? Or are they unrelated to economic performance and competitiveness? An American scholar, Mark Roe, maintains that corporate governance is not closely connected to the economic performance of nations in comparison to other factors such as product, capital and labour markets.[6]

In contrast, William Lazonick and Mary O'Sullivan argue that the A-B model may impair competitiveness and that the G-J model can realize good performance by encouraging long-term investment policies and strengthening R&D activities.[7] Whereas the A-B model fits a market-control hypothesis of innovative enterprise, the G-J model suits the organizational hypothesis. Undoubtedly, R&D activities can be essential to manufacturing firms, and long-term investment is indispensable to fruitful results. In these respects, the corporate governance structures of two countries, Germany and Japan, supported better records, and Lazonick and O'Sullivan's conclusions seem persuasive in this one regard. Yet their argument pays little attention to the recent stagnant economies of Germany and Japan. US and British 'success', not 'failure', and German and Japanese 'distress' seem the appropriate words of the moment. Evaluating the USSR's collapse in 1990, an American journalist, Michael Prowse, wrote in the *Financial Times*: 'Now Pax Americana will begin just as Pax Britannica began after the victory of the Napoleonic War.'[8]

While the American and British economies are in relatively good shape, Germany and Japan require changes in their economic systems and corporate governance. Is their adverse situation temporary? Or is it a long-lasting phenomenon? If so, should the G-J model, thought to be better than the A-B model throughout the 1970s and 1980s, move towards the A-B model?

A positive answer to the second question suggests that corporate governance globally will converge towards the A-B model. Or will the specific arrangements of countries be preserved? If we consider the conclusions of William Baumol and Leslie Hannah that levels of GDP per capita in developed countries show a tendency to converge, regardless of differences in economic systems, a dual convergence may arise.[9] In one instance, the absolute level of GDP per capita may be similar; in the other, corporate governance may be comparable. The globalization of firms may give further cause for convergence since international firms prefer to operate within the same structures. The regional and worldwide integration of company laws and auditing, as in the case of the EU, acts as another spur. German and British corporate governance will come under the same, homogenized company laws of the EU in the future.

Another question is: how different are the US and Britain, even though they are called forms of Anglo-Saxon capitalism? Britain has been characterized as 'family capitalism' by Chandler, and as 'gentlemanly capitalism' by Coleman, who sees its firms as once controlled by amateur 'gentlemen' and, to a lesser extent, by professional 'players' (in a sense not to be confused with the work of Cain and Hopkins).[10] Historically, Britain would be quite different from the USA, the paragon of managerial capitalism. To clarify the similarities and differences of corporate governance, we will survey its historical development in Britain and Japan, simultaneously placing the USA and Germany in perspective.

The British Case

In the mid-19th century, due to the passing of company acts, a host of joint stock enterprises appeared in Britain. Yet, along with many public limited companies, private limited companies came into being and became the typical form of British joint stock enterprises. These businesses remained, in general, small in scale compared to US counterparts, and they did not they integrate forwards and backwards extensively.

Consequently, relatively small and un-integrated firms were a marked British characteristic, despite their adopting joint stock company forms. The original owners' power persisted, and, in the case of the large holding firms created around the turn of the century, the power of constituent firms and their owners was dominant in decision-making. According to Chandler, the British economy was an example of 'personal capitalism', in which internal organization and managerial hierarchies were weak. In also referring to 'family capitalism', he is stressing family ties and the proprietors' influence. The larger British firms were no longer partnerships but joint stock companies. Nonetheless, management and ownership were not separated, and owner-managers continued to govern.

In the inter-war period, large companies such as ICI, Unilever, Imperial Tobacco, J. & P. Coats, and Dorman Long emerged, and they demonstrated to a certain extent a transformation in the relationship between ownership and management. Professional and salaried managers appeared on a significant scale in a variety of industries. Their new role was often coupled with the holding company form, examples being Imperial Tobacco and United Steels, which preserved the owners' power.

After the Second World War, the British economy experienced an all-time high growth rate, and the trend towards the managerial firm continued. At the same time, institutional investors such as pension funds and insurance companies began to acquire a large quantity of shares, and transformed the ownership of joint stock companies. Approximately 60 per cent of shares were held by insurance companies and pension funds in 1992. By contrast, although there are influential pension funds such as CalPERS in the US, they account for a more modest 35 per cent of shares nationally. It should be acknowledged that the British economy is especially dominated by institutional investors.

Given the enhanced role of institutional investors, what kind of changes took place in British corporate governance? In the 1960s and 1970s, the British economy faced a worsening situation, evidenced by high unemployment and low growth rates, or even, sometimes, negative growth rates. Yet, in the 1980s, and notably in the 1990s, the British economy seemed revitalized, having moved towards US-style managerial hierarchies and governance structures predicated on market control. Is the historical relic of family or gentlemanly capitalism still working in Britain today? Or is it dead?

The Japanese Case

The development of joint stock companies in Japan began during the late 19th century, mainly in the railways, cotton spinning, and banks. Most of these firms became big, independent enterprises, and were basically isolated from the *zaibatsu*.[11] On the other hand, these business groups - such as Mitsui, Mitsubishi and Sumitomo - emerged as a particularly Japanese feature. At first, they were controlled by associations of families, then became a form of partnership with corporate status, and eventually, around 1920, evolved into holding companies with family ties. But, within Mitsui and Sumitomo, traditionally salaried managers had exercised a large degree of the power and decision-making. This tendency was fortified by the demands generated by the growth of the *zaibatsu*, and by the fact their activities in mining, banking, trading and manufacturing required professional knowledge and expertise. Families could not have a large enough pool of capabilities, and, instead, salaried managers with qualifications from higher education were employed. In the Mitsui and Sumitomo *zaibatsu*, the separation of ownership and management proceeded over time.

Mitsubishi was different because its origins were more recent in comparison to its Mitsui and Sumitomo rivals with histories amounting to hundreds of years.[12] Its founders - Yataro and Yanosuke Iwasaki, and their sons - had decision-making roles, although they also hired a number of university graduates. But, even at Mitsubishi, the rise of professional managers became undeniable because its huge business needed professionals. All three *zaibatsu* built large-scale organizations and internal capabilities. In the wartime economy, around 1940, military agencies exerted strong pressure on the *zaibatsu* to invest in armaments production, but the parent companies did not have the required funds. They were obliged to turn to external financing, and their subsidiaries came under strong governmental control. Each company was ordered to transact with a designated bank, so foreshadowing the post-war main bank system. As a consequence, the power of the families decreased and the centrifugal tendency accelerated, making subsidiaries and associated companies more independent of their parent companies.

After the Second World War, the US Occupation forces dissolved the *zaibatsu*, but they were shortly re-established as *keiretsu*, whose key feature was mutual shareholding.[13] These groups can be termed horizontal *keiretsu* or bank-centered, financial *keiretsu*, because they have no distinct headquarters. Banks have a strong say in the operations of *keiretsu*, but trading companies and even heavy industry enterprises can exercise considerable powers of decision-making. Although they are called the Mitsubishi, Mitsui, or Sumitomo group, family control no longer exists. Each member company has become a thorough managerial firm, but they are not typical since mutual shareholding ties them to the group.

Vertical or hierarchical *keiretsu* were also formed, and examples include large industrial firms such as Japan Steel, Matsushita, Hitachi, Toshiba, Toyota and Nissan. They have all constructed extensive networks composed of several hundred subsidiaries and associated firms.[14] At the same time, most of these parent firms belong to horizontal *keiretsu*. As a result, Japan has overlapping structures of vertical and horizontal *keiretsu*, in which each parent business is a managerial firm with mutually-held shares.

In the vertical *keiretsu*, suppliers and customers are important stakeholders as well as major parties to transactions, and such partners hold shares in each other and compose a stable shareholding structure. It is said that 60 per cent of shares may be held in this manner, making unfriendly acquisition impossible in Japan. It should be noted that a stable shareholding structure is recognizable not only in *keiretsu* firms, but also in firms not belonging to either vertical or horizontal *keiretsu*.[15]

As well as businesses originating in the pre-war period, new firms such as Sony and Honda built vertical *keiretsu*. Both types generally belonged to the first generation of founders, yet, as such founders did not have a large proportion of shares, they became in the main managerial rather than entrepreneurial. The post-war period did, nonetheless, produce a number of entrepreneurial firms, including Seibu, Daiei and Kyocera. Newly-established companies were as instrumental as older firms in developing the post-war Japanese economy.

Within the horizontal *keiretsu*, banks played a critical role in financing companies and monitoring their performance. As they provide funds together with other banks, through *kyocho yushi* or cooperative financing, they are in the position of main banks, although this role is not limited to *keiretsu* companies only.[16] Like stable shareholding, it was extended to non-*keiretsu* companies like Honda and Sony, so that it became a rule for every company to have a main bank. Aoki, furthermore, maintains that the main bank system has an institutional complementarity with the long-term employment system.[17] Between the 1960s and 1980s, the two forms of *keiretsu* were thought to be a major driving force behind Japan's economic development, the vertical form in particular encouraging long-term investment. Accordingly, Japanese corporate governance was thought to be a contributor to economic performance and strong competitiveness in overseas markets. To some, it seemed to be the *Pax Japonica*.

With the collapse of the boom in 1990, judgement on the Japanese system, especially corporate governance and its characteristic relational stakeholders, changed. There was a preference for 'agile' management, implicitly criticising long-termism in favour of fluid management structures, and underlining market principles rather than organizational coordination. Privatization and deregulation have boosted the market principles espoused during the period. Arguments for the horizontal *keiretsu* seemed to have lost their momentum, and the vertical *keiretsu* are censured because of their slowness to adapt and because of their exclusiveness. The management structures of large firms are criticized, due to their inability to restructure with speed. Outside interests also query the lack of openness and disclosure, and there are arguments to build shareholders' power along the lines of the US system.

The US Exemplar

The US, historically at the vanguard of capitalism, is now regarded as the exemplar of market control. But, before the rise of institutional investors, between the 1930s and 1960s, its managerial capitalism displayed organizational control, in a period viewed as the *Pax Americana*. Managerial firms separated management from ownership, possessed relatively long-term employment systems, and dispersed shareholding amongst hundreds of thousands of investors. Under this situation, top managers had autonomous power over decision-making, and organizational control coincided with prosperity.

However, changes began to occur. Institutional investors increased their shareholding from a marginal ratio in the 1950s to approximately 40 per cent in 1990.[18] During the mergers and acquisitions boom of the 1980s, many firms were traded like commodities. As US growth rates were comparatively low, corporate governance structures were criticized. Under the anti-monopoly acts, including those of Glass-Steagall and Macfadyen, *keiretsu*, close bank-industry relations, and nationwide commercial banks were not possible. Some businessmen and scholars appealed for the abolition of the Glass-Steagall Act, which prohibited the union of commercial banking and the securities business. To enable the formation of *keiretsu* in the US, some businessmen urged the mitigation of anti-trust legislation.

Major reform proposals were not realized, although Glass-Steagall and other acts were changed. The US economy, nonetheless, rebounded from the low point of the 1970s and 1980s. But, despite these clear indications, a range of questions remains. Is the US recovery in comparison with Germany and Japan merely temporary? Has long-term 'decline' in Britain been reversed? Will Japanese corporate governance structures have to change fundamentally? Most intriguingly: whither do we all go?[19]

Notes

1   M.Albert, *Capitalism vs. Capitalism: How America's Obsession with Individual Achievement and Short-Term Profit Has Led It to the Brink of Collapse* (1991).

2   A.A.Berle and C.G.Means, *The Modern Corporation and Private Property* (1932); A.D.Chandler, *The Visible Hand: The Managerial Revolution in American Business* (1977), pp.1-12.

3   For a general discussion on corporate governance, see J.Charkham, *Keeping Good Company: A Study of Corporate Governance in Five Countries* (1994); W.C.Kester, 'Industrial Groups as Systems of Contractual Governance', *Oxford Review of Economic Policy*, vol.8, no.3 (1992).

4   M.Roe, *Strong Managers, Weak Owners: The Political Roots of American Corporate Finance* (1994); M.Fukao and Y.Morita, 'Koporeto Gavanansu ni Kansuru Ronten Seiri' ('Some Issues on Corporate Governance'), *Kinyu Kenkyu (Finance Studies)*, vol.13, no.3 (1994).

5   On the German system, see E.R.Schnieder-Lenne, 'Corporate Control in Germany', *Oxford Review of Economic Policy*, vol.8, no.3 (1992); T.Baum, 'Takeovers Versus Instituions in Corporate Governance in Germany', in D.D.Pretile and P.R.J.Holland (eds), *Contemporary Issues on Corporate Governance* (1994); J.Edwards and K.Fisher, *Banks, Finance and Investment in Germany* (1994).

6   Roe, *Strong Managers, Weak Owners*.

7   W.Lazonick and M.O'Sullivan, 'Big Business and Corporate Control', in M.Warner (ed.), *International Encyclopedia of Business and Management* (1996), pp. 365-385; W.Lazonick and M.O'Sullivan, 'Organization, Finance and International Competition', *Industrial and Corporate Change*, vol.5, no.1 (1996); W.Lazonick and M.O'Sullivan, 'Financial Commitment and Economic Development', *Financial History Review*, Vol.4, no.1-2 (1997); M.O'Sullivan, 'Corporate Governance and Industrial Development' (Harvard Ph.D., 1996).

8   *Financial Times* (1993).

9   W.J.Baumol, S.A.B. Blackman, and E.N.Wolff, *Productivity and American Leadership: The Long View* (1991); L.Hannah, 'The American Miracle, 1875-1959, and After: A View in the European Mirror', *Business and Economic History*, vol.24, no.2 (Winter 1995), pp.197-220; L.Hannah, 'The Joint Stock Company, Concentration and the State, 1894-1994', in A.Allan (ed.), *Proceedings of the Annual Conference 1994*, Business Archives Council, 1995, pp.52-75.

10 A.D.Chandler, *Scale and Scope: The Dynamics of Industrial Capitalism* (1990); D.C.Coleman, 'Gentlemen and Players', *Economic History Review*, vol.26 (1973); P.J.Cain and A.G.Hopkins, 'Gentlemanly Capitalism and British Expansion Overseas: New Imperialism, 1850-1945', *Economic History Review*, vol.40, no.1 (1987); P.J.Cain and A.G.Hopkins, *British Imperialism: Innovation and Expansion* (1993); *British Imperialism, Crisis and Deconstruction, 1914-1990* (1993).

11 On *zaibatsu*, see H.Morikawa, *Zaibatsu: the Rise and Fall of Family Enterprise Groups in Japan* (1992); J.Hirschmeier and T.Yui, *The Development of Japanese Business* (1981); E.Abe, 'Japanese Business History', in M.Warner (ed.), *International Encyclopedia of Business and Management*; E.Abe, 'The Development of Modern Business in Japan', *Business History Review*, vol.71 (Summer 1997).

12 For a history of the Iwasaki Family, see E.Abe, 'Iwasaki, Yataro', in Warner, *International Encyclopedia*, pp.2407-9.

13 On the *keiretsu*, see W.C.Kester, *Japanese Takeovers: The Global Contest for Corporate Control* (1991); T.Kikkawa, 'Kigyo Shudan: the Formation and Function of Enterprise Groups', in E.Abe and R.Fitzgerald (eds), *The Origins of Japanese Industrial Power* (1995); M.Shimotani, 'The Formation of Distribution *Keiretsu*: the

Case of Matsushita Electric', in Abe and Fitzgerald, *Origins of Japanese Industrial Power*. On corporate governance in Japan, see H.Miyajima, 'The Privatization of Ex-*Zaibatsu* Holding Stocks and the Emergence of Bank-Centered Corporate Groups in Japan', in M.Aoki and H.K.Kim (eds), *Corporate Governance in Transitional Economies: Insider Control and the Role of Banks* (1995), pp.361-403; T.Okazaki, 'Nihon ni Okeru Koporeto Gavanansu no Hatten' ('Development of Corporate Governance in Japan'), in M.Aoki and R.Dore (eds), *Shisutemu to Shiteno Nihon Kigyo* (*The Japanese Firm as a System*) (Tokyo, 1995), pp.437-84; T.Hoshi, 'The Economic Role of Corporate Grouping and the Main Bank System', in M.Aoki and R.Dore, *The Japanese Firm: The Sources of Competitive Strength* (1994), pp.285-309; P.Sheard, 'Interlocking Shareholdings and Corporate Governance in Japan', in Aoki and Dore, *Japanese Firm*, pp.310-349.

14   M.W.Fruin, *The Japanese Enterprise System* (1992).
15   Stable shareholding structures seem to stem not only from cultural factors but also from the long-term economic benefits.
16   On the main bank system, see P.Sheard, 'The Main Bank System and Corporate Monitoring and Control in Japan', *Journal of Economic Behavior and Organization*, vol.11 (1989), pp.399-422; Hoshi, 'Economic Role'.
17   M.Aoki, 'The Contingent Governance of Teams: Analysis of Institutional Complementarity', *International Economic Review*, vol.35, no.3 (August 1994), pp.657-676.
18   S.D.Prowse, 'Institutional Investment Patterns and Corporate Financial Behavior in the United States and Japan', *Journal of Financial Economics*, vol.27 (1990), pp.43-66.
19   For a more recent discussion, similar to the above views, see R.Dore, *Stock Market Capitalism: Welfare Capitalism; Japan and Germany versus the Anglo-Saxons* (2000).

Chapter 2

The Corporate Governance of Japanese Firms at the Early Stage of Industrialization: Osaka Cotton Spinning and Nippon Life Assurance

Matao Miyamoto and Takeshi Abe

Introduction

In recent years, much discussion has taken place on the corporate governance structure of Japanese firms, and this has led to general agreement on their characteristic features. Firstly, both the board of directors, assigned the task of strategic decision-making, and the executives, responsible for carrying out management policy, are composed of almost the same members, having climbed the executive ladder after entering the company as new university graduates. Secondly, supported by mutual stockholding between firms, as well as the stabilization manoeuvres of such stockholding, company management has a considerably free hand, independent of the stock market. Thirdly, employees, as stakeholders, have a substantial influence upon the decision-making of firms. Fourthly, owing to the great weight of indirect finance in corporate fund-raising, banks, especially main banks, function as an effective monitor of firm management.

So, when did this type of corporate governance structure emerge? One of the prevailing views, asserted by Tetsuji Okazaki and other scholars, is that the structure has its origin in the institutions introduced under the wartime economic regime between 1937 to 1945.[1] On the other hand, Hideaki Miyajima presents an alternative view, stating that Japanese-type corporate governance fully developed in the postwar period, even if its proto-type was invented during wartime.[2]

What these two views share in common is their regard for the Japanese-type corporate governance as a relatively new system. Therefore, as Okazaki wrote, 'the classical type of corporate governance, under which the stockholder's rights were respected, prevailed in pre-war Japan', that is the years before 1937, meaning that corporate governance of an entirely different nature was previously dominant.

However, one wonders if an Anglo-Saxon style of corporate governance was widely present at the early stage of Japanese industrialization. Is it true that a drastic change occurred in corporate governance during wartime? Is it not necessary to re-examine how today's corporate governance structure was formed within a longer historical context? This paper is an attempt to shed light upon the changing structure of corporate governance in early Japanese companies through an examination of the relationship between owners, that is stockholders, and salaried managers.

Once Japanese industrialization began around the mid-1880s, the number of joint-stock companies rapidly increased, in part due to the progress of company legislation, and modern company institutions prevailed within Japanese big business by the early 1900s.[3] Joint-stock companies in those days, however, had some peculiarities in their methods of raising capital and in their stockholders' involvement with company management. Because of the undeveloped stock market, these companies were obliged to rely heavily on a small number of company promoters in order to raise their capital. These promoters, being the powerful business leaders of each local community, usually had an informal group of subordinate investors who were willing to join in their leaders' venture. Therefore, early Japanese joint-stock companies were often established as joint ventures by investor groups, each of which was headed by a business leader. In these joint investments, each group was asked to subscribe an amount of shares equal to those of the other groups. The boss of each group assumed a position on the board of directors, as a representative, in order to maintain the balance of power.[4] In the sense that the major stockholders sat on the board of directors, the early Japanese joint-stock companies might be regarded as owner-controlled firms.

Their position as directors was, however, quite nominal. As it was common for one group to invest in various companies, the boss frequently held multiple directorships concurrently. Therefore, they were no more than part-time directors for each company. In addition, they seldom had professional or technical knowledge relevant to the companies in which they were involved. It might be said that their interest in a specific firm was solely the return on investment. Under this situation, the delegation of management to administrative staff was widely adopted. Being entrusted with a wide range of authority, from policy-making to daily management, administrative staff - including chief engineers, plant managers, and managers in charge of commercial affairs - virtually filled the role of top management.

The administrative staffs were, however, often reprimanded for their policies and business performance by the major stockholders, who held the posts of directors, because of a lack of established rules concerning delegation. Nevertheless, as Hidemasa Morikawa points out, salaried managers with high education qualifications gradually came to hold real management control by around the early twentieth century, reducing the pressure from major stockholders.[5]

Why and how were salaried managers able to grasp actual business power? What kind of changes occurred in ownership structure, therefore, during the process? We would like to discuss this topic, with special reference to the cases of Osaka Cotton Spinning Company (*Osaka Boseki Kaisha* or *Osakabo*, and, hereafter, referred to as OCS), and Nippon Life Assurance Limited (*Nippon Seimei Hoken Kaisha*, or NLA). These two companies were chosen not only because archival material was available, but because they were considered to be representative of joint stock companies at the early stage of Japan's industrialization.

Firstly, as examples, both were vanguard enterprises in their respective fields, having great entrepreneurial success shortly after their establishment. Secondly, both were large-scale joint stock companies in terms of paid-up capital and the number of investors: OCS raised 280 thousand yen from 95 subscribers, while NLA raised 60 thousand yen from 244 subscribers. Thirdly, both OCS and NLA, when raising their capital, relied heavily upon a small number of company promoters under whom investors grouped to make joint investments. The two companies were a 'motley combination' made up of various investors' groups. Fourthly, although the major stockholders or their deputies occupied seats on the board of directors at the time of establishment, most of them did not work as such, and played only a nominal role. Instead, salaried managers or administrative staff substantially controlled the business of these companies. Fifthly, such structures of ownership and corporate governance led to some form of management instability in both companies. Repeated disputes among stockholders and between employed managers and stockholders arose. The efforts made for resolving such problems gave birth to changes in ownership structure and in corporate governance.

Table 2.1 Osaka Cotton Spinning: Concentration of Stockholding, 1882-1914

Date	(A)	(B)	(C)	(D)
April 1882	2,500	80	31.3	49.7
Dec 1883	2,800	95	29.5	46.1
June 1886	6,000	202	29.7	37.1
Dec 1889	12,000	384	31.3	30.7
June 1893	24,000	479	50.1	24.5
June 1898	24,000	607	39.5	22.5
June 1901	32,000	662	48.3	22.2
Dec 1905	48,000	756	63.5	16.4
Nov 1907	75,000	1,163	64.5	14.4
May 1905	100,000	1,450	69.0	20.8

Notes: (A) Number of stocks issued; (B) Number of stockholders; (C) Number of stocks per head; (D) Percentage of stocks held by ten largest shareholders.
Source: N.Takamura, *Osaka Boseki Kaisha* (1970).

The Osaka Cotton Spinning Company

Osaka Cotton Spinning Company, now Toyo Cotton Spinning Company (or *Toyobo*), was established in Osaka in 1882, and was the first mechanized cotton spinning enterprise in Japan to become an entrepreneurial success.[6] Its main promoter was

Eiichi Shibusawa, who, as one of the most powerful business leaders of those days, contributed to setting up a number of modern companies in Japan.

As shown in Table 2.1, the 280,000 yen raised in 1883 from 95 subscribers included former feudal lords (*daimyô*) and well-known merchants in the big cities. A sum of 106.5 thousand yen was raised from 17 feudal lords, 86.5 thousand yen from 56 Osaka merchants, 80.2 thousand yen from 17 Tokyo merchants, and 6.8 thousand yen from 5 other people. Taking advantage of their position as the most powerful business leaders of the day in Osaka, Denzaburo Fujita and Jyutaro Matsumoto cooperated with Shibusawa. They contributed greatly to the raising of initial capital funds from Osaka merchants in a variety of fields, many of whom were reluctant to invest in a new business such as cotton spinning. Stockholding was highly concentrated when the company was established, with the top ten stockholders holding 46.1 per cent of the total stocks issued.

This form of capital-raising and ownership structure was reflected in the appointment of directors (see Table 2.2). As major stockholders, Fujita (the tenth largest stockholder) and Matsumoto (the fifth largest stockholder) were elected as the first president and director respectively. Tatsutaro Kumagai, who was the Osaka branch manager of the First National Bank (*Dai-Ichi Kokuritsu Ginkô*), was appointed as another director. The First National Bank was under the control of Shibusawa. As the largest stockholder, Shibusawa joined the board of directors as a counsellor, along with two other major stockholders, Bunsaku Fujimoto and Sakuro Yajima, both of whom were from Tokyo.

The directors were re-elected in 1887. Fujita stepped down as president, and Matsumoto succeeded him. Seiichiro Saeki, who was also a major stockholder, replaced Matsumoto as a director. Then, in 1892, Sadatake Iba, who was a representative of the Sumitomo *zaibatsu*, which had invested in OCS, took Kumagai's place. With the enforcement of the Commercial Law in 1893, three persons from among the major stockholders were appointed as auditors.

Therefore, the major stockholders occupied the board of directors, and, in this sense, OCS looked like an owner-controlled company. However, all the directors, including Shibusawa, were too busy to devote themselves to the duties of top management. Shibusawa seldom came to Osaka, because he held similar posts in many other companies, most of which were located in Tokyo. Fujita and Matsumoto had diverse businesses in various fields. Beginning with shoe-making, Fujita expanded into purveyance to the Ministry of Defence, mining, trading, civil engineering and construction, shipping, railroad, and sulphuric chemicals manufacturing. In addition, he was the president of the Osaka Chamber of Commerce at the time he was president of OCS. Matsumoto ran an extensive business ranging from drapery, grocery, banking, railroad, brewery and sugar-refining. Other directors, counsellors and auditors had other main occupations. Moreover, none of them possessed any professional knowledge of the modern cotton spinning industry, the machinery and technological know-how of which had been transplanted from the West following the Meiji Restoration of 1868.

Under these circumstances, the delegation of management affairs to administrative staff became inevitable. Takeo Yamanobe, the chief engineer, had been dispatched to Blackburn in Lancashire, England, in order to learn the techniques of cotton spinning. He played the most important role in management, along with the sales manager, Seizo Kamata, who had previously worked as the chief manager for a silk fabric wholesaler in the Kyoto Prefecture. Rihei Kawamura joined OCS from a raw cotton wholesaler, after Kamata resigned in 1891. These men received higher salaries than those paid to the directors, revealing that they virtually functioned as top management, although the most important decision-making still remained in the hands of Shibusawa and the directors. The administrative staff mentioned above received 50 yen as a monthly salary, while the president and directors received 30 and 20 respectively.

Table 2.2 Osaka Cotton Spinning: Board of Directors, 1893-94

Position	Name and Occupation	July 1893
President	Jutaro Matsumoto. Retailer, western cloth. President, 130th National Bank, Muslin Spinning & Weaving Co., Nankai Railway, Japan Sugar Refinery Co., Osaka Canal Co.	
Director	Seiichiro Saeki. Chairman, Cotton Thread & Cloth Exchange. Director, Nankai Railway, Osaka Alkali Co.	
Director	Sadatake Iba. General Director, Sumitomo House.	
Auditor	Bunsaku Fujimoto.	
Auditor	Ichitaro Abe. Wholesaler, silk fabric. President, Shirt Weaving Co.	
Auditor	Tokubei Taku. President, Taku Co. Managing Director, Sakai Sake Brewing Co. Director, Naniwa Bank, Osaka Beer Co.	

Position	Name and Occupation	January 1894
President	Takeo Yamanobe. Engineer.	
Director	Mitsumasa Hirose. Former General Director, Sumitomo House.	
Director	Tokubei Taku. As above.	
Auditor	Ichitaro Abe. As above.	
Auditor	Seijyuro Shibuya. Wholesaler, raw cotton.	
Auditor	Genjyuro Koezuka. Sake brewer.	

Sources: Minutes, General Meetings; N.Takamura, *Toyo Boseki Kabushiki Kaisha* (1986).

However, these administrative staff or salaried managers were not necessarily given a free hand, but came under pressure from the major stockholders and directors. There is evidence to support this interpretation. The general meeting of stockholders seems to have worked effectively, quite different from the situation seen in Japan today. According to the minutes of general meetings, the original documents of which remain in Toyo Cotton Spinning Company, and date back to 1893, the percentage in attendance was relatively high (see Table 2.3).

Yamanobe recorded in 1890 the following on the tendencies of stockholders of joint stock companies, and on the duties of managers in light of these tendencies.[7]

> Being dazzled by the huge profits of other existing companies, a number of investors are hastily planning to set up new companies, expecting similar high profits as those gained in other companies, without deliberation over the uncertainty of profitability in a new company. Being captivated by a temporary boom in the stock market, some investors become the stockholders of companies purely for speculative purposes without any interest in the long-term prospects of the company, and thereby easily change their mind, depending on dividends and stock prices. It is very natural and inevitable for investors to behave in this way. Therefore, persons in charge of management, and responsible for the future prosperity of the company, have a duty to please stockholders by keeping dividends as high as possible. They understand the situation under which the company was set up, and make efforts to strengthen the foundation of the company from the perspective of long-run development.

Yamanobe, who looked upon himself as 'a person in charge of management and responsible for the future prosperity of the company', drew a clear line between himself and the investors who 'become stockholders purely for speculative purposes'. He, therefore, tried to satisfy stockholders and their natures. It was perhaps a reflection of this that both dividend rates (dividend as a percentage of capital) and payout ratios (dividend as a percentage of profits) were quite high, at the sacrifice of capital reserves and depreciation, in the several years following OCS's establishment.

This dividend policy, favourable to stockholders, contributed to a sharp rise in the stock price of OCS, which soared to some 230 yen for the face value of 100 yen in the years from 1885 to 1889. The company increased paid-up capital from 280,000 yen in 1884 to 1.2 million yen in 1889, with a simultaneous increase in the number of stockholders from 98 to 384. Yamanobe succeeded in gaining a good reputation in the eyes of stockholders.

The situation changed after 1892, when OCS lost half of its plant through fire damage. The 650,000 yen expenses for damage reconstruction, which was covered by reserves and issuance of company bonds, weakened the company's financial condition and affected its profitability. Moreover, OCS was confronted with fierce competition from other spinning companies entering the field in the 1890s. OCS was often behind other companies from the latter half of the 1890s in such areas as profitability, growth, and market share. In particular, OCS was losing its competitive edge in the cotton yarn market. Yamanobe, as virtual top manager, had entered the board of directors in 1895, thereby gaining increasing responsibility. He was obliged to maintain the dividend rate at levels as high as those in other major companies, in spite of the fact that OCS's rates of return on total assets were lower than those of its rivals.

Table 2.3 Osaka Cotton Spinning: Stockholding and Attendance at General Meetings, 1893-1914

Date	(A)	(B)	(C)	(D)	(E)	(F)	(G)	(H)
July 1893	504	24,000	239	32	3,717	47.4	53.8	15.5
July 1895	580	24,000	209	15	16,600	36.0	38.6	69.2
Dec 1900	565	24,000	127	240	14,576	22.5	65.0	60.7
July 1905	756	48,000	137	348	29,491	18.1	64.2	61.4
Dec 1910	1,443	100,000	n/a	786	69,163	n/a	54.4	69.2
June 1914	1,450	100,000	n/a	276	35,042	n/a	19.0	35.0

Notes:
(A) Total number of stockholders at end of the year
(B) Total number of stocks issued at the end of the year
(C) Number of stockholders in attendance at general meeting
(D) Number of stockholders submitting power of attorney at general meeting
(E) Number of stocks held by stockholders in attendance and submitting power of attorney
(F) Stockholders attending as percentage of total stockholders (C/A)
(G) Stockholders attending and submitting powers of attorney as percentage of total stockholders (C+D/A)
(H) Stocks held by those at general meeting or submitting power of attorney as percentage of total number of stocks (E/B)

Source: Minutes, General Meetings.

The Japanese cotton spinning industry, which had grown rapidly in the 1890s, met with a major obstacle as it entered the 20th century. In the recession that began around 1897, the price of cotton yarn dropped substantially. In the years 1900-1901, the depression began in earnest, and output and sales plummeted. A contemporary Business Report of OCS stated that the cotton yarn division faced its greatest predicament since its establishment. The stock price of OCS fell sharply.

This situation created some discord in managerial echelons, and Yamanobe was attacked by the major stockholders, especially from those close to the president Matsumoto. Eiichi Shibusawa testified as follows.[8]

There were also troubled times for the Osaka Cotton Spinning Company. Perhaps finding it difficult to overcome these, Yamanobe dropped in to Tokyo one day, and things had reached a point that even the indefatigable Yamanobe was unexpectedly thinking to quit the company. Although I was not unaware that the spinning industry was in dire straits as a result of the current economic situation, such action would burst the bubble that our efforts had created so far. So, I said that I was irrevocably opposed to this, and gave him words of encouragement.

Katsumasa Okamura, who worked as an engineer under the supervision of Yamanobe, adds the following.[9]

> In 1897, the reaction to the postwar boom set in, and, with the fall in the value of silver and the upheaval in the exchange rate with China, there were troubled times for the spinning industry. Osaka Cotton Spinning Company also made big losses. The Osaka directors around the current president, Jutaro Matsumoto, who had been hostile to the real power held by Mr. Yamanobe in the company, began to say that, because they were losing with Yamanobe as chief, they would like to have him resign. Defamed and attacked in various ways at stockholders' meetings, Mr. Yamanobe was embittered and seems to have wanted to quit the company. He even consulted me. It was probably about this time that he went to Mr. Shibusawa's residence to ask to be able to resign. But, in the following year, when the situation became disadvantageous for Mr. Matsumoto's group, they were in turn attacked, and in 1898 Mr. Yamanobe became president instead. With the commercial recovery of 1899, considerable profits were made and Mr. Yamanobe was triumphant.

Yamanobe thus assumed the office of president in 1898, following this ordeal. As shown in the following words recorded by Matsumoto on his retirement, this was significant as the beginning of a change from the main form of Meiji period stock companies, in which the major stockholders acted concurrently as directors, to a form in which professional managers were appointed to directors.[10]

> I have held the post of president for more than five years, but today, when the industry has advanced conspicuously, it has become difficult for someone like me who has interests in other companies to act as president in name only. From now on, someone must be chosen as president who can devote himself to this company alone, and supervise management and production by himself, in order to reduce costs and increase productivity.

Matsumoto continued to hold his position as a major stockholder in the company and was president of the 130th Bank, a main bank of OCS along with the First Bank. It is likely that he maintained an influence in the management of OCS even after his resignation. The stockholders did not necessarily leave every aspect of management to the directors either. A substantial number of stockholders were still present at the general meetings of stockholders and asked to speak about dividend policy, the movement of stock prices, the pecuniary burden of stockholders, and other matters, although the percentage of attendance was declining over time.

At the extraordinary general meeting of stockholders in January 1900, for example, a proposal from the managers requested the issuance of company bonds to the amount of 400 thousand yen for the purpose of a weaving plant expansion. It was approved. The managers proposed to raise funds through the issuance of company bonds because they considered it difficult, under the current business conditions of OCS, to persuade stockholders to accept a capital increase, which posed an additional burden to stockholders. However, the issuance of company deposits later turned out to be quite difficult due to the severe depression. So, in March of the following year, an extraordinary meeting was again called, and, with the cancellation of the previous decision, a capital increase to the amount of 400 thousand yen by way of allotment of preferred stock to existing stockholders was proposed as an alternative.

The meeting became an imbroglio. Despite the fact that, in the new plan, the minimum dividend rate of preferred stock was promised at 12 per cent, many stockholders were opposed, and asked for an amendment. One stockholder, Ginjiro Higuchi, insisted that the company borrow money from a bank under promise of future company bonds. Two stockholders, Shobei Tamura, a gold and silver foil merchant in Osaka, and Kyuichi Komuro, a bill broker in Osaka, argued that, from the viewpoint of maintaining the price of old stocks, the company should make every effort to raise funds by the issuance of company bonds. Another stockholder, Hisashi Yamano, demanded that, if any stockholders did not want to accept the preferred stock, they should be allowed to transfer it to other stockholders. Yamanobe accepted this proposal.

The meeting eventually ended with the adoption of the original proposal, accepting Matsumoto's opinion that, for the purpose of strengthening the foundation of the company, it would be better to introduce preferred stocks. To borrow money from banks would injure the company's reputation. Yet the fact that a heated debate developed at the stockholders' general meeting illustrates the position in which the manager was placed at that time.

Yamanobe's attitude towards the stockholders is also noticeable. At the 43rd regular meeting in January 1905, Shozaemon Kubota, a druggist claiming to be representative of the major stockholders in Kyoto, was against the managers' proposal of profit disposal. He strongly insisted that the company increase the dividend rate in the current term to 9 per cent by cutting the profit to be carried forward to the next term. Although many other stockholders felt this to be too demanding, Yamanobe asked the attendants to accept the suggestion, and Kubota's proposition was ultimately approved. This episode reveals Yamanobe's deliberate consideration of stockholders.

As has been shown in the examples noted above, top managers tended to be caught in a dilemma between the interests of stockholders and those of the company as a whole. Nevertheless, generally speaking, it can be said that they came to have stronger power in the company as time passed. Under the presidency of Yamanobe, OCS began to adopt new strategies. First, after the appointment of Yamanobe as president, OCS shifted its emphasis from the production and sale of low counts of yarn. These had been profitable in the early days, but suffered from the competition of other major spinning companies in the 1890s. The company moved to ancillary weaving and cloth exports after the first decade of the 20th century. A 120-loom expansion in 1898 was undertaken, and this was followed, in 1901, by the introduction of 500 'new-type power looms', namely Northrop automatic power looms, which were purchased when Yamanobe went to the U.S. Moreover, in 1906, OCS merged with the Kanakin Cotton Cloth Company, which ranked third at that time in the scale of its weaving plants, with the result that OCS became the number one weaver in Japan.

Second, this sort of aggressive investment in plant and equipment, which had never been seen before, could not be undertaken without a change in the company's financial policy. As we have seen, OCS realized high dividend rates and high pay-out ratios at the sacrifice of depreciation and reserves in the several years following its establishment. However, after the Russo-Japanese War, dividends fell, while reserves apparently increased. The managers tried to raise funds through various means such as an increase in capital, including the issuance of preferred stocks, the issuance of company bonds, borrowing from the First Bank, Hypothec Bank and other banks, and the drawing of promissory notes. These policies undermined the financial condition of the company, so that the company became obliged to accept directors sent from First Bank. In fact, OCS was confronted with severe financial difficulties in the first half of the 1900s. But, these efforts began to produce fruit after the Russo-Japanese War. If the managers of the company had been much more sensitive to stockholders' interests, such a positive business strategy, as noted above, would not have been adopted.

In concluding this section, we must pay attention to the changes that occurred in the ownership structure with the emergence of salaried managers. As has been noted, Osaka Cotton Spinning Company was established as a motley combination of various investor groups. This ownership structure had an influence on the corporate governance structure of the company. However, these investor groups gradually disposed of their stocks. Most of the old feudal lords' groups, who had invested in the company through Shibusawa's persuasion, had left the company as early as 1890, and the Tokyo merchants' groups followed immediately afterwards. On the Osaka side, Denzaburo Fujita, who became the first president of the company as the tenth largest stockholder, rapidly disposed of his stocks after he resigned from his position. Matsumoto continued to hold his stocks until the turn of the century, but parted with them after he resigned as counsellor to the company in 1904.

Instead, many Osaka merchants acquired the company's stocks. The number of stockholders increased from 95 at the company's establishment to some 500-600 in the 1890s; to 600-700 in the 1900s; and finally to more than 1500 in the years from

1911 to 1914, when OCS merged with Mie Cotton Spinning Company to become Toyo Cotton Spinning Company. The degree of concentration in stockholding also lessened. In addition, the major stockholders frequently reshuffled. From this, it is suggested that increasing numbers of stockholders lost their interest in the company's management. A declining trend in the percentage of attendance at stockholders' meetings can be said to show this (see Table 2.3).

Nagging major stockholders, such as the bosses of investors' groups present in the early days, gradually disappeared, and silent stockholders relatively increased in number. This may have produced a more favorable situation for salaried managers like Yamanobe. However, another noteworthy fact is that the core stockholders did continue to exist. Of such core stockholders, Shibusawa held the greatest presence for a long time. He maintained his position as the first and largest stockholder until the mid-1900s, when he retired from business. He continued to support Yamanobe, as illustrated by the episode noted earlier. Shibusawa, with his charisma, was the most influential figure throughout the country at that time, and must have supported the triumph of salaried managers over the stockholders.

Another person who became a major stockholder was Yamanobe himself. He gradually acquired stocks to emerge as the seventh largest stockholder by 1898, when he took the presidency. This no doubt reveals that, in those days, stockholding on a relatively large scale was a requirement for a salaried manager to be appointed as president of the company. In addition, after the beginning of the 20th century, an association to promote stockholding was set up by the staff of OCS, and Yamanobe was elected as the chairman. The association, named *Yushukai*, functioned as a major stockholder on behalf of salaried managers.

Naigai Cotton Trading Company, Hikotaro Abe, Kihei Seo, and Masajiro Tazuke were the other major stockholders at OCS after 1900. Naigai Cotton Trading, which was a supplier of raw cotton to OCS, came to hold stocks when it assisted OCS with financing. The latter three people had been former stockholders of Kanakin Cotton Cloth Company, which had merged into OCS. So, they were 'stable' stockholders for OCS as well.

As seen in Table 2.3, the number of stockholders who submitted a power of attorney letter to the stockholders' meeting increased over time, suggesting that an growing number of stockholders became indifferent to the role of management. On the other hand, the percentage of attendance in terms of stocks, including the number of power of attorney letters, showed an increase. This probably means that the managers succeeded in acquiring a kind of *carte blanche* from many stockholders.

In this way, the Osaka Cotton Spinning Company carried out stabilization manoeuvres in stockholding on the one hand, and the dispersion of stock holding on the other. A change in ownership structure was the result, and formed a background against which salaried managers gained real power within the Osaka Cotton Spinning Company.

Nippon Life Assurance

Nippon Life was a life insurance company established in the city of Osaka in 1889.[11] The main promoter was Sukesaburô Hirose, who was one of the wealthy merchants in Ômi, the eastern part of the Shiga Prefecture. Hirose, in cooperation with Jisuke Okahashi, who was a famous cotton cloth merchant and banker in Osaka, raised their capital from 244 subscribers, including bankers and merchants, both in Osaka and Ômi. Naoharu Kataoka, the vice-president at the founding of the company, reminisced later in life about the company's raising of capital.[12]

> In those days, in Osaka, there were several businessmen's cliques, such as the Matsumoto clique, Okahashi clique, Tanaka clique, etc., and they were likely to be hostile to each other. However, we persuaded all the cliques to participate in the company, on the grounds that in such an undertaking as life insurance, which deeply involves public welfare, the monopolization of the business by one particular clique should be avoided and would not bring about business success. In addition, we did not allow a stockholder, regardless of whether they were a promoter or not, to subscribe for more than 50 stocks, with the intention of offering the stocks to the general public.

Careful consideration was given to maintaining the balance of power among investors' groups as well as to the appointment of directors. As is shown in Table 2.4, the representatives of major stockholders, in most cases the bosses of investor groups, occupied almost all the positions on the board of directors. Most of them held similar posts in other companies and, therefore, did not work as full-time managers at Nippon Life. In particular, Zen'emon Konoike, well-known throughout the country as a man of wealth, was invited to be president in the expectation that his fame would enhance business creditability. But his role was a nominal one. The administrative staff, such as the vice-president, Naoharu Kataoka, whose previous post was chief superintendent of Shiga Prefecture, and Seisuke Izumi, who was sent from the 136th National Bank, had much more important management roles.[13]

Let us examine the relationship between the employed managers and stockholders by looking at the nature of discussions at general meetings of stockholders. In NLA, fifteen regular meetings and twelve special meetings were held from 1890 to 1905.[14] The president Zen'emon Konoike attended only four times during the period. Even when he was present, he never took the chair, and the vice-president, Naoharu Kataoka, did so instead. In addition, there is no evidence that Konoike ever gave an important speech at the meetings until he handed over the presidency to Kataoka in 1903. Jisuke Okahashi, Ichibei Tanaka, and Kichirobei Yamaguchi, who as powerful business leaders played an important role in establishing the company, also seldom expressed their opinions. Although such people as Jirosaburo Naniwa, Tatutarou Kumagai, Sadataro Kusama, Seichoku Matsumoto and Eisuke Nishida, all of whom were Osaka bankers, were appointed to the posts of director as representatives of the major 'investors' groups', their roles in the management team were limited. They were too busy to devote themselves to the company, as was the case with their counterparts in the Osaka Cotton Spinning Company. It was Sukesaburo Hirose, an owner-manager, and Naoharu Kataoka and Seisuke Izumi, as salaried managers, that held real power in management. In particular, Kataoka, who was called 'a driving force', and other administrative staff around him demonstrated strong leadership, and developed an aggressive strategy, which enabled the company to become the top insurance company in Japan in a decade after its establishment.

The regular stockholder meetings usually proceeded in the following way. They began by reporting on the annual business performance, the balance sheet, the profit and loss statement, and the inventory of property. Next, proposals for dividend distribution were discussed. Election of directors and revision of the company's article were taken up frequently as agenda items both in regular and extraordinary meetings, held every year for the former and a total of eleven times for the latter between 1890 to 1905. Frequent discussions on the company's articles can be said to reflect the business environment for life insurance in those days, when legislation of the Old and New Commercial Codes, and enactment of the Insurance Business Law were being implemented.

Table 2.4 Nippon Life Assurance: Board of Directors, 1889-1918

Name	Position and Occupation
Zen'emon Konoike	President, 1889-1903. Konoike group. 13th National Bank.
Naoharu Kataoka	Vice-President, 1889-1903. President, 1903-19. Director, Police Force, Shiga Prefecture.
Sukesaburo Hirose	Director, 1889-98. Hirose group. 133rd National Bank.
Jirosaburo Nanba	Director, 1889-92. 22nd National Bank.
Tatsutaro Kumagai	Director, 1889-93. 1st National Bank.
Sadataro Soma	Director, 1889-93. Konoike group. 13th National Bank.
Masanao Matsumoto	Director, 1889-1904. 130th National Bank.
Seisuke Izumi	Director, 1889-96. Executive Director, 1896-97. Director, 1897-1909.
Jisuke Okahashi	Auditor, 1899-1903. Okahashi group. 34th National Bank.
Eisuke Nishida	Auditor, 1889-95. Yamaguchi group. 34th National Bank.
Chusaku Takeda	Auditor, 1891-1914. 121st National Bank.
Michio Doi	Counsellor, 1892-93. Director, 1893-1917. Konoike group. 13th National Bank.
Kin'ichiro Tani	Counsellor, 1893-94. Director, 1894-97. NLA employee.
Gonbei Koya	Auditor, 1896-98. 32nd National Bank.
Yasusaburo Ashida	Auditor, 1899-1914. Konoike group. Konoike Bank.
Yasujiro Inoue	Director, 1903-10. 136th National Bank.

Kasuke Koshino	Director, 1903-17. Yamaguchi group. Yamaguchi Bank.
Ichibei Tanaka	Director, 1903-10. 130th National Bank.
Shigeyuki Hashimoto	Director, 1908-19. Kataoka group. NLA employee.
Suketaro Hirose	Director, 1908-19. Hirose group. 133rd National Bank.
Tamemi Kawai	Auditor, 1911-14. 51st National Bank.
Kanemichi Banno	Auditor, 1941-31. Yamaguchi group. Yamaguchi Bank.
Chugo Ohashi	Auditor, 1914-15.
Kihei Seo	Auditor, 1914-20. Wholesaler, cotton and cloth.
Genjiro Koezuka	Auditor, 1916-20. Sake brewer.
Kichirobei Abe	Director, 1918-42. Wholesaler, rice.

Source: NLA records.

With the exception of a few meetings, such as that of 1903, when the resignation of the president, Konoike, and embezzlement by an employee were taken up as major issues, the meetings seldom became imbroglios. Proposals submitted by the managers were usually approved without strong objection. In the regular meeting of 1900, a stockholder successfully proposed omitting the reading of the biannual company report, and this procedure became a convention in subsequent years. For the election of directors, nomination by the chairman rather than voting was adopted.

However, the stockholders were sensitive to dividends and the business performance of the company. At its establishment, NLA had promised to produce a supplementary settlement of accounts every eight years. This constituted a periodic review of the annual business reports. It was based on a deferred dividend plan, under which profits resulting from lower than expected expenses plus profits from lower than expected mortality rates were identified. They were placed in the reserves, distributed as dividends to the insured, or used as supplementary dividends to stockholders or as supplementary bonuses to the directors, manager and employees. Because more dividends to policyholders or more supplementary bonuses to company staff meant fewer dividends to stockholders, stockholders were naturally anxious about the settlement. At the extraordinary meeting of stockholders in 1897, when NLA planned to announce the first supplementary settlement of accounts, a stockholder asked a question regarding the special dividends to stockholders. In the regular meeting in 1903, another stockholder raised a similar question to managers, concerning the second supplementary settlement of accounts. In the case of NLA, a stockholder who continued to hold his stock for an eight-year period, during which there was a supplementary settlement of accounts, would receive both annual dividends and supplementary dividends at the end of the period. So, if we calculate dividend rates, in terms of all the dividends received by him divided by paid-up capital, they were high. On average, they were as high as 14.5 per cent in 1889-97; 23.8 in 1898-1905; 40.0 in 1906-13; and 29.1 in 1914-18. As was the case in OCS, the managers of NLA had to pay special attention to stockholders' interests.

The stockholders sometimes demanded returns other than dividends. In 1911, the stock price of the company rose sharply from 200 yen to some 400 yen, on the grounds of its excellent business performance and large accumulation of both policy reserve and forward surplus. Under the circumstances, not a few stockholders of the company asked for the free distribution of stocks to be made as a way of sharing profits. Responding to this, Kataoka stated the following in the meeting of stockholders in February 1911.[15]

> Some stockholders might consider the rise in the stock price of our company as the result of a remarkable increase in forward surplus in our company. However, I must say that such a view has arisen from a misunderstanding of the nature of the surplus in our company. This surplus has been forwarded as funds for dividends to policyholders, supplementary dividends to stockholders and supplementary bonuses to company staffs under the supplementary settlement of accounts to be carried out every eight years. Therefore, all of it does not necessarily revert to the stockholders. Moreover, although it may seem that the policy reserves of an insurance company are equivalent to reserves in companies in other fields, this is misleading. Policy reserves do not belong to the stockholders' account, but are a liability reserve provided for the payment of insurance. I do hope that stockholders will hold the stocks of our company while understanding the nature of our company.

Ordinary stockholders, however, did not necessarily understand Kataoka's assertion. As they entered the Taisho Era (1912-1926), some of them began to demand an increase in capital on the grounds of growing company reserves, and frequently sent letters to managers such as Kataoka. As the management team did not agree to this demand, the group of stockholders asking for the capital increase organized the Council of Major Stockholders, probably an informal organization. The Council adopted a resolution demanding that capital move from 30,000 to 1.5 million yen. Then, seven delegates entered into negotiations with management, and campaigned among other stockholders. All the seven delegates elected by the Council - Tomozo Nishimura, Chugo Ohashi, Shinjiro Masuda, Jinyomo Terada, Genjiro Koezuka, Kihei Seo and Zengoro Shiroyama - were major stockholders, or 'the bosses of investors' groups' in the sense noted earlier. Some of them had also invested in Osaka Cotton Spinning Company as men of wealth.

In response, management held several meetings with those major stockholders holding more than 50 stocks, in order to explain that an increase in capital was of no use under the company's current situation. The major stockholder group insisted that '...our claim does not mean the sacrifice of policyholders'. Kataoka refuted their argument: 'under the current situation in which everything is going well with our company, not only is there no strong reason for an increase in capital, but it would also give society an impression that stockholders might monopolize the profits that should be distributed to policyholders'. The controversies were heated.

As long as a number of major stockholders maintained their demands, managers could not resist a change in policy, and eventually announced to the Council of Major Stockholders in March 1914 that the company would carry out a four-fold increase in capital at the end of that year. Although newly-issued stocks, which were offered to the existing stockholders, were paid out of the stockholders' own funds, the company distributed additional dividends from its surplus in response to demands for a free distribution. Later, around 1920, further friction arose between stockholders and managers with regard to a second increase in capital. Stockholders linked the proposal to good business performance and the accumulation of large reserves. Yet the top managing director, Suketaro Hirose, asserted that the profits and reserves in an insurance company were produced not necessarily from stock-capital but from lower expenses, lower mortality, and higher than expected yields from investment of its assets. Hence, there was no need for an increase in capital. However, once more, the company responded to stockholders' claims by doubling its capital. These episodes are very suggestive of the deep divisions between a management that emphasized the peculiarity of an insurance company, and stockholders that placed much more emphasis on investment returns.

The stockholders frequently discussed the asset management of the company. At the stockholders' meeting in 1901, Tokutaro Kameoka, who was also one of the powerful investors in Osaka, raised specific questions.[16] He stated:

> According to the tables prepared by management, dividend rates of the stocks held by NLA are between five and six per cent, while the interest rate of loans is 8 per cent. Although I know that the statutes of our company permit the buying of sound stocks, I hope that our company uses as minimal funds as possible for investment in stocks with lower dividend rates, given that the profitability of providing loans is higher than that of investment in stocks.

Kataoka answered:

> Mr Kameoka's opinion is plausible, but I would like to ask you to understand that the comparison of profitability among various forms of assets is not necessarily relevant, due to the omission of interest rates for bank deposits, securities and demand deposits in the table, omitted for fear that disclosure might hinder banking business. We do not hold risky securities…Thus, annual returns on investment in stocks are on average 6.88 per cent. While it is true that providing loans is more profitable than securities investment at this time, I feel that a disproportionate emphasis on loans is rather unsound. Of most importance is to keep a balance between the two. Of the stocks we are now holding, those of Kiwa Railroad may become problematic from the viewpoint of certainty, but stocks like those in Hokkaido Railroad Company are held for the reason that this company was set up by people, including the three governors of Osaka, Kyoto and Shiga

Prefectures, to whom we are greatly indebted for their assistance at the establishment of our company. Some people may have some objections to our holding such stocks, given current economic conditions. However, even if this is so, in so far as it is obvious that a railroad is profitable due to its indispensability for a national economy and its promise as an enterprise, no one can assert that our holding of stock would bring disadvantage to our company.

Kameoka's speech, encouraging short-run returns without an understanding of the nature of asset management in an insurance company, which should be made from a long-run perspective, reveals the mindset of rentier-type stockholders in those days. The stockholders also carefully observed where the funds were directed. One typical example was the Saiga Company's default case, which occurred in the first half of the 1910s.[17] Saiga Company was a kind of venture business in the electric power industry and railroads, established by Tokichi Saiga in the mid-Meiji Period. The company had diversified from its business of electric machinery and equipment to almost all businesses related to electricity and railroad, including the contractual business of construction, the establishment of companies, the issuing and underwriting of stocks, and participation in management. Saiga had become known as 'the king of electricity' because of his aggressive business activities and his success. Although the company's business had expanded so much that it had more than 100 related companies, the company was confronted with financing difficulties due to rapid expansion. Under this situation, it was rumored that NLA was giving financial support to Saiga Company due to Kataoka's personal connection. In the stockholders' meetings during the early 1910s, the stockholders repeatedly asked managers to disclose the truth of the matter. As Kataoka replied, 'there is no unfair dealings in our investments and loans', referring to the fact that NLA did not invest in or provide loans directly to Saiga Company. Nevertheless, it was true that NLA had given financial support to Saiga, to those personally related to the firm, and to its affiliated companies. For this reason alone, stockholders were suspicious of management, and eventually it became difficult for NLA to continue its support. Judging from this, it might be said that the stockholders' meeting worked to monitor the behaviour of managers.

As we have seen, Kataoka was not beyond criticism, but he did understand the peculiarities of the life insurance business, and he was different from ordinary stockholders, whose central concerns were the profitability and safety of investments. He made various efforts to introduce modern insurance theory and to bring specialists of the life insurance business into the company. NLA, for example, set up a research department in the company as early as 1894. The department was under the direct control of Kataoka, and was assigned such duties as research into the insurance industry in Japan and foreign countries, translation of foreign books, journals and papers, scientific studies of modern insurance, the collection of foreign and domestic books, and information related to life insurance. Company staff that were 'proficient in jurisprudence, medical science, mathematics, economics and foreign languages' were assigned to the department. The head, Yonejiro Hitomi, was one such staff member who had studied life insurance science under Professor Rikitaro Fujisawa of Tokyo Imperial University, known as a leading scholar in the insurance field. Another member of staff, Shigeyuki Hashimoto, was a bachelor of law graduate from the university. Among a number of foreign books and papers collected by the department, important ones were translated and distributed to staff in the company and to its agents. It is said that the activities of the department greatly contributed to the progress of insurance management in NLA and to the diffusion of modern insurance knowledge.[18]

Also, Kataoka was enthusiastic about introducing actuarial science to insurance calculations, such as determining the basis for premiums and policy reserves. The actuary department was set up in 1895, and trained staffs were assigned to it. At the stockholders' meeting in 1896, Kataoka discussed actuarial practice.[19] This episode suggests that Kataoka attached great importance to these methods at NSL.

> Concerning calculation methods, since they must be based on the principle of insurance, we have appointed two learned staff members as the head and sub-head of the actuary department, one of whom we sent to Tokyo in order to study insurance science, the other of whom is a graduate of the Imperial University. Based on the importance of actuarial science, we should offer them the same benefits as a manager or a deputy manager. However, if we appoint them formally to the posts of manager or deputy manager, the number of managers becomes too many. Therefore, I would like to propose that the head of the actuary department be informally treated the same as a manager and the sub-head the same as a deputy manager.

In addition, in almost every year from 1897, NLA dispatched one or two of its company staff abroad for the purpose of studying the insurance business in advanced economies. At the stockholders' meeting in 1897, Kataoka said 'the life insurance industry is developing remarkably in foreign countries. I fear that we will be left behind the stream unless we observe the real state of overseas affairs. Therefore, we are planning to dispatch two company staff members to Germany and the United Kingdom this year, with the aim of developing our company'.[20] In 1907, NLA provided 1,800 yen in annual extra benefits to those company staff studying abroad, while Kataoka's annual salary was only 480–600 yen, reflecting the company's expectations of its staff. Kataoka, who himself had little education, understood that it was indispensable for modern management to possess staff with formal higher education.

Kataoka's influence had penetrated deeply into the company by the end of the 19th century. He was inaugurated as president following the resignation of Zen'emon Konoike in 1903, and, thereafter, for 16 years assumed the role of top manager. Significant changes in the ownership structure of the company occurred simultaneously. As we have noted, the stocks of NLA at its establishment were scattered amongst many investors. Of the 244 original stockholders, with the exception of Jisuke Okahashi, who kept 12,000 stocks for late-comer subscribers, 13 stockholders, including Sukesaburo Hirose and Zen'emon Konoike, held 130 stocks each; of the rest, 230 had less than 50 stocks per person. As discussed earlier, this policy imposed restrictions on the power of major stockholders in particular, and so the ownership structure may have brought instability to the management of the company.

On the board of directors at the time of establishment, Kataoka was the only person appointed from the administrative staff. In this sense, his position in the company was similar to that of Yamanobe in Osaka Cotton Spinning Company. But the former differed from the latter in the respect that Kataoka was within an ownership structure without core stockholders, and he did not have a charismatic supporter such as Eiichi Shibusawa. These circumstances might have given Kataoka a greater degree of freedom on the one hand, but paradoxically a weaker control over the exercise of power on the other.

Owing to scattered stockholding and distant directors, the stock of NLA became around the turn of the century a target for people centred around one Hiroshi Okabe, who was the owner-manager of the Osaka Life Insurance Company.[21] Even stockholders on the board of directors did not necessarily understand that most of the funds used in a life insurance company were gained not from capital stock but from premiums paid by policyholders; that, therefore, profits resulting from asset management should be distributed more to policyholders than to stockholders. Yet groups around Okabe became interested in these funds.

Table 2.5 Nippon Life Assurance: Concentration of Stockholding, 1889-1914

Year	(A)	(B)	(C)	(D)	(E)	(F)	(G)	(H)	(I)	(J)
1889	12,000	374	32.1	28.2	1.1	0.4	3.2	2.8	19.6	27.1
1890	12,000	438	27.4	16.3	1.8	1.2	4.8	5.2	3.0	16.0
1893	12,000	413	29.1	18.2	1.8	1.5	4.5	4.8	2.3	14.9
1898	12,000	383	31.3	20.2	1.8	2.5	4.4	5.3	2.3	16.3
1904	12,000	256	46.9	27.2	6.1	3.9	6.4	26.9	2.3	45.6
1906	12,000	231	51.9	44.8	9.5	10.3	6.4	17.8	2.8	46.8
1911	12,000	201	59.7	46.7	10.0	10.3	6.4	17.8	2.8	47.3
1914	60,000	347	172.9	41.3	9.4	10.3	2.8	16.3	2.2	41.0

Notes: (A) Number of stocks issued; (B) Number of stockholders; (C) Number of stocks per head; (D) Percentage of stocks held by largest ten shareholders; (E) Percentage of shares held by Hirose group; (F) Kataoka group; (G) Koinike group; (H) Yamaguchi group; (I) Okahashi group; (J) Total percentage of stocks held by major shareholders' group (E+F+G+H+I). *Source*: NLA records.

Against this background, Kataoka and a few stockholders, who were much more interested in the management of an insurance company, began at the turn of the century to perform stabilization manoeuvres. As a result of this, the Kataoka, the Hirose and the Yamaguchi groups continued to purchase NLA stocks in the market, and these three groups came to far surpass other stockholders in their levels of stockholding. Due to these actions, the number of stockholders of NLA declined, in contrast to the case of OCS. The ownership structure of NLA changed from that of scattered stockholding in the early days to oligopsonistic stockholding by the early 1910s, in which the core three groups had the greatest presence (see Table 2.5).

Accordingly, those who were representatives or deputies of the three groups began to dominate the board of directors. In addition, those people such as Sukesaburo Hirose, Jisuke Okahashi, Seisuke Izumi, Yasujiro Inoue and Ichibei Tanaka, who had greatly contributed to the establishment of the company, retired or left during the first two decades of the 20th century. Kataoka, Kasuke Koshino from the Yamaguchi group, Suketaro Hirose and the son of Sukesaburo Hirose, and Shigeyuki Hashimoto, who had climbed the executive ladder since entering as a new university graduate, and was regarded as Kataoka's confidant, gained control of the management. In particular, supported by the three major stockholders' groups, Kataoka, who had become the second largest individual stockholder by 1903, when he took the presidency, reigned over the company as the top manager both in name and in reality.[22] Trends in the percentage of attendance at stockholders' meetings, in terms of both attendants and stocks (see Table 2.6), suggest that increasing proportions of stockholders had an interest in management. The numbers of shareholders also decreased. In both the cases of Yamanobe and Kataoka, there had been some friction between stockholders and themselves until they finally gained real power in their respective companies. Their triumphs were not realized until the structure of stockholding was stabilized.

Table 2.6 Nippon Life Assurance: Stocks and Attendance at General Meetings, 1890-1905

Date	(A)	(B)	(C)	(D)	(E)	(F)
Nov 1890	438	12,000	80	3,026	18.3	25.2
Jan 1895	385	12,000	110	6,518	28.6	54.3
Jan 1900	307	12,000	203	7,555	66.1	63.0
Feb 1905	226	12,000	150	9,140	66.4	76.2

Notes: (A) Number of stockholders at end of year; (B) Number of stocks issued at end of year; (C) Number of stockholders attending; (D) Number of stocks held by those attending; (E) Number of stockholders attending as a percentage of total stockholders (C/A); (F) Number of stocks held by those attending as a percentage of total stocks (D/B). *Source*: NLA records.

Conclusion

This article has discussed the Japanese corporate governance structure in the period from the end of the 19th century to the First World War, when Japan's industrialization successfully began, through the case studies of OCS and NLA. First, in the early days, both companies were obliged to rely heavily on a small number of company promoters in order to raise their capital, partly because of the undeveloped stock market. These promoters, being the powerful business leaders of local communities, usually had informal groups of subordinate investors who were willing to join in their leaders' venture. In these joint investments, each group was asked to subscribe for an amount of shares equal to those of other groups, and the boss of each group assumed a position on the board of directors as the representative of each group, so keeping the balance of power. The position and roles of the directors were, however, quite nominal. The boss of a group frequently held the post of director in other companies concurrently. Therefore, they were only part-time directors, and they seldom had professional or technical knowledge relevant to the companies. It might be said that their interests in a specific firm were solely in the firm's return on investment.

Second, under this situation, the delegation of management to administrative staffs was widely adopted both in OCS and NLA. Being entrusted with a wide range of authority, from policy-making to daily management, administrative staffs, including chief engineers or plant managers and managers in charge of commercial affairs, virtually filled the role of top management. At OCS, an engineer, Yamanobe, who was often reprimanded for his policies and business performance by the major stockholders, such as the president Matsumoto, was gradually promoted. He finally rose to the position of president in 1898, being supported by the founder of the company, Shibusawa, the national business leader of Japan. Although Yamanobe as the president came under pressure from the major stockholders and directors, he accomplished various business innovations both in production methods and marketing. He did succeed in strengthening the managerial foundations of OCS. At NLA, Kataoka, as vice president of the company, played a role in top management from the beginning, and he was inaugurated as the president in 1903, without support from a charismatic stockholder such as Shibusawa at the OCS. These circumstances might have given Kataoka a greater degree of freedom. He understood the modern life insurance business and the indispensability of company staff with higher formal education.

Third, during the period from the late 19th century to the First World War, such managers as Yamanobe and Kataoka carried out stabilization manoeuvres in stockholding, and succeeded in creating ownership structures favourable to salaried managers. In OCS, the early investor groups gradually disposed of their stocks on the one hand, and the number of stockholders increased on the other. As a result, the degree of concentration in stockholding lessened. Nagging major stockholders, such as the bosses of investors' groups, whose presence was conspicuous in the early days, gradually disappeared, and silent stockholders relatively-speaking increased in number. However, such core stockholders as Shibusawa, Yamanobe, Naigai Cotton Trading Company, and a few persons from Kanakin Cotton Cloth Company did continue to exist. The managers succeeded in acquiring support from many stockholders. The change in ownership structure brought about this outcome, and created a situation in which salaried managers gained real power within the OCS. At NLA, although the number of stockholders was declining after 1890, in contrast to the case of OCS, the Kataoka, the Hirose and the Yamaguchi groups continued to purchase NLA stocks in the market from the beginning of the 20th century. Consequently, these three groups came to far surpass other stockholders. So, in NLA as well, an ownership structure favourable to the salaried managers was intentionally created.

Finally, there is the relation between recent discussions on the corporate governance structure of Japanese firms and the above-mentioned facts. Such scholars as Okazaki and Miyajima seem to assume that an Anglo-Saxon style of corporate governance was widely present in pre-war Japan. It was true that the large stockholders had effective power at the early stage of these companies' history. In this sense, the corporate governance of early modern Japan was similar to that of the Anglo-Saxon model. But the governance of large stockholders had ended by the late 19th or early 20th century, and the governance of salaried managers was established by the First World War. What enabled this change were the stabilization manoeuvres in stockholding, often associated with the wartime or post-war periods. Although we could add topics such as mutual, inter-firm stockholding, employee stockholding, or the main bank system for a complete understanding of Japanese corporate governance, our study reveals that Anglo-Saxon structures did not necessarily prevail within pre-war big businesses. Contemporary corporate governance in Japan did not emerge suddenly under the wartime regime, but needs to be understood in its much longer historical context.

Notes

1   T.Okazaki and M.Okuno (eds), *Gendai Nihon Kezai System no Genryu* (*The Origin of the Contemporary Japanese Enterprise System*) (1993); T.Okazaki, 'Nihon ni Okeru Corporate Governance no Hatten' ('The Development of Corporate Governance in Japan'), in M.Aoki and R.Dore (eds), *System Toshiteno Nihon Kigyo* (*Japanese Enterprise as a System*) (1995).

2   H.Miyajima, 'Zaikai Tuiho to Keiesha no Senbatsu' ('The Purge of Managers and the Selection of Managers'), in J.Hashimoto (ed.), *Niohon Kigyo System no Sengo-shi* (*Post-War History of the Japanese Enterprise System*) (1996).

3   M.Miyamoto and T.Abe, 'Meiji no Shisan-ka to Kaisha Seido' ('Wealthy Persons and the Company System in the Meiji Period'), in M.Miyamoto and T.Abe (eds), *Nippon Keiei-shi 2: Keiei Kakushin to Kôgyôka* (*Business History of Japan, II: Innovation and Industrialization*) (1995).

4   T.Imuta, 'Meiji-ki ni Okeru Kabushiki Kaisha no Hatten to Kabunushi-sô no Keisei' ('The Development of Joint-Stock Companies in the Meiji Period and the Formation of Shareholding'), in Institute of Economics, Osaka City University (ed.), *Meiji-ki ni Okeru*

Keizai Hatten to Keizai Shutai (*Economic Development in the Meiji Period and its Promoters*) (1968); H.Morikawa, *Nippon Keiei-shi* (*Business History of Japan*) (1981); M.Miyamoto, 'Sangyô-ka to Kaisha Seido no Hatten' ('Japanese Industrialization and the Development of the Company System'), in S.Nishikawa and T.Abe (eds), *Nippon Keizai-shi 4: Sangyô-ka no Jidai* (*Economic History of Japan, iv: The Age of Industrialization*), vol.1 (1990).

5   Morikawa, *Nippon Keiei-shi*; H.Morikawa, 'Salaried Managers', in W.D.Wray (ed.), *Managing Industrial Enterprise* (1989).

6   For the history of Osaka Cotton Spinning Company in the Meiji period (1868-1912), see N.Takamura, 'Osaka Bôseki Kaisha', in K.Yamaguchi (ed.), *Nippon Sangyô Kinyû-shi Kenkyû: Bôseki Kinyû Hen* (*The Study of Industrial Finance in Japan: the Volume on Spinning Firms*) (1970); M.Miyamoto, 'The Products and Market Strategies of the Osaka Cotton Spinning Company, 1883-1914', in *Japanese Yearbook on Business History, Vol.5.* (1988); Tôyô Bôseki Kabushiki Kaisha (ed.), *Hyaku-nen-shi: Toyobo* (*100 Years' History of Toyobo*), vol.1 (1986).

7   T.Yamanobe, 'Bôseki-gyô Kochaku Shihon Shôkyaku oyobi Son'eki Keisan ni Kansuru Shisetsu' ('My Opinions on the Depreciation of Fixed Capital in the Spinning Industry and the Profit and Loss Account'), in *Bôseki Rengô Geppô* (1889), 2.

8   Y.Uno (ed.), *Yamanobe Takeo Kun Shôden* (*Short Biography of Mr Takeo Yamanobe*) (1918).

9   Interview of Mr. Katsumasa Okamura in Shibusawa Seien Kinen Zaidan Ryûmonsha (ed.), *Shibusawa Eiichi Denki Shiryô* (*Materials for the Biography of Eiichi Shibusawa*), vol.10 (1956).

10 Minutes, General Meeting of Stockholders of Osaka Cotton Spinning Company (Toyo Cotton Spinning Company Archives).

11 For the history of Nippon Life Assurance, see Japan Business History Institute (ed), *The 100-Year History of Nippon Life* (1991).

12 Interview of Mr.Naoharu Kataoka (Nippon Life Insurance Archives).

13 For the history of this company in the Meiji period, see the Japan Business History Institute (ed.), *100-Year History.*

14 Minutes, General Meeting of Stockholders of NLA (Nippon Life Insurance Archives).

15 Minutes, General Meeting of Stockholders of NLA (Nippon Life Insurance Archives).

16 Minutes, General Meeting of Stockholders of NLA (Nippon Life Insurance Archives).

17 For more on this affair, see Nippon Life Insurance Company (ed.), *Nippon Seimei Hyaku-nen-shi* (*The 100 Years' History of Japan Life Insurance Company*), vol.1 (1992).

18 Nippon Life Insurance Company, *Nippon Seimei Hyaku-nen-shi.*

19 Minutes, General Meetings of stockholders of NLA (Nippon Life Insurance Archives).

20 Minutes, General Meetings of stockholders of NLA (Nippon Life Insurance Archives).

21 For more on this affair, see Nippon Life Insurance Company, *Nippon Seimei Hyaku-nen shi*; I.Ogawa, 'Osaka Seimei no Seiho Nottori to Nippon Seimei no Taiô' ('The Takeover of Life Insurance Companies by Osaka Life Insurance Company and the Countermeasures of NLA'), *Hoken-gaku Zasshi* (*Journal of Insurance Studies*) (1987).

22 One person who entered NLA in the Taisho Era and was later appointed as a managerial staff member testified as follows: 'We must recognize that thirty years in the eighty-year history of NLA were entirely the age of Kataoka. During this age, the company was reigned over by Kataoka and the managers of Kataoka's subordinates.' See H.Nagao, 'Ichi Seiho Shain no Kaiso' ('Memoir of a Salaried Man in a Life Insurance Company'), *Inshuaransu* (*Insurance*) (1978).

Chapter 3

Corporate Governance, Business Organization and Competitiveness: British Business in the Inter-War Period

Robert Fitzgerald

Introduction: Firms, Structures, and Capabilities

The notion of corporate governance has emerged as an issue of far-reaching import, dealing with the proper and efficient conduct of individual businesses, and arguing the virtues and vices of the differing national systems and the circumstances that shape such conduct. Economic questions about finance, ownership, and management are intertwined with political dimensions, such as laws, regulation, and government policy; there are, additionally, the many social dimensions, as represented by notions of responsibilities and fair rewards. The importance of governance rests on its ability to embrace many aspects of business, and codes of best-practice conduct reflecting the breadth of these concerns have sought to cope with the consequences of spectacular corporate failures. Beyond consideration of individual firms, commentators have noted variations in national models of capitalism, seeking links with the long-term performance of whole economies. Britain and the US are seen as similar enough to contrast with Japan and Germany, the benefits of external shareholding, capital markets, and the profit-motive competing with committed investors, insider control, and the mixed objectives of several stakeholders. The range of arguments and perspectives can, therefore, be confusing, and the definition of 'corporate governance' uncertain. Nonetheless, the political and economic significance that has been attached to the issue is undeniable.[1]

One influential assessment of corporate governance and its implications is derived from the work of economists, and concentrates on the ownership of giant, dominant companies, the rights of shareholders, and on their ability to instil profit-maximising disciplines. By focusing on the nature of financial markets, it is concerned with the mobility of capital and investor incentives. Shareholders will, it is argued, switch their capital whenever resources are under-utilised or more profitable opportunities arise. As a result, their decisions maximise efficiency and output for a given set of technological or economic conditions. To achieve these desirable objectives, knowledge within financial markets about investment opportunities and the internal competencies of companies is, in the accepted jargon, 'perfect'. Such an analysis, of course, is best suited to the cases of large, private corporations operating in Anglo-American style economies, in which shareholders, following a profit-motive, use their control of ownership to motivate and influence appointed managers. It tends to overlook the governance of public and mutual organizations; partnerships, smaller firms, and family enterprises; and subsidiaries. It ignores also the contribution of networks, business groups, and cross-shareholdings, and, finally, the role of laws, regulation and government in the maintenance of governance. By focusing on the relationship between 'external' owners and 'internal' executives, this influential perspective conceals the detail and complexities of management and operational process, and the connections with competitiveness and innovation are not demonstrated evidently and specifically.[2]

Criticisms of this standpoint on corporate governance are well known. Schumpeter noted that technologies could not axiomatically be assimilated by every firm in presumed optimum market conditions, because they were the product of complex organizations and firm-specific skills that are difficult to replicate.[3] Companies use technologies with a strategic and entrepreneurial intent, and, in seeking to dominate as well as transform an industry, they do not willingly reveal or share their competitive advantages. The emphasis on financial markets and external funding, by overlooking the central role of the companies themselves, provides a scant portrayal of strategy formation, decision-making, and governance structures within firms themselves. The rights, influence and control of one interest group, shareholders, are too narrow a base to determine the sources of economic growth and welfare. Market equilibrium outcomes for a given set of technologies and conditions ignore the crucial question of innovation and change, and their relationship to the corporate resource allocation devised by management. Productivity stems from an investment in firm-specific, not predominantly market-accessible, assets; it emerges more directly from organizational control, as opposed to market-based incentives.

Companies succeed by accruing expertise and competencies in particular technologies and processes, and devise approaches that cope with uncertainty, the perfect knowledge of markets and other enterprises being unobtainable. They acquire these competencies over a long period, and use them to entrench a specific strategic or market position that distinguishes them from competitors. It is corporate-based expertise, established procedural routines, and learning capabilities that achieve rising productivity, economic change, and growth. These competencies are not easily altered; nor are commitments and mistakes easily reversible. The complexity behind the creation and management of capabilities places responsibility and control with insiders and employees. For many, therefore, the link between shareholder value, competitiveness, and economic development is too readily accepted, and governance within businesses has a greater significance than the agency problems encountered by shareholders. It also clear, moreover, that the 'irreversibility' of numerous corporate capabilities makes the sequence of decision-making and resource-allocation a vital research topic, and their accretion has to be understood over a substantial period of time. For both these reasons, the subject of business history can make a unique contribution to debates on corporate governance and its implications.

When considering the relevant issues, business historians frequently refer to the work of Penrose. She focuses in the main on the topic of insider control and on the development of professional management. Penrose views the firm as a pool of resources operating in an administrative framework; internal management is chiefly responsible for developing and utilising a unique set of capabilities; and any lack of managerial resources or talent will place constraints on growth.[4] Her ideas find echoes in those of Chandler, a business historian who has made an unquestionable contribution to our understanding of corporate governance. He links the success of growth industries with the emergence of large-scale, joint stock enterprises, the strategic control of managers, and hierarchical, coordinated structures. The investment in managerial resources enabled the full exploitation of new technologies, and captured the rising returns to scale and scope in both production and marketing.[5] O'Sullivan, in turn, draws upon the Chandler thesis, but explores the theoretical issues of governance and their consequences more explicitly. She considers the relationship between economic development, innovation, organizational coordination, and the strategic outcomes of corporate resource allocation. There is an emphasis on the making of investment decisions; the nature of those investments; and the use of returns for further investment versus their use for other purposes, including shareholder dividends.[6]

Historians, economists, students of management, and policy-makers have particular interests, but identify a number of interrelated topics. There are, firstly, the rights, duties and functions of owners, and the degree to which such owners should or can interfere in the management of firms, or, alternatively, the extent they might determine managerial objectives. Answers depend on the appropriate boundaries between investors and managers, but, in addition, on the 'balancing' role of other 'stakeholders', such as government, communities, employees, suppliers, distributors, and customers. The nature of ownership influences its functions: in the Anglo-American system, shareholding came to provide the needed investment funds and long-term finance; in Japan and Germany, on the other hand, banks and other financial institutions became committed investors in enterprises. From the 1960s onwards, the rise of the institutional investor on the British and US stock markets has exerted sway over corporations, creating an environment proportionately more favourable to financial engineering and short-termism. For many commentators, it also encouraged non-synergic mergers. Such trends weakened, it is contended, insider control, organizational integration, financial commitment, and the affinity between strategy, learning processes, research, training, and entrenched routines within companies. For a while, competitive advantages appeared to pass to the so-termed 'stakeholding' forms of capitalism in Germany and Japan. To understand the full implications of ownership, governance, and management, business historians, ultimately, added comparative insights to their longitudinal perspective on the nature of control, strategy, and decision-making, most obviously in the work of Chandler, Cassis and O'Sullivan.[7] The causal link between insider control, innovation, and competitiveness – strongly advocated by O'Sullivan in her preference for the German model over the US – seems less certain with the passing of the 1990s and the reversal in national economic fortunes. For many others, the adaptability offered by stock markets, corporate restructuring and profit incentives – the much criticised short-termism – has been the source of recent Anglo-American strength. We are left, then, not with a preference for one system over another, but with the need to understand the role of differing systems according to stages of economic development, historical circumstances, technological requirements, economic climate, and a range of other factors.

Another key element of the corporate governance debate is, secondly, the question of monitoring, disclosure, the assessment of decision-making, and guarding against the possibilities of 'moral hazard' or corporate collapse. Shortcomings have been found in almost every type of business and in most leading economies, although wrong-doing and deception have to be separated from the mistakes and risks entailed in every business enterprise. In the Anglo-US systems, the reporting mechanisms available to shareholders are pivotal here; in Germany and Japan, banks and other financial institutions have been allotted monitoring duties. The need for such scrutiny is associated with the separation of ownership and direct control, the growing size and complexity of business, and the professionalization of management. It is linked, thirdly, to the more overlooked aspect of corporate governance: the quality of personnel; management hierarchy; and the nature and processes of decision-making. As O'Sullivan and others have argued, it is this dimension that determines the ability of large-scale companies to undertake organizational learning, innovation, and change; the integration and motivation of all employees; and the assimilation of innovation, strategy and operational routines. It is a perspective that accords with current resource-based interpretations of the firm.[8] The character of ownership and financing controls the ways in which management is externally accountable, and also influences the objectives and capabilities of management. Yet, whatever the impact, it is the internal elements of the firm that are central to its long-term competitiveness.

This paper focuses on a set of inter-related issues: the organization and leading personnel of certain highly-criticised, large-scale British companies during the inter-war period; the connections with ownership; the monitoring of decision-making; internal control mechanisms; the relationship between these factors and competitive success; and the extent a possible 'failure' in governance and management contributed, comparatively speaking, to British industrial decline. The control of British businesses in the first half of the twentieth century has been assailed emphatically. Chandler argues that, in general, founding families and owner-managers remained in control longer than their US compettitors, and that their companies failed to develop the professionalism and managerial hierarchies associated with increasingly-complex technological and organizational demands. The inability to distinguish between strategy-formulation and operations, it is stated, especially hindered the ability of British manufacturers to undertake long-term planning and corporate change. Interestingly, O'Sullivan follows Lazonick's greater stress, not on the insufficiently-clear separation of direction and routines, but on the need for these functions to be organizationally integrated.[9] The two positions are not mutually exclusive, but may suggest some imprecision or difference in the case against British industry. Chandler believes, therefore, that the external dimensions of corporate governance were influential, because ownership was not distinguished from management. On the other hand, the principal-agency dilemmas of shareholders, so prominent in theoretical terms, appear barely relevant to this portrayal of British industry before the Second World War. In many important cases, the poles of insider versus external control did not exist; instead, the rise of powerful institutional investors within the stock exchange was, as in the US, a marked occurrence of the post-war years. There were, however, examples of tensions and difficulties between criticised executives and other interested 'insiders', including partner companies and banks, notably in the 1920s.

However, as we legitimately give due weight to the insider dimensions of governance, questions about the historical evidence remain. It is not entirely clear how the concept of governance and managerial control might fill the empty 'black box' supposedly at the centre of neo-classical, market-orientated views of economic efficiency. Theories advocating the importance of administrative frameworks and integrated structures have to be linked to evidence showing their impact on crucial competencies, such as strategic planning and implementation, decision-making, research and development, the enhancement of human resources, or operational systems. They must, additionally and ultimately, affect a firm's ability to innovate, adapt and compete. Each example would by necessity be a complex story of many factors, and conclusions are rarely exact or beyond interpretation, including those to be made about Britain. Furthermore, notions of 'organizational integration' or 'managerial resources' are too generalised to cope with the reality of differing governance types, each suited to specific periods, countries, product markets, or even firms. The support for 'integrated managerial enterprise' or 'multidivisional hierarchy' as the basis for competitive success is more precise, but, as we shall argue, more easily challengeable. To appreciate the aptness of an ownership and managerial structure, the history, competitive position, and product markets of each enterprise should be assessed. Lastly, the stress on governance and insider control means that the context of business and economic conditions is ignored, and, however strong the strategic intent, the ability of firms to transform markets has natural and variable limitations.

Many key firms located in Britain's staple industries, it is stated, could not fully adapt to changes in international and domestic demand during the 1920s and 1930s, because loosely-coordinated structures and a weak strategic, headquarters function hindered schemes of rationalization. These British holding companies have been reproached as the worst examples of such weaknesses, because inadequate central direction and integration enabled uncompetitive constituent firms and detrimental family-control to continue. As a group, they are seen as handicapped in comparison to international competitors and to the rising model of integrated, managerial enterprise; a lack of professional personnel, organizational hierarchy, and formal procedures were inappropriate to the challenges of modern industry.[10] It follows, too, that ownership and governance structures did not provide the means or the incentives to improve capabilities and performance. Other judgements have been less definitive or condemnatory, noting improvements to early administrative failings.[11] In several key cases, multiple directorships and particular personalities increased the influence of parent firms within the subsidiaries of holding companies, and the gradual evolution of centralized personnel and accounting policies had a similar effect. The pattern of practice across firms became, in fact, complex to interpret. By the 1920s, the textile firm of Coats had a noticeably 'hybrid' structure: it had defined product and geographical divisions, as would a managerial enterprise, yet they oversaw legally-separate subsidiaries, as would a holding company.[12]

Two prominent cases of the holding company form in Britain were the shipbuilding, engineering and armaments sector and the textile industry. These examples have been depicted as monopolistic in intent, inhibiting industrial rationalization, and, by implication, the consolidation of managerial enterprises. Criticisms have emerged from our growing understanding of the importance of managerial enterprise. The successful businesses described by Chandler contain an organizational hierarchy governing an incorporated, unitary enterprise capable of achieving economies of scale and scope.[13] Others hold that the perceived utility of managerial enterprise has tended to disregard the advantages of family firms, business groups, alliances, and holding companies, through a stress on their negative aspects. It might be argued that the pervasiveness of the holding structure in large-scale British companies – or, indeed, in Japanese or German businesses – suggests the possibility of advantages. To what extent does the evidence validate criticism of a deficiency in organization and managerial competence? Did a system of inter-connected firms, subsidiaries and personal networks provide some form of supervision and monitoring by various 'insiders'? Did governance mechanisms allow or prevent corrective measures in instances of failure?

The Shipbuilding and Engineering Industry

The British shipbuilding, engineering and armaments industry of the inter-war period is often and justifiably paraded as an example of competitive nemesis. The firm of Beardmore has become well-known for the commercial difficulties that challenged its existence and for the ineffectiveness of its managerial response in the 1920s. It cannot be criticised as unwilling to invest and build modern facilities; this is not a case of enterprise conservatism, but arguably one of incautious risk-taking. Beardmore began the construction of its Dalmuir shipyard, near Glasgow, in 1900, and, having run out of credit, it was compelled to bring in the Sheffield firm of Vickers, Son & Maxim, as it was then called.[14] The new site was well-equipped and designed on a grand scale, mainly to meet Royal Navy orders, and it allowed the assembly of whole ships, from hulls to fixtures and ordnance. Dalmuir also had the world's largest fitting-out basin. While building these marine engineering facilities, Beardmore diversified further: it opportunistically bought shares in Masons Gas Power Company, and, in a move intended to assist expansion, it secured supplies through the purchase of the Mossend steel works. Vickers, which on paper had a controlling interest, was worried by the growth and expenditure plans, and attempted to impose restraints.[15] By the end of the First World War, William Beardmore, Lord Invernairn, had forced through expansion via subsidiaries into aircraft manufacture, locomotives, steam and oil-powered engines, buses, lorries, taxis, motor-cycles, automobiles, and steel, as well as mining and quarrying.[16]

Powerful owners failed, therefore, to control its executive and management, possibly, according to the principles of corporate governance, to the long-term detriment of their investment. On the other hand, the strategy of diversification had a commercial logic for contemporary heavy industry firms, and Vickers itself, ironically, was one of Britain's biggest examples of conglomeration. The tensions were matters of personality and trust, and worries over the scale and financial implications of William Beardmore's policies in relation to his resources, not the underlying principle of rapid diversification through the flexible investment and management mechanisms of the holding company. The post-war boom and declining military orders seemingly justified Beardmore's acquisition of subsidiaries and its multiple product markets. But the unforeseen economic circumstances of the 1920s soon left it over-capitalized and unprofitable, even compared to local rivals, and the well-documented sequence of events that beset the company took place during 1926-29. Vickers sold its interest, the Treasury used its leverage under the Trade Facility Acts, and Invernairn was ousted.[17]

The government, as keeper of the tax revenues, was, like Vickers, a major and influential stakeholder. If the personal capitalism prevalent at Beardmore did not demonstrate a lack of entrepreneurship or investment – that is, innovation – the owner's autocratic, unbending style was inappropriate in the depressed conditions of the 1920s. The company was unable to achieve adequate throughput in its subsidiaries, and soon suffered from its policy of diversification. As an armaments manufacturer, Beardmore had been faced with the cessation of hostilities, and been presented with the opportunities of the post-war boom. The firm formed a number of vertical and horizontal corporate links, and these offered numerous potential advantages to shipbuilders. The unpredictable and uneven nature of the industry favoured diversification into related or even unrelated products, and the creation of forward and backward networks facilitated supplies in good times and sales orders when conditions were bad.[18] Group structures and holding companies potentially offered economies of scope, secured markets, assisted control over materials and costs, dispersed risks, and enhanced financial stability. The uncertainty of markets did not fit well with the 'perfect knowledge' models of economists.

Despite the advantages of a conglomerate strategy, especially for a capital goods or heavy industry firm, specific charges can still be levelled at Beardmore:

that managerial resources were inadequate for a firm of its size and diversity, and that, as well as the chairman having no personal office, there was no headquarters function. As 'outsiders' could not easily appreciate the range of its business activities, 'insider' control mechanisms obtained greater import. It is worth noting that the main company did have a managing director, a secretariat, and an accounting section by the 1920s.[19] In these measures, therefore, there is some recognition of the need to monitor the performance of subsidiaries, but, unfortunately, the level of evidential detail means conclusions are elusive. Yet the headquarter's role may be reasonably judged as unsophisticated compared even to other contemporary conglomerates, where greater degrees of synergy and cohesion were created by the centralization of specific managerial and monitoring functions.

As we shall see, these mechanisms supported the aims of diversified business interests, effective plant-level management, and a network of cooperative institutional links, which could all provide vital organizational capabilities. Once more, whether Beardmore had appropriate levels of managers and technicians within its operational units is an open question, for which there is little documentary evidence. Slaven characterises shipbuilding firms on the Clyde as possessing estimating and costing departments, and a works department or a number of production departments. In 1899, the Sheffield firm of John Brown bought the Clydebank shipyard, near Glasgow, and, before the First World War, it was organized functionally with nineteen departments, and, below them, the engine works alone had sixteen separate units. Qualified people included draughtsmen, naval architects, and engineers, and line management came under the departmental heads, some of whom were appointed to the main board. Thomas Bell, a major figure in the company, emerged as managing director at Clydebank in 1909, and held the post for twenty-six years.[20] He seems to have been regarded as an example of professional and effective management. In a final assembly process such as shipbuilding, flow and coordination at the level of individual plants was a major task for management. Operating and tactical decisions required to implement policy were clearly delegated to departmental heads, and below them in the yards were hierarchies of supervisors and workers.[21] Like Beardmore at Dalmuir, John Brown at Clydebank became the shipbuilding section of a vertically-integrated industrial empire.

Beardmore's decline and financial pressures undoubtedly stirred personal conflicts and a bitter battle for control, damaging the main company and relations with and between subsidiaries.[22] The dismissal of Invernairn was drawn out, and his removal from the boards of minor companies was even more complex and difficult.[23] Low demand and a lack of throughput seriously weakened several of these subsidiaries, and the uncompetitive prices they quoted as suppliers to associated firms disrupted agreements and mutual relations within the group.[24] Debtors were finally forced to act, and the Bank of England, representing the banking industry and the government, was amongst the stakeholders. They appointed Hans Reincke as chairman in February 1930, and he summed up nearly a decade of failings by pointing to the old guard's lack of foresight, poor management, and the failure to rationalize.[25] In assessing the Beardmore firm over a longer term, however, some acknowledgement should be given to later reforms, which were based on a general reorganization of Glasgow shipbuilding, and the reinforcement of management within the Parkhead steel forge and other subsidiaries.[26] Under Reincke, the functions and purposes of all linked firms and major manufacturing investments were investigated and stated; departments overseeing operations such as Locomotives or Commercial Vehicles did exist, and were administered by designated managers; and revitalization plans were devised for each department.[27] During the 1930s, stakeholders had been able to change Beardmore's executive control, and, as a consequence, planning, monitoring, personnel, and administration were all improved.

Vickers, intimately connected with the history of Beardmore, had its origins in steel and armaments, then engaged in naval engineering, and became during these years one of Britain's largest conglomerates. It shared Beardmore's strategy of manufacturing everything needed for a warship, ultimately moving into many forms of ordnance, and it anticipated the military use of motorised vehicles by buying car-maker Wolseley. Vickers was one of Britain's most active multinationals in the years before the First World War, establishing overseas plants to meet the orders of host governments. In the immediate period after 1918, its operations in Britain included locomotives; boilers; turbines; engines of all kinds; machinery and machine tools; gas meters; furniture; and toys; in addition to ships, ordnance, and cars. It acquired, additionally, train-lighting, refrigerator, and electric cable companies, and then Metropolitan Carriage & Wagon and British Westinghouse, both by themselves huge concerns that were merged into Metropolitan-Vickers.[28] Economic conditions and the low throughput prevalent in so much of British heavy industry troubled the conglomerate during the 1920s, although Chandler accepts that the company had a well-established tradition of hiring experienced and talented executives and technicians, whilst remaining a family firm.[29]

In the restructuring of 1925, subsidiary boards were founded to coordinate the three major activities of armaments and shipbuilding, other industrial products, and finance, and, over the next three years, the firm underwent a period of disinvestment.[30] Able, non-family managers were recruited to take control from the family, and Vickers re-appeared as a profitable and financially-strong company, despite the difficulties of its previous ventures. The company fails to concord with suggested British stereotypes, and relied on interlocking managerial skills and a cabinet-style governance, as opposed to the flair of any individual.[31] In October 1927, it was merged to form Vickers-Armstrong, through which it could bolster the weaker Armstrong-Whitworth, and gain from the rationalization of armaments manufacture.[32] Gauging the depth and quality of Vickers' management at plant-level remains as difficult as other cases, but Chandler presents British Westinghouse, an acquired subsidiary with US origins, as a benchmark by which to judge British companies in the inter-war years.[33] Certainly, ownership factors or holding company structures did not inhibit the development or maintenance of professional management and administrative systems. Yet, as ever, Britain offers mixed evidence, and Armstrong-Whitworth's lack of success, even during the favourable years before the Great War, contrasts with the case of Vickers. It had been weakened by an autocratic management style, until administrative reforms modelled on its rival were introduced in 1911. Diversification into hydroelectricity and Canadian pulp and paper milling further complicated the difficulties confronting its traditional steel and engineering businesses in the 1920s.[34]

Insider networks were important in an industry in which regional concentration, vertical interdependence, horizontal diversification, rationalization, and merger were characteristic. As noted earlier, boards had connections with banks, which sometimes assumed the role of creditors and stakeholders, and with government departments, including the Treasury as well as the Admiralty. They all influenced the nature of corporate governance. Furthermore, through a series of acquisitions and rationalizations over the inter-war period as a whole, the role of the professional manager increased. From the turn of the century to the years following the First World War, several British steel, shipbuilding and armaments manufacturers had founded diversified conglomerates, firstly in response to growing naval and military expenditure, and subsequently in an effort to transfer wartime profits to peacetime commerce. At first, inter-firm cooperation was necessary to joint ventures and projects, supported the utilization of technology and labour, and assisted negotiations with government; ultimately, it might lead to mergers and rationalization, whilst securing supplies and smoothing the volatile nature of demand. The Clydebank shipyard operated within the John Brown combine, but existed in a wider network. Before the First World War, the group undertook cooperative ventures with Cammell Laird, Fairfield, Vickers, and Armstrong-Whitworth; cultivated independent and joint contacts at the Admiralty; and merged with the Belfast shipbuilders of Harland & Wolff. Whatever the assumed weaknesses of the headquarters function, John Brown's fortunes, institutional relationships, and reputation were all inextricably linked, and the soundness of the Clydebank management was quoted as a source of strength.[35] The Scottish shipbuilders, Lithgow, moved into steelmaking during the 1920s, and extended its engineering interests, finally buying Fairfield, a competitor, in 1935. Fairfield was, in turn, connected to the Anchor Line, which provided links with the maritime transport industry.[36] In a parallel to the close relationships between Japanese shipping, shipbuilding, and metal manufacturing firms, Lord Inchcape's Peninsular and Oriental line acquired the Glasgow yard of Alexander Stephen and the Steel Company of Scotland just after the First World War. It is fair to add that Stephen's link with a major customer hardly sustained adequate throughput in the subsequent, depressed decade, when only one third of its capacity was used, even if its commonplace troubles would have been difficult to deflect.[37]

Harland & Wolff, with its well-connected chairman Lord Pirrie, established connections with Lithgow and the marine engineering company of Weir, and also joined with the Royal Mail Shipping Group.[38] It has been said that the expertise and focus of the Harland & Wolff management were located at the level of the plant, and this should be viewed as a strength, not as an automatic deficiency. Colville, a family-owned but professionally managed enterprise, emerged as a formative influence in the restructuring of the Scottish steel industry. By 1920, it was wholly owned by Harland and Wolff, yet it was under the direction of the well-respected Sir John Craig, a career manager.[39] In 1930, it acquired a competitor, John Dunlop & Co., from Sir James Lithgow and his brother, Henry, who then both joined the Colville board, and the shipbuilding firm later used its position as a major customer to merge the Steel Company of Scotland and the Lanarkshire Steel Company with Colville.[40] The reconstruction of the Royal Mail Group between 1931-36 is quoted as an example of a committed relationship between industry and financial institutions. The Midland Bank provided substantial credit, and, as a consequence of events rather than intention, it became deeply involved in business strategy and plans.[41] Sir James Lithgow, moreover, had been a leading figure in the reorganization of Beardmore in the late 1920s, and his appointments as its director and finally as chairman were merely further confirmation of his pivotal role in the business world of Glasgow.[42] Clearly, his personal reputation in the industry and within a network of insiders assisted the stabilization and development of the business.

Cross-ownership, multiple directorships, banking links, and government contacts constituted a business and information network, and the 'insider' control of owners and executives provided some form of monitoring, and, in some key cases, mechanisms for rectifying policies. With the growth of conglomerates, from the turn of the century, the connections between businesses grew, although it is economic difficulties from the later 1920s onwards that drew in the banks and government, so instigating rationalization schemes and several changes in board membership. Despite being a family firm, Vickers is credited with showing especially early signs of professionalization, which assisted its internal governance, decision-making, and growth strategies within a holding company structure. Across many large companies, by the end of the 1930s, the appointment of professional managers complemented improved administrative procedures that could monitor and assist the operations of the subsidiaries.[43] The firm of Beardmore, in particular, indicates the extent of change in personnel and practice. Consideration of internal governance and systems did not alter the overall holding company structures, because they suited the product markets of shipbuilding and armaments. They assisted rapid expansion in the growth period to 1920, and supported the development of non-armaments businesses in the immediate post-war depression. Diverse operations seemingly enabled companies engaged in capital goods projects and fluctuating export markets the possibility of spreading risks and balancing cash-flows. In terms of furthering new businesses and products, British conglomerates had been ambitious, and it is interesting that, for their reluctance to develop the heavy and chemicals industries of Japan, the old *zaibatsu* of the inter-war period have, perhaps ironically, been described as 'conservative'.[44] Ownership and governance had not limited the capacity for entrepreneurial change and commercial innovation. The continuing length and the depth of the problems confronting the industry in the inter-war period, however, required more than an improvement in management, organization, or governance. Although the industry had furthered these capabilities by the middle or late 1930s, it is arguable that better trading conditions, tariff protection, and war preparations had the greater impact on its fortunes.

Management and the Textile Industry

The sudden decline in markets and the problems of rationalization and management were 'much the same', says Chandler, in British textiles as they were in shipbuilding and steel.[45] It has been noted, not unfairly, that some of the federations that were created at the turn of the century were collusive in intent and lacking in internal dynamism.[46] So, early judgements of these textile conglomerates were harsh: the majority of mergers, seeking to protect the vested interests of unreformed firms, were seen as failing to produce any fundamental internal and organizational changes.[47] The continuation of family ownership, entrenched within monopolistic but poorly-functioning federations, prevented the professionalization of management. Confusion seems to have infused policy-making and central administration at the Bleachers Association, and its board of directors apparently imitated an assembly devoid of any unified purpose.[48] As Chandler is highly critical of British corporate structures and the holding company in particular, he contends that their legal consolidation did not in general promote administrative coordination, investment, or managerial recruitment, despite instances of joint purchasing, research, accounting procedures, or overseas transplants. He acknowledges that the Bleachers Association, Calico Printers Association, Bradford Dyers, J. & P. Coats, and the Linen Thread Company all enlarged 'their small corporate offices' in the inter-war years, but blames them for leaving constituent firms in charge of purchasing, processing and sales. In integrating spinning with weaving, and in founding marketing networks, Whitworth & Mitchell, Joshua Hoyle, and Horrocks, Crewdson are quoted as exceptional.[49] They are, nonetheless, significant exceptions. Chandler admits that the potential returns to scale in natural fibre manufacturing were not extensive, but looks for vertical integration and coordination between production-stages as a means of increasing throughput and lowering costs. On the other hand, as he states, mergers followed by rationalization were not used to found successful textile enterprises in either the U.S. or Germany.[50] Were British firms, nonetheless, slow in unifying the manufacture of yarn and cloth? Did this greatly affect the competitiveness of the whole cotton textile industry, or were there counterbalancing efficiencies in regional clustering, efficient market mechanisms, and international trading networks? Smaller scale, family businesses did not necessarily gain from firm-specific marketing channels. All of these issues are, in fact, part of a contentious debate, but we can more easily ask if the combines were able to gain the benefits of vertical integration and coordination between production-stages.[51]

The Linen Thread Company was founded between 1898-1900, and eventually linked six British and Irish firms and their U.S. subsidiaries. At the main holding company, board committees were formed to oversee sales, finance, or manufacturing, and a variety of departments were established to oversee selling, bookkeeping, commercial information, invoicing and other functions. There was an early intention to systematize gradually any activity that might benefit from centralization, although the combine was wary of 'drastic changes' that could cause greater disorganization. In 1898, the several sales offices inherited from the constituent companies were rationalized, and, when sales staff were placed under the control of the new Glasgow headquarters, resistance was encountered. As a result, it was decided to consider 'steps to secure, without further loss of time, the advantages that the formation of the Linen Thread Company Ltd was intended to secure'. In order to improve the coordination of national and international sales and invoicing, member firms were ordered to bring their books to the central office, and a Statistical and Information Department was founded. Although individual factory managers continued to arrange their own purchasing, they were not allowed to hold more than six months of stock without the prior permission of the central Manufacturing Committee. The headquarters determined the remuneration of salaried mill staff, and output was rationalized to a small extent by the closure of the Springburn Mill in Ireland in 1899. Although a holding company, LTC was managed through a mixture of decentralized production and centralized support functions, and this structure remained in force during the inter-war years.[52] From an early point, therefore, the new holding company established extensive monitoring mechanisms across the subsidiaries, and developed the ability to disseminate administrative information. Staffing policy and pay were placed within the ambit of the headquarters function, and resources were devoted to obtaining economies of scope in the function of marketing and, to a lesser extent, purchasing. Despite complex ownership and external governance structures, and continued family and vested ownership, internal management and control were extended. From an early point in LTC's history, there appears a strong desire to gain the advantages of a large-scale organization, while the holding company structure accounted for product diversity and technologies within separate production units.

Additional, if not conclusive, evidence suggests that early changes at Calico Printers Association, Bradford Dyers Association, English Sewing Cotton, and Tootal, Broadhurst and Lee addressed significant managerial issues.[53] Furthermore, Payne believes that another large, merged company, J. & P. Coats, evolved a 'highly efficient bureaucratic structure', and that its board oversaw the central direction of statistical information, buying, selling, and accounting. Coats is an example of British success, and, ignorant of the strictures against personal capitalism, it fused family ownership with professionalized management, as, indeed, had Vickers.[54] The firm was converted into a limited company in 1890, the same year in which its marketing branch, the Central Agency, was founded. Five years later, Coats bought up its main rivals in Scotland and England, and owned mills in the U.S., Canada and Russia. With seventeen production units, 150 selling depots, and 21,000 employees across the globe, it was one of Britain's largest companies. Its reputation for efficiency and competitiveness made it a formative influence on the structure and organization of the textile combines that were established by 1900. Chandler acknowledges the achievements of its international joint sales agency, and the fact that, like the Fine Cotton Spinners and Doublers Association, it recruited non-family managers.[55] Coats was a cotton thread manufacturer, located in Paisley, near Glasgow, which under the chairmanship of Archibald Coats and his sales director, Ernst Philippi, built a worldwide reputation. The amalgamation of Coats was followed by the merger of fifteen other cotton, linen and silk threadmakers in 1897-99 to form the English Sewing Cotton Company, which was, in turn, linked to the American Thread Company. Coats was quick to invest in ESCC, and, in the early 1900s, it seconded Philippi to implement much-needed managerial reforms. At ESCC itself, the continued involvement of particular men from the constituent firms was recognized as a mistake, and some mills were rationalized. Its sales organization was placed within the Central Agency, which gained further from the enhanced market power and throughput.[56]

The linking of Coats, ESCC and American Thread created a powerful alliance within the international cotton thread industry, although disputes did arise between the parties concerned. Coats, moreover, secured its raw materials of cotton yarn by owning shares in the Fine Cotton Spinners and Doublers Association, and purchased a coalmine that provided energy supplies. FCSDA, founded in 1898, united some thirty-one Lancashire cotton firms, and followed the usual pattern of centralizing buying, selling and distribution functions. Executive power seems to have rested with the headquarters, which decided prices and allocated orders. The production mills retained their original identity, and their names were seen as carrying repute and customer confidence.[57] Coats held shares in the Calico Printers Association, where Philippi served as chairman of its Reconstruction Committee, introducing effective reforms out of initial organizational chaos, and finally being appointed a director. CPA's use of managerial expertise from Horrockses, Crewdson and the Bleachers Association, as well as Coats, was illustrative of the importance of vertical links.[58] Interestingly, when the Linen Thread Company was formed, it too sought advice from Coats and Philippi on matters of managerial organization. As well as arranging a loan, Philippi advised on the centralization of administrative and selling activities, and LTC's sales department was consequently modelled on the Central Agency. Coats, moreover, appointed a board member to LTC.[59] From its inception, Philippi's famed marketing subsidiary effectively replaced informal price and market share agreements between firms, and it acted to maintain the relative position of its constituent producers through an efficient, integrated, and rationalised selling system. In gaining the even and enhanced throughput of vertical integration, Coats and ESCC bolstered and facilitated the position of the production units and their managers within their respective holding companies.[60] Institutional links with linen thread companies, cotton manufacturers and calico finishers enabled the diversification of investments, but served, simultaneously, as a means of exchanging commercial and organizational information. They extended, furthermore, the number and nature of stakeholders with an interest in specific firms, so ultimately including allied manufacturers, suppliers, and buyers, all offering advice and appraisal.

Coats's continued interest in managerial structure, during the inter-war period, has received less attention than its earlier innovations. By the 1920s, Coats had a number of operating 'divisions', each supervised by an executive committee, and numerous sub-committees of the board oversaw matters such as cotton buying, training, employee welfare, capital expenditure, and advertising. In 1930, it was investigating the position and role of the subsidiaries, and it was intent on 'important internal changes in the organization of the parent Company'. The overall aim of reform was to improve managerial control and general efficiency, by formally deciding on the balance of responsibilities between the Glasgow headquarters and the constituent firms. Whilst central functions such as purchasing, finance, accounting, and technical assistance were to be improved, a holding company structure, it was decided, would continue to offer authority and operational freedom to the production units and the Central Agency. Nonetheless, the constitutions of local mill committees were re-drafted to comply with overall objectives, and a Quality Sub-Committee was charged with imposing production and product standards. The mills at Paisley and in England were grouped into a single subsidiary, United Thread Mills Ltd, which formed a new division alongside the businesses in Vienna, the US companies, the wholly-owned overseas subsidiaries, and associated foreign companies. Their policies were coordinated through separate executive committees. At Glasgow, a Merchandising Department was formed to consider those issues that fell between production and marketing, since this aspect of product differentiation, packaging and advertising had been poorly done, 'if at all'. The Central Agency was instructed to improve the flow of information on sales estimates, so that manufacturing output could be better planned, and the new Merchandising Department, taking over the central warehouse, sought to focus the mills on production issues. Crucially, Heads of Department were appointed to manage the new functionally-defined central activities. At the Glasgow headquarters, expenditure was subjected to more detailed scrutiny, and the Cost Section was converted into a separate department to service both the Finance and the Budget and Costs Sub-Committees.[61]

Despite Coats being, once more, an example of a family firm, the owners had overseen increasing levels of professionalisation and organizational complexity within their businesses, including a hierarchy of reporting and control. Through these mechanisms, they were able to enhance operations and decision-making, and, in turn, notable product and marketing improvements. In other words, and on the evidence available, external governance characteristics were in accord with insider control capabilities and requirements, and, therefore, facilitating strategic change. For what it is worth, Coats in this period seems in compliance with several theoretical perspectives on corporate governance, with the shareholders seemingly protected, and insider control producing effective managerial practice. Nonetheless, during the inter-war period, the Lancashire cotton industry did not in general demonstrate the same capacity for product and organizational innovation as the threadmakers, whose markets were more buoyant and less dependent upon batch production. The integration of spinning and weaving continued to lag behind the rising competitors of Japan and elsewhere. The establishment of the Lancashire Cotton Corporation in 1929 was partly brokered by the Bank of England, and its aim was to rationalize spinning and increase throughput. Because the LCC was not universally welcomed, the relationship between the main company and the mills was tense. As so much case evidence from many sources suggests, enforced merger was slow to achieve the anticipated synergies and associated scale and scope economies. Parliamentary legislation and compulsory levies did obtain, by the later 1930s, considerable progress in the concentration of the industry, but questions about Lancashire's ability to absorb new technology and co-ordinate overseas sales remained.[62] A large and important section of the cotton industry appeared unable to fulfil its organizational requirements, although its experience was not typical of other textile firms or sectors.

Authors have rightly stressed the role of horizontal merger in the formation of British textile holding companies, but acquisition did occur; and so, too, did vertical integration, chiefly through the coordination of production and marketing. Overall, claims of administrative failings appear exaggerated. Support activities such as accounting, finance, purchasing, and sales functions were centralized, when deemed beneficial. The control of production management at the level of mills may be explained by institutional legacy, but was sometimes counterbalanced by the involvement of board committees, divisions or a designated subsidiary at a higher level of managerial supervision. The economies of vertical integration and limited opportunities for scale returns were additional reasons. British textile companies proved able to adapt, and, through holding company structures, gained advantages from the coordination of support functions, the centralization of purchasing and marketing, and from vertical links between firms. There is extensive evidence of cross-ownership and multiple directorships, bringing, in several key examples, the direct transfer of managerial expertise and organizational reform. They reveal a network of owners and executives capable of providing a degree of monitoring, and, from the turn of the century onwards, the greater levels of professionalization within the large holding companies can be seen.

Holding Companies Compared

Were the organizational solutions of international competitors in the shipbuilding and textile sectors distinct from those of British companies? Although improvements can be illustrated, were these measures inadequate by comparison to solutions overseas? In fact, parallels in business strategy and structure can be found in Japanese enterprises, even though their success in the inter-war period is often contrasted. Differences in economic circumstances and in the role of government seem more determinant. The major *zaibatsu* that came to dominate the Japanese economy and its heavy industry were holding companies, within which managerial practices, authority structures, and levels of family involvement varied. But, generally, their headquarters operated only loose control over the many satellite subsidiaries that made up these business groups.[63] As in the case of British shipbuilding, the themes of diversification, batch production, inter-firm connections and works-level management influenced organizational structures. The *zaibatsu* were not predominant in cotton textiles, but scope economies, vertical linkages, and local control were factors which similarly maintained the holding company form.

One important example of business organization in the Japanese shipbuilding industry is Mistsubishi Goshi Kaisha, established as a public company in 1893. Operations were originally organized centrally, but what Morikawa calls 'operationally defined divisions' slowly evolved. Shipbuilding was encouraged by naval orders and successive wars, and by government legislation in the 1890s that subsidized long-distance shipping routes and technologically-advanced vessels. Links with shipping firms were important in assisting the growth of the industry. A major reorganization in 1908 changed the system of 'operationally defined divisions' into a system of formal 'operating divisions', which implemented their own regulations, accounting procedures, and personnel management, and were able to act in an independent manner. As it became involved in power plant, automobiles, heavy equipment, and planes, Mitsubishi Goshi founded a holding company structure, in which the key role of the subsidiary management was acknowledged. In 1917, it transformed its subsidiaries into public companies, and these were responsible for shipbuilding, iron and steel, banking, and trading. A further subsidiary in automobiles and aircraft was founded in 1920, and, in 1934, it was merged with the shipbuilding interests into the famed Mitsubishi Heavy Industries (MHI).[64] With its interests in banking and trading, the Mitsubishi group differed from the holding companies and networks of British shipbuilding, but organizational structures and principles had much in common.

By different route and timings, Mitsui came to be based on the holding company form. In 1893, Mitsui organized its diversified enterprises into four unlimited partnerships that recognized the long-established independence of the units. Centrifugal tendencies were accentuated by the greater willingness of the Mitsui family, compared to the Iwasakis, to release control to salaried managers, and the *zaibatsu* developed as a number of somewhat autonomous corporations.[65] In 1909, Mitsui Gomei Kaisha was officially founded as a means of consolidating the operationally-independent subsidiaries, which were changed over the next two years from unlimited partnerships to public concerns. Reformers at the main company had sought to imitate Mitsubishi Goshi, which was at this point controlled more centrally. Yet, ironically, it was Mitsubishi that in 1917 followed the holding company form established at Mitsui.[66]

Interestingly, Mitsubishi Shipbuilding (MSC) and Mitsui were the two shipbuilding firms that best weathered the economic travails of the 1920s, and they respectively benefited from close links with NYK and the shipping division of Mitsui Bussan. Kawasaki Shipbuilding had connections with Kawasaki Steamship, and the larger lines of NYK and OSK, but it carried other comparative disadvantages.[67] Its investments, overcommitment in a particular shipbuilding sector, and failure to rationalize hampered its competitive and financial performance. The resources and opportunities of the established *zaibatsu* were undermined in the 1920s by a sharp decline in their major areas of trading, mining, and marine and general engineering.[68] To stimulate a moribund shipbuilding sector, the government began in 1932 to subsidize the scrapping of old vessels and the building of modern ships. It was these policies, as well as military and naval orders, that transformed the Japanese industry and offered adequate throughput, not any major change in the nature or structure of management.[69]

Mitsubishi and Mitsui, as family owned but gradually professionalized, large-scale businesses, were not unusual. Suzuki states that the holding company became the dominant form in Japan between 1920 and 1930. He notes the devolution of managerial functions within these enterprises, and he argues that dynamism emerged from the individual firms, not the groups themselves.[70] The managerial and staffing resources available to Mitsubishi Goshi and Mitsui Gomei were parlous compared to the operational subsidiaries or their plants, where policy as well as production decisions were formulated. Diverse interests, the spreading of risks, vertical linkages along the production value chain, and the sharing of information and managerial expertise all supported the emergence of large business federations. Takeda agrees that the headquarters functions in the *zaibatsu* were, as in British holding companies, too small to exert direct influence and regular control, but adequate enough for the purposes of monitoring.[71] In Japan, militarization and war-time administration of the economy subsequently instigated direct dealing between government and subsidiary management, and the growing power of the state weakened the coordinating role of the main *zaibatsu* or their head offices.[72]

The nature of production and operational scale in the cotton textile industry were less complex than the case of shipbuilding, but, as in Britain, a number of giant concerns did emerge in Japan by the 1920s. Yui notes the prominence of merger activity in this decade, as 40 per cent of the cotton industry came under the control of three companies, Kanegafuchi Spinning, Toyo, and Dai Nippon.[73] Organizational gains were found in the vertical linking of purchasing and sales through group structures, just as the holding company in Britain made these advantages possible. When Mitsui Bussan progressively acquired Kanegafuchi, the subsidiary was granted access to a vast trading network. Within the industry as a whole, there was no widespread effort to place merged interests within single integrated businesses that were strategically controlled by a headquarters function or operational divisions. Historical focus upon the horizontally-diverse *zaibatsu* tends to underplay the crucial relations between the subsidiaries and their component suppliers, in addition to the vertical connections of prominent new *zaibatsu* companies, such as Nissan and Nitchitsu.[74] Similarly, links along the value chain between manufacturing units, suppliers and buyers offered economies of scope, purchasing power, and marketing access to the Japanese cotton textile industry. Despite the mergers of the 1920s, therefore, Suzuki acknowledges the role and relative independence of functionally-orientated management structures within many textile factories, and he notes the smallness of company headquarters. As in the case of the British combines, it proved easier to consolidate commercial activities than the manufacturing units, the result being centrifugal tendencies that resisted the creation of centralized production departments.[75] But monitoring and control procedures were available, and, through the sogoshosha or general trading companies, economies of scale and market opportunities were available, as in Britain, through the coordination of marketing activities.

Governance and Competitiveness

There are, of course, important differences that explain the rising international competitiveness of the Japanese cotton textile businesses and the declining fortunes of British companies. The achievements of the heavy sector in Japan – the investment in technical and managerial expertise in the furtherance of rapid development – are also noteworthy. Across many products and markets, challenges to the pre-eminence of Britain's staple industries enforced a painful process of restructuring. Yet, in trying to locate or understand the contributory factors, the combined issues of ownership, corporate governance and internal management do not suggest immediate solutions.

Firstly, the divorce of ownership and management, and the ability of shareholders to exert market disciplines or profit-maximising efficiencies appear hardly relevant to the historical evidence. For many large businesses of inter-war Britain, ownership and management were often not separated, and, even where professionalization and the deepening of administrative structures occurred, important owners remained influential.

Secondly, taking a very different perspective, the failure to end family ownership is suspect for inhibiting the process of professionalization, often through the creation of loose federations without suitable managerial hierarchies, coherent strategies, effective structures for decision-making or operations, and scale or scope economies. By affecting the culture and the nature of management, personal or family ownership harmed the utilisation of corporate resources and the implementation of business change. Yet this interpretation ignores or underestimates evidence of administrative organization and reform in many large British holding companies. The centralization of key functions, such as finance and accounting, assisted monitoring procedures; coordinated marketing and purchasing brought available synergies, and augmented the advantages of vertical integration; and, in some cases, all these activities were able to enhance the capabilities of diverse production units. In the case of the shipbuilding and armaments industry, product and market diversity offered strategic as well as operational advantages. British companies had organizational characteristics shared by successful competitors, including Japanese businesses, with their examples of family ownership and involvement, holding company structures, and light central control of subsidiaries.

Thirdly, international comparisons highlight the greater importance of factors other than governance and managerial organization, when explaining business performance. These characteristics may have been detrimental in the British context, but they were not so unique or marked internationally, nor fatal to numerous firms. Economic conditions at home and overseas, levels of market maturity, labour skills and costs, military expenditure, and tariff protection are all part of the equation, and the limits as well as the possibilities of managerial initiative should be considered.

Lastly, if we turn our attention to the key issue of internal governance structures, we can ask if the 'classic' model of managerial enterprise is universally suitable. Does the holding company form – so prevalent geographically and historically – offer particular advantages?

Within British textiles, as we have seen, merged enterprises brought the centralization of purchasing, marketing, and support activities such as accounting, invoicing and commercial information. As well as having some impact on costs, efficiency, and planning, throughput in an industry where the scale of each production unit was relatively small could consequently be improved. In theory, the skills and flexibility of the British labour force at this time would have further facilitated scope economies, in addition to customization and the production of high quality goods, just as international competitors gradually benefited from new technologies and greater technological integration. Multi-subsidiarity and holding company structures secured supplies and markets, and improved contacts with domestic and overseas customers. Institutional links and alliances between the different combines themselves further enhanced these advantages.

While natural textile firms gave priority to scope economies, returns to scale were more easily available in shipbuilding and engineering. Those industries that were capital-intensive and subject to large fluctuations in orders and markets could gain the greatest advantages from business groups and inter-firm connections. Security of supply was needed during good trading conditions, although high material costs were a long-term danger, and trusted customers were an asset in poor economic circumstances. Shipbuilding, mechanical engineering, steelmaking, ordnance, and shipping were associated businesses, and upstream and downstream partners counterbalanced inherent commercial difficulties and assisted fluctuations in throughput.[76] The infrequency of large capital orders additionally encouraged involvement in less directly-related operations, such as automobiles, transportation, and electrical engineering, in the hope they could provide alternative cash-flows. Holding company structures were suited to the maintenance of these linkages and to the supervision of a highly-diversified enterprise.

If we compare the reality to the abstract advantages, we should acknowledge that particular institutional legacies and difficult economic conditions shaped the potential capabilities of holding company in inter-war Britain. Undoubtedly, textile combines were formed as defensive postures against international competitors and as attempts to reap monopolistic advantages. Equally, many founding families retained their established role and vested interests, despite the harsher competitive environment and the increasing administrative complexity and scale of business. Whatever these influences on strategy, ownership and managerial practice, the Linen Thread Company – as well as Calico Printers, Bradford Dyers, English Sewing Cotton, and Fine Cotton Spinners and Doublers – demonstrated a capacity for organizational change, so gaining some of the advantages available to a holding company. Coats in particular – but also Whitworth & Mitchell, Joshua Hoyle, and Horrocks, Crewdson – did not fit this pattern, as a successful family business grew through acquisition and diversification and not merger. It employed the holding company form in order to transfer its managerial capabilities to a larger enterprise, and, subsequently, consolidated its growth through further organizational reforms. Before 1914, bulk purchasing, the centralization of support services, and mass distribution brought benefits not so easily acquired, for a variety of reasons, in the scale of production. In the 1920s and 1930s, contracting markets accelerated the search for efficiencies, improved management, and effective marketing channels. During the post-war boom of 1918-21, the holding company clearly enabled shipbuilding and engineering companies to diversify rapidly into related, non-military products; with the arrival of economic difficulties, vertical linkages and product diversity protected sales and cash-flows. In general, shipbuilding and armaments companies established business groups through acquisition rather than merger. In the well-cited case of Beardmore, crisis eventually brought significant changes in administration and control.

What type of governance structure can we associate with holding companies, and, consequently, to the various large-scale businesses of inter-war Britain? Because there is no pattern in the link between family enterprise, organizational structure, or levels of professionalization, the major issue is not one of ownership or external control. On the question of internal governance, how can the characteristics of holding companies utilize organizational capabilities and strategic circumstances? In answering this question, among the numerous analyses of management models, the work of Grant is especially relevant, because he distinguishes between the various advantages held by diversified and other large-scale companies. He notes the potential of 'corporate relatedness', from which businesses can benefit from risk-avoidance, commonality in decision-making and implementation, and the utilisation of core skills in strategy, finance and control. Grant is seeking to explain the rationale of unrelated diversification within conglomerates. 'Operational relatedness', on the other hand, arises from technological, operational and scale synergies, and may encourage unitary, multidivisional structures, as well as related diversification. In realising these specific benefits, a company has to bear considerable costs in vertical coordination and horizontal interaction, while corporate relatedness emphasises transferable knowledge and skills. The levering of core competencies, in other words, may have alternatives in more diverse market opportunities, commercial information, and entrepreneurial initiative.[77] Kay also adds support for the conglomerate and its profitability, and he concentrates particularly on the spreading of risks. He argues that, once formed, the costs and danger of integration explain the long-term robustness and longevity of conglomerates.[78]

Certainly, the strategies, organization and managerial initiatives of British holding companies reveal an intention and ability to exploit the competitive and institutional advantages listed by Grant, but also Kay. A system of subsidiaries offered the benefits of rapid growth, diversification, and risk-aversion. It allowed synergies in purchasing, marketing and administration; enabled effective plant-level or business unit management and initiative; and assisted throughput and vertical integration of the value chain. There were advantages that explain why British businesses, like their Japanese and European competitors, chose the holding company form. They, therefore, enhanced them through increasing headquarters coordination and professionalization. National and local business networks, acting as sources of commercial information, trust relationships, and deal-making, encouraged and supported the institutional arrangements of groups. Alongside multiple directorships and cross-shareholdings, they assisted to some degree with the monitoring of firms, representing the various interests of financial institutions, debtors, government, buyers, suppliers, and shareholders. The evidence and detail available about so many individual cases prohibits absolute certainty on the quality of corporate governance, taken from a contemporary perspective, in key sectors of the British economy. There are further complications, because theories and debates on governance are not well attuned to the specific historical circumstances. Management within the British inter-war industries of shipbuilding, armaments and textiles has revealed its numerous deficiencies, yet, on the inter-linking issues of governance, strategy and operational control, it deserves a balanced critique rather than wide-ranging condemnation.

Notes

1   See, for example, J.Charkham, *Keeping Good Company: A Study of Corporate Governance in Five Countries* (1994).
2   See K.Keasey and M.Wright, 'Issues in Corporate Accountability and Governance: An Editorial', *Accounting and Business Research*, 23, no.91A (1993); R.I.Tricker, *Corporate Governance: Practices, Procedures and Powers in British Companies and their Boards of Directors* (1984).
3   J.A.Schumpeter, *Capitalism, Socialism and Democracy* (1942); *The Theory of Economic Development* (1949).
4   E.T.Penrose, *The Theory of the Growth of the Firm* (1949).
5   A.D.Chandler, *Scale and Scope: the Dynamics of Industrial Enterprise* (1990).
6   M.O'Sullivan, *Contests for Corporate Control: Corporate Governance and Economic Performance in the United States and Germany* (2000).
7   Chandler, *Scale and Scope*; O'Sullivan, *Contests for Corporate Control*; Y.Cassis, *Big Business: the European Experience in the Twentieth Century* (1997).
8   See, for example, D.J.Teece, 'Economic Analysis and Strategic Management', *California Management Review* (1984), vol.26, pp.87-110; C.K.Prahalad and G.Hamel,

'The Core Competencies of the Corporation', *Harvard Business Review* (1991), vol.99; J.A.Kay, *Foundations of Corporate Success* (1993).

9   O'Sullivan *Contests for Corporate Control*; W.Lazonick, *Corporate Governance and Sustainable Prosperity* (1997).

10 See A.D.Chandler, *Scale and Scope*, and, also, W.Lazonick, *Business Organization and the Myth of the Market Economy* (1991).

11 J.F.Wilson, *British Business History, 1720-1994* (1995), pp.106-10,154-5; M.W.Kirby and M.B.Rose, 'Introduction', in *Business Enterprise in Modern Britain* (1994), pp.17-18. See also L.Hannah, *The Rise of the Corporate Economy* (1983), p.87.

12 See below.

13 A.D.Chandler, *Strategy and Structure: Chapters in the History of Industrial Enterprise* (1962); A.D.Chandler, *The Visible Hand: the Management Revolution in American Business* (1977); Chandler, *Scale and Scope*; A.D.Chandler, F.Amatori, and T.Hikino, *Big Business and the Wealth of Nations* (1997); A.D.Chandler and H.Daems (eds), *Managerial Hierarchies: Comparative Perspectives on the Rise of the Modern Industrial Enterprise* (1980); A.Chandler, 'The Emergence of Managerial Capitalism', in M.Granovetter and R.Swedberg (eds), *The Sociology of Economic Life* (1992), pp.131-58; D.F.Channon, *The Strategy and Structure of British Enterprise* (1973); L.Hannah, ed., *Management Strategy and Business Development: an Historical and Comparative Study* (1976); Hannah, *Rise of the Corporate Economy*; C.Schmitz, *The Growth of Big Business in the United States and Western Europe, 1850-1939* (1993).

14 Vickers bought a 50 per cent stake.

15 Glasgow Business Records Centre (GBRC), UGD100/1/1/1, Beardmore, Board Meeting, 15 Jan 1906; UGD100/1/1/15, Beardmore, Meeting of Directors, 19 Feb 1929, 3 May 1929. See also Tolliday, *Business, Banking and Politics*, pp.87-8. Beardmore acquired shipbuilders R.Napier & Sons in 1900. See Macrosty, *Trust Movement in British Industry*, p.42.

16 J.R.Hume and M.S.Moss, *Beardmore: the History of a Scottish Giant* (1979), p.88.

17 'William Beardmore, Jnr, Lord Invernairn', *Dictionary of Scottish Business Biography*, Vol.I (1986), pp.91-3.

18 D.Todd, *The World Shipbuilding Industry* (1985), pp.36-42,162,252-86. See also J.R.Parkinson, *The Economics of Shipbuilding in the United Kingdom* (1960); J.R.Parkinson, 'Shipbuilding', in N.Buxton and D.H.Aldcroft (eds), *British Industry between the Wars: Instability and Industrial Development* (1979), pp.80-4.

19 'William Beardmore, Jnr, Lord Invernairn', *Dictionary of Scottish Business Biography*.

20 'Sir Thomas Bell', Dictionary of Scottish Business Biography, Vol.I (1986), pp.207-211.

21 A.Slaven, 'Management and Shipbuilding, 1890-1938: Structure and Strategy in the Shipbuilding Firm on the Clyde', in A.Slaven and D.H.Aldcroft (eds), *Business, Banking and Urban History* (1982), pp.35-53; E.Lorenz and F.Wilkinson, 'The Shipbuilding Industry, 1880-1965', in B.Elbaum and W.Lazonick, *Decline of the British Economy*, pp.110-12.

22 GBRC, UGD100/7/1/17, Beardmore, Notes for M.Norman, 16 June 1929.

23 GBRC, UGD100/1/1/15, Beardmore, Meeting of Directors, 4 Sept 1931, 1 June 1931, 27 Nov 1931.

24 GBRC, UGD100/1/1/15, Beardmore, Meetings of Directors, 8 Dec 1930, 27 Nov 1931.

25 GBRC, UGD100/1/1/15, Meetings of Directors, 15 Feb 1928, 7 Feb 1930, 28 Feb 1930, 27 June 1930.

26 Tolliday, *Business, Banking and Politics*, pp.237-47; Chandler, *Scale and Scope*, pp.341,343-4; GBRC, UGD100/1/13/19, Beardmore, Meetings of Directors, 31 Dec 1942; UGD100/1/1/3. Board Minutes, 5 Jan 1950.

27 GBRC, UGD100/1/1/15, Beardmore, Meeting of Directors, 20 Sept 1929, 5 Feb 1930, 28 March 1930, 4 Sept 1931, 16 Dec 1931.

28 'Vickers, Thomas Edward (1833-1915) and Vickers, Albert (1838-1919)', *Dictionary of Business Biography*, Vol.V (1986), pp.622-8.

29 Chandler, *Scale and Scope*, pp.341-4.

30 As is well known, Wolseley was sold to Morris Motors in 1925; the electrical equipment section of Metro-Vick was bought by General Electric in 1928, which merged it with British Thomson-Houston to form Associated Electrical Industries (AEI); the carriage section of Metro-Vick was joined with a similar Cammell Laird operation to form Metro-Cammell Carriage Railway & Wagon Company; the steel-making plants of Vickers and Cammell Laird became the basis of the English Steel Corporation.

31 Chandler, *Scale and Scope*, 341-4; J.D.Scott, *Vickers: a History* (London, 1962), pp.76-94,137-68,158-9. See also C.Trebilcock, *The Vickers Brothers: Armaments and Enterprise, 1854-1914* (London, 1977), pp.ix-xl,26-51,142-52.

32 Tolliday, *Business, Banking and Politics*, pp.191-7.

33 Chandler, *Scale and Scope*, pp.241-2.

34 Scott, *Vickers*, pp.88-94,152-5,161-8; Chandler, *Scale and Scope*, pp.340-5; W.J.Reader, *Bowater: a History* (Cambridge, 1981), pp.32-59; Tolliday, *Business, Banking and Politics*, pp.192-7; Trebilcock, *Vickers Brothers*, pp.xxvi-vii, 146-8. See also S.Pollard and P.L.Robertson, *The British Shipbuilding Industry, 1890-1914* (London, 1979); and R.J.Irving, 'New Industries for Old? Some Investment Decisions of Sir W.G.Armstrong, Whitworth & Co. Ltd, 1900-1914', *Business History*, vol.27 (1975).

35 'Sir Thomas Bell', *Dictionary of Scottish Business Biography*, Vol.I (1986), pp.207-11.

36 'Sir James Lithgow', *Dictionary of Scottish Business Biography*, Vol.I (1986), pp.222-7.

37 GBRC, UGD4/12/3, A.Stephen & Co., Minute Book, 30 July 1919, 19 Aug 1920, 20 July 1922, 21 Aug 1922, 20 July 1926, 6 July 1927, 27 June 1929. See also S.L.Jones, 'The Overseas Trading Company in Britain: the Case of the Inchcape Group', in S.Yonekawa and H.Yoshihara (eds), *Business History of General Trading Companies* (1987), pp.131-69; S.L.Jones, *Two Centuries of Overseas Trading: the Origins and Growth of the Inchcape Group* (1986); 'Sir Alexander Murray Stephen', *Dictionary of Scottish Business Biography*, Vol.I (1986), pp.238-40.

38 See W.J.Reader, *The Weir Group: A Centenary History* (1971). See E.H.H.Green and M.Moss, *A Business of National Importance: the Royal Mail Shipping Group, 1902-1937* (1982). Royal Mail owned a number of lines, including White Star, and accounted for 15 per cent of Britain's merchant fleet by the early 1930s.

39 M.Moss and J.R.Hume, *Shipbuilders to the World: 125 years of Harland and Wolff, Belfast, 1861-1986* (1986), pp.92,96-7,132-3,135,173-4,244-50,270,278,282-3,285-321; T.R.Gourvish, 'British Business and the Transition to a Corporate Economy: Entrepreneurship and Management Structures', *Business History*, vol.29 (1987), p.32.

39 See 'Sir John Craig', *Dictionary of Scottish Business Biography*, Vol.I (1986), pp.101-104.

40 P.L.Payne, *Colvilles and the Scottish Steel Industry* (1979), pp.188-9,191-3,220-2,238-49,356. By 1935, Colvilles controlled 80 per cent of Scottish steel output.

41 See A.R.Holmes and E.Green, *Midland. 150 Years of Banking History* (1986), pp.184-5.

42 'Sir James Lithgow', *Dictionary of Scottish Business Biography*, Vol.I (1986), pp.222-7; Chandler, *Scale and Scope*, pp.327-8; GBRC, UGD100/1/1/18, 13 April 1939.

43 Chandler, *Scale and Scope*, pp.320-5,327; 'Sir John Craig', *Dictionary of Scottish Business Biography*, Vol.I (1986), pp.101-104; 'Sir Allan Campbell Macdiarmid', *Dictionary of Scottish Business Biography*, Vol.I (1986), pp.121-5; P.W.S.Andrews and E.Brunner, *Capital Development in Steel: a Study of the United Steel Companies* (1951), pp.119-21,123-4,156-8,162-5,167-9,208,234,355; R.Peddie, *The United Steel Companies Ltd, 1918-1968* (1969), pp.13-15,18-19,26; F.Scopes, *The Development of*

the Corby Works (1968), pp.110-18,129-31,237; R.Fitzgerald, *British Labour Management and Industrial Welfare, 1846-1939* (1987), pp.89-114,164-72,184-95.

44 Morikawa, *Zaibatsu*, pp.1-2,43,114,215.

45 Chandler, *Scale and Scope*, p.341.

46 Hannah, *Rise of the Corporate Economy*, pp.8-40. 330 of the 895 firms affected by mergers between 1887-1900 were to be found in the textile industry: see L.Hannah, 'Mergers in British Manufacturing Industry, 1880-1918', *Oxford Economic Papers*, vol.xxvi (1974), p.22.

47 Payne, 'Family Business in Britain: an Historical and Analytical Survey', in Okochi and Yasuoka (eds), *Family Business*, p.181.

48 D.J.Jeremy, 'Survival Strategies in Lancashire Textiles: Bleachers' Association Ltd to Whitecroft plc, 1900-1980s', *Textile History*, vol.24 (1993), pp.163-209. See also Macrosty, *Trust Movement*, pp.124-32.

49 Horrockses, Crewdson & Co. was itself an amalgamation of two concerns in 1887. See Macrosty, *Trust Movement*, p.125.

50 Chandler, *Scale and Scope*, pp.22-4,45-6,288-9,332-4.

51 See, for example, C.Clark, 'Why Isn't the Whole World Developed? Lessons from the Cotton Mills', *Journal of Economic History*, vol.xlvii (1987), pp.141-73; M.Mass and W.Lazonick, 'The British Cotton Industry and International Competitive Advantage: the State of the Debates', in M.B.Rose (ed.), *International Competition and Strategic Response in the Textile Industries since 1870* (1990), pp.9-65; J.Singleton, *World Textile Industry* (1997), pp.98-101,127-31. It is worth mentioning that the international trading network characteristic of the British textile industry in general appeared by the inter-war years a poor competitor to larger scale, more organized marketing by other countries. See Department of Overseas Trade, *Report of the British Economic Mission in the Far East* (HMSO, 1931), pp.240-1.

52 GBRC, UGD143/1/1/1, Linen Thread Company, Copies of Agreements, 17 Dec 1897, 19 May 1898; UGD143/1/3/1, Committee Minutes, 6 July 1898, 23 Sept 1898, 14 Oct 1898, 22 June 1898, 30 Dec 1898, 26 Jan 1899, 22 Feb 1899, 7 March 1899, 27 April 1899, 6 July 1899, 7 July 1899; UGD143/1/3/2, Committee Minutes, 9 Aug 1899, 13 Sept 1899; UGD143/5/4, Executive Committee, 1901-46, 24 Dec 1901, 13 June 1902, 9 Dec 1902. See also Linen Thread Company, *The Faithful Fibre* (privately published, 1951). Further reorganization occurred in 1953, when the company and its subsidiaries were placed in groups based on products. See UGD143/1/3/47, Board Minutes, 16 April 1953, 16 July 1953.

53 J.Clapham, *An Economic History of Modern Britain*, Vol.III (Cambridge, England, 1951), pp.229,231,289; 'Sir Alfred Herbert Dixon, Bart (1857-1920)', *Dictionary of Business Biography*, Vol.II (1984), pp.107-10; 'Broadhurst, Sir Edward Tootal', *Dictionary of Business Biography*, Vol.V (1984); 'Douglas, George', *Dictionary of Business Biography*, Vol.II (1984); 'Lee, Henry (1817-1904), and Lee, Sir Joseph Cocksey (1832-1894)', *Dictionary of Business Biography*, Vol.III (1985), pp.703-14; 'Lee, Lennox Bertram (1864-1949)', *Dictionary of Business Biography*, Vol.III (1985), pp.715-25; P.L.Cook and R.Cohen, *Effects of Mergers: Six Studies* (1958), pp.151-68.

54 Payne, 'Emergence of the Large-Scale Company in Great Britain'; Payne, 'Family Business in Britain', in Okochi and Yasuoka (eds), *Family Business*, p.181; D.W.Kim, 'From a Family Partnership to a Corporate Company: J. & P. Coats, Thread Manufacturers', *Textile History*, vol.25 (1994), pp.185-226; A.K.Cairncross and J.B.K.Hunter, 'The early growth of Messrs J. & P. Coats, 1830-1883', *Business History*, vol.29 (1987).

55 Chandler, *Scale and Scope*, p.289.

56 'Archibald Coats', *Dictionary of Scottish Business Biography*, Vol.I (1986), pp.329-35; 'Sir James Henderson', *Dictionary of Scottish Business Biography*, Vol.I (1986),

pp.363-6; 'Otto Ernst Philippi', *Dictionary of Scottish Business Biography*, Vol.I (1986), pp.389-92; Macrosty, *Trust Movement*, pp.144-54.

57 Macrosty, *Trust Movement*, pp.121-36,137-49,151.

58 'Archibald Coats', *Dictionary of Scottish Business Biography*, Vol.I (1986), pp.329-35; 'Sir James Henderson', *Dictionary of Scottish Business Biography*, Vol.I (1986), pp.363-6; 'Otto Ernst Philippi', *Dictionary of Scottish Business Biography*, Vol.I (1986), pp.389-92; Macrosty, *Trust Movement*, pp.144-54.

59 GBRC, UGD143/1/3/1, Linen Thread Company, Committee Minutes, 26 June 1898, 7 March 1899; Macrosty, *Trust Movement*, pp.136-7.

60 'Otto Ernst Philippi', *Dictionary of Scottish Business Biography*, Vol.I (1986), p.391.

61 GBRC, UGD199/1/1/5, J. & P. Coats, Directors' Minute Book, 1928-38, 27 July 1928, 9 Oct 1930, 12 & 13 Nov 1930, 11 June 1931, 25 May 1933, 19 July 1934, 11 June 1936, 16 July 1937, 7 Dec 1936; UGD199/1/1/14, General Purposes Committee, 1930-1936, 23 & 24 Oct 1930, 21 Nov 1930, 27 Nov 1930; UGD199/1/1/59, Organisation Committee, 14 Oct 1931, 11 Nov 1931, 9 & 29 Dec 1931, 13 Jan 1932, 4 & 17 March 1932, 7 Dec 1932, 14 March 1933, 18 April 1933, 13 June 1933, 19 Dec 1933; UGD199/1/1/74, Executive Committee: Division 1, 1930-1945, 9 Dec 1930.

62 W.Lazonick, 'The Cotton Industry', in Elbaum and Lazonick (eds), *Decline of the British Economy*, pp.18-50; W.Lazonick, 'Industrial Organization and Technological Change: the Decline of the British Cotton Industry', *Business History Review*, vol.107 (1983), pp.230-6; M.W.Kirby, 'The Lancashire Cotton Industry in the Inter-War Years: a Study in Organizational Change', *Business History*, vol.26 (1974), pp.145-59; J.H.Bamberg, 'The Rationalization of the British Cotton Industry in the Interwar Years', *Textile History*, vol.19 (1988), pp.83-102.

63 Morikawa, *Zaibatsu*, pp.1-2,43,114,215; Suzuki, *Japanese Management Structures*, pp.50,54

64 Morikawa, *Zaibatsu*, pp.1-24,57-92,146-7; 'Mitsubishi Heavy Industries', *International Directory of Company Histories*, Vol.4 (1991), pp.577-9; 'Kawasaki Heavy Industries Ltd', *International Directory of Company Histories*, Vol.4 (1991), pp.538-40.

65 Morikawa, *Zaibatsu*, pp.1-24,57-92,106-14,126,128,130,145-6,183,192; M.Miyamoto, 'The Position and Role of the Family Business in the Development of the Japanese Company System', in Okochi and Yasuoka (eds), *Family Business*, pp.39-94; M.Shimotani, 'History and Structure of Business Groups', in Shiba and Shimotani (eds), *Beyond the Firm*, p.17.

66 Morikawa, *Zaibatsu*, pp.106-14,183,192; M.Miyamoto, 'The Position and Role of the Family Business in the Development of the Japanese Company System', in Okochi and Yasuoka (eds), *Family Business*, pp.39-94; M.Shimotani, 'History and Structure of Business Groups', in Shiba and Shimotani (eds), *Beyond the Firm*, p.17.

67 See 'Kawasaki Kisen Kaisha, Ltd', *International Directory of Company Histories*, Vol.4 (1991), pp.457-60.

68 Y.Fukasaku, *Technology and Industrial Development in Pre-War Japan: Mitsubishi Nagasaki Shipyard, 1884-1934* (1992), pp.12-42; Morikawa, *Zaibatsu*, pp.121-130,140-158; Todd, *World Shipbuilding Industry*, pp.286-96. See also 'Sumitomo Heavy Industries Ltd', *International Directory of Company Histories*, Vol.4 (1991), pp.634-5; 'Mitsui O.S.K. Lines Ltd', *International Directory of Company Histories*, Vol.4 (1991), pp.473-6.

69 Morikawa, *Zaibatsu*, pp.1-24,57-92,146-7; 'Mitsubishi Heavy Industries', *International Directory of Company Histories*, Vol.4 (1991), pp.577-9; 'Kawasaki Heavy Industries Ltd', *International Directory of Company Histories*, Vol.4 (1991), pp.538-40. See also T.Chida and P.N.Davies, *The Japanese Shipping and Shipbuilding Industries* (1990).

70 Suzuki, *Japanese Management Structures*, pp.33-6. See also T.Yui, 'Development, organization, and business strategy of industrial enterprises in Japan, 1915-1935', *Japanese Yearbook on Business History*, vol.5 (1988).

71 See Haruhiro Takeda in this volume.
72 Morikawa, *Zaibatsu*, pp.182-248; Shimotani, 'History and Structure of Business Groups in Japan'; K.Suzuki, 'From *Zaibatsu* to Corporate Complexes'; and T.Shiba, 'A Path to the Corporate Group in Japan: Mitsubishi Heavy Industries and its Group Formation', in Shiba and Shimotani (eds), *Beyond the Firm*, pp.5-28,59-87,167-84; T.Okazaki, 'The Japanese Firm under the Wartime Planned Economy', in Aoki and Dore (eds), *The Japanese Firm*, pp.350-78.
73 Yui, 'Development, Organization, and Business Strategy'; D.Farnie and S.Yonekawa, 'The Emergence of the Largest Firms in the Cotton Spinning Industries of the World, 1883-1938', *Textile History*, vol.19 (1988).
74 Yui, 'Development, Organization, and Business Strategy'; T.Yui, 'The Enterprise System in Japan: Preliminary Considerations on Internal and External Relations', *Japanese Yearbook on Business History*, vol.8 (1991); Shimotani, 'History and Structure of Business Groups', pp.2,5-7,11-14.
75 Suzuki, *Japanese Management Structures*, pp.26-8,33,35-6.
76 See J.Pfeffer and G.Salancik, *The External Control of Organizations: A Resource Dependence Perspective* (1978); A.Goto, 'Business Groups in a Market Economy', *European Economic Review*, vol.19 (1982), pp.53-70.
77 R.M.Grant, 'On Dominant Logic, Relatedness and the Link between Diversity and Performance', *Strategic Management Journal*, vol.9 (1988), pp.639-42.
78 N.M.Kay, *Pattern in Corporate Development* (1997).

Chapter 4

Corporate Governance in the Inter-War *Zaibatsu*

Haruhito Takeda

Introduction

The *zaibatsu* were a predominant form of business organization amongst large enterprises in Japan during the inter-war years. It is generally agreed that, since the end of the Second World War, all the stakeholders of Japanese enterprises - shareholders, financial institutions, managers, employees, and customers - have exercised some degree of influence on corporate governance. Among the *zaibatsu* of the inter-war period, however, the power of the holding company as shareholder was virtually absolute, and employees had no influence on corporate governance. Similarly, *zaibatsu*-affiliated financial institutions were subservient to the will of the holding companies, and had little power on *zaibatsu* subsidiary companies.

The analysis of *zaibatsu* corporate governance during the pre-war period must necessarily focus on the relationship between managers and shareholders. In addition, the influence of business associations as a stakeholder needs to be discussed. Because Japan's business activities before the end of the Second World War were often based on cartel agreements, *zaibatsu* subsidiaries faced conflicts between the will of the holding company and cartel regulation.

To understand the characteristics of the *zaibatsu* system during the inter-war period, therefore, it is necessary to distinguish between two relationships: one between the family and the holding company, and the other between the holding company and its subsidiaries. Without this distinction between families and holding companies as shareholders, the discussion of *zaibatsu* corporate governance becomes problematic, and risks overlooking the peculiar characteristics of shareholders in Japan before 1945.

The Position of Zaibatsu Affiliated Companies

Table 4.1 shows the distribution of big business by size and by economic sector.[1] The important share of the holding companies sectors within this distribution is consistent with other data for this period, and demonstrates the need to focus on the *zaibatsu* and holding companies. Table 4.2 shows the position of the three largest *zaibatsu* - the Mitsui, Mitsubishi and Sumitomo-related companies - within the total population of Japanese companies with total assets in excess of 100m yen. Among the financial institutions with assets over 1bn yen, *zaibatsu*-affiliated banks and government-related financial institutions occupied an important position. Half of the manufacturing and mining companies with assets in the 200-500m yen range were *zaibatsu*. Affiliated companies weigh heavily in each category of Table 4.2. They represented 30 per cent of the companies with over 1bn yen of assets, and 50 per cent if one excludes government-related financial institutions; 40 per cent of the companies in the 0.5-1bn yen range; 33 per cent of those between 200-500m yen; and 11 per cent of those between 100-200m yen.

Table 4.1 Japanese Big Business According to Size, Sector and Type, 1937

(A)	(B)	(C)	(D)	(E)	(F)	(G)	(H)	(I)	(J)	(K)
Over 1 bn	-	-	-	-	10	-	-	-	10	20
Over 500m	1	-	-	-	1	1	1	1	-	5
Over 200m	4	-	-	1	7	7	9	1	4	33
Over 100m	3	1	3	2	14	7	6	2	3	41
Over 70m	5	1	4	-	9	5	3	1	1	29
Over 59m	2	1	4	-	13	5	9	2	4	40
Total No. Companies	15	3	11	3	54	25	28	7	22	168
% of Big Business	8.9	1.8	6.5	1.8	32.1	14.9	16.7	4.2	13.1	100.0
Total Assets Ym	3,195	237	1,004	485	6,021	19,803	5,473	1,540	1,846	39,604
% of Assets	8.1	0.7	2.5	1.2	15.2	49.9	13.8	3.9	4.7	100.0

Notes: (A) Total assets in yen; (B) Number of electric power companies; (C) Gas power companies; (D) Railways; (E) Merchant Shipping; (F) Manufacturing and mining; (G) Banks; (H) Insurance; (I) Miscellaneous; (J) Holding companies; (K) Total number of companies in each category of asset values.
Source: *General Financial Directory of Banks and Companies*.

Two points are to be noted regarding these tables. Firstly, the holding companies and financial institutions, which provided capital to companies in other sectors (see Table 4.1), are as a whole overwhelmingly larger than the companies engaged in manufacturing and mining. Secondly, the financial and holding companies of the *zaibatsu*, which were essentially 'in-house' investment banks, occupied an important position within the overall financial sector. In addition, compared with the post-war period, when the Antimonopoly Law of 1947 prohibited the establishment of holding companies, their existence was a distinctive feature of the pre-1945 Japanese economy.

Table 4.2 Japanese Companies with Assets Larger than 100m Yen (1937)

Over 1bn Yen
Finance and Insurance: Bank of Japan, Nippon Kangyo Bank, Yokohama Specie Bank, Sanwa Bank, Yasuda Bank, Dai-ichi Bank, Bank of Sumitomo, Mitsui Bank, Mitsubishi Bank, Industrial Bank of Japan

Over 500m Yen
Finance and Insurance: Dai-Hyaku Bank, Mitsui T & B
Commerce: Mitsui Bussan
Public Utilitties: Tokyo Electric
Manufacturing and Mining: Light Nippon Steel

Over 200m Yen
Finance and Investment: Nippon Life Insurance, Rokujuku Bank, Mitsubishi T & B, Nomura Securities Co., Sumitomo T & B, Meiji Life Insurance, Jugo Bank, Dai-ichi Life Insurance, Teikoku Life Insurance, Chiyoda Life Insurance, Hokkaido Takushoku Bank, Kobe Bank, Yasuda T & B, Aichi Bank, Kyodo T & B, Nagoya Bank
Holding Company: Mitsui, Mitsubishi, Sumitomo, Toyo-Takushoku
Commerce: Mitsubishi Trading
Public Utilities: Toho Electric, Daido Electric, Nihon Electric, Ujikawa Electric, Nippon Mail Steamship Co.
Manufacturing and Mining: Oji Paper Mfg. Co., Kanegafuchi Cotton Spinning, Nippon Chisso Hiryo, Mitsubishi Heavy Ind. Co., Nippon Mining Co., Kawasaki Shipbuilding Co., Mitsubishi Mining Co.

Over 100m Yen
Finance and Investment: Tokyo Marine Insurance
Holding Company: Oji Securities
Commerce: Toyo-Menka
Public Uitlities: Osaka Shosen
Manufacturing and Mining: Mitsui Mining, Sumitomo Steel Manufacturing, Hokkaido Coal and Steam

Note: T&B means Trust and Banking.
Source: General Financial Directory of Banks and Companies.

Characteristics of Company Ownership

There was a major change in company ownership during the inter-war years. Table 4.3 shows the change in dominance from individual to corporate shareholders. The share in the number of 'large shareholders' decreased from 0.59 to 0.36 per cent of the total during 1919-36, while issued shares held by 'large shareholders' increased from 21.0 per cent to 37.4 per cent. The fundamental cause of this increased concentration was the rise in corporate shareholdings.

Table 4.3 Share Ownership of Japanese Companies, 1919 and 1936

No. of Companies	379	477
Large Shareholders as % of Total Shareholders	0.59	0.36
% of Stocks Held by Large Shareholders	21.0	37.4
Including:		
Individuals	15.5	5.9
Banks	0.8	2.1
Insurance, Securities and Trusts	3.1	20.7
Corporations	1.6	8.7
Average No. of Shareholders per Company	2,040	3,589
Average No. of Stocks per Shareholder		
Large shareholders	4,644	17,434
Others	103	95

The basis for the shift is as follows. Firstly, there was a growth in insurance and trust companies as investment institutions. Secondly, holding companies grew under the influence of a revised taxation system. At the end of 1936, of the 20.7 per cent of total shares owned by corporations, 11.2 per cent or over half of the corporation shares were in the hands of holding companies. Thirdly, industrial companies increased company ownership by transforming their divisions into subsidiary companies or by acquiring shares of independent firms (*keiretsu*). For example, during this period, Mitsui Trading Company and Mitsui Mining increased their investments in subsidiary companies. Within the large companies that occupy the upper half of Table 4.2, many expanded their assets through corporate stocks.

Among large shareholders, the largest were the *zaibatsu* holding companies, which shared a unique relationship with the owner family. The principle of ownership was based on investment exclusivity, the limiting of investors to the same family, and the tendency to exclude potential sources of capital from outside the family. As evidence of this closely-held family investment structure, it was not until the Second World War that holding companies became publicly-quoted on the stock market. Within the *zaibatsu* umbrella, all the stocks of pivotal businesses such as Mitsui Trading Company and Mitsui Mining were completely held by holding companies. Because of this exclusive ownership, the shareholders of *zaibatsu* did not demand an increase in the pay-out ratio in order to realise a high dividend rate. To allow business growth, while also maintaining exclusive ownership, the requisite capital had to be obtained through the reinvestment of business profits.

From 1909 until the first half of the 1920s, between 20 and 30 per cent of the net profit of *Mitsui Gomei* (the holding company of Mitsui) was paid to the Family Council, and a large portion of this amount was placed in an internal reserve. In 1925, the income tax law was revised to make reserves liable, and *Mitsui Gomei* changed its approach. Though 70 per cent of profits were paid to the Family Council from 1925 onwards, family members could not access this increased dividend payment, because the Family Council kept it in *Mitsui Gomei*'s accounts as the family's deposit. As a result, less than 15 per cent of the net profit was distributed to family members. According to data between 1925 and 1931, the net profit of this period was 21m yen per year, while the income of the 11 families was only 3.3m yen (some 15 per cent of the total).

Similarly, the dividend rate of the holding company Mitsubishi Ltd was 6 per cent during the First World War and between 1-4 per cent during the 1920s. A sum of 172m yen was paid to the family between 1913-40, while capital at Mitsubishi Ltd increased by about 180m yen. That is to say, the holding company demanded capital reinvestment equal to its capital return.

Zaibatsu shareholders were absolutely 'stable', and did not to demand a high dividend rate. The appearance of this characteristic was brought about by the peculiar attitude of the family to the business, as they observed unique restrictions on the use of ownership. Family members were neither allowed to sell their own equity, nor to become independent from the family business. Their ultimate obligation was to take the family business that had been inherited from their parents' generation, develop it, and pass it on to their children. In order to achieve this, strong guidelines were set out by the family. For example, in Mitsui's case, in order to avoid the loss of family assets and to keep the reputation of the family business, a Family Constitution was established which prescribed how family members should avoid extravagance and refrain from involvement in other businesses.

The Relationship between Family and Holding Company

Formally speaking, apart from the last few years of the Second World War, *zaibatsu* families did not abandon exclusive ownership of their holding companies. As investors, they had absolute freedom of action over their holding companies. However, according to contemporary research, *zaibatsu* salaried managers, who moved up the company hierarchy through internal promotion, grasped real managerial control. The family members' participation in the management of holding companies seems of no importance.

Looking at the inter-war period, it is thought that Dan Takuma of Mitsui *zaibatsu* and Suzuki Masaya of Sumitomo *zaibatsu*, both salaried managers, held control and real leadership. In the case of the highest decision-making organ of *Mitsui Gomei*, for example, the family members attended general membership meetings only a few times a year. In most cases, their attendance was merely ceremonial, in order to acknowledge the half-year accounts.[2] Considering the frequency and composition of these meetings, family members could not exercise supervision. With regards to the Board of Directors of *Mitsui Gomei*, it is pointed out that 'family members were often absent from their meetings. For instance, Mitsui Hachiroemon Takamine, *Mitsui Gomei* president and head of the senior main family, attended less than half of the active partners' meetings each year'.[3] The fundamental relationship between the business and the family can be summed up as 'reigning without governing'.

There is one point to be added. It is known that Iwasaki Koyata who took command of Mitsubishi administration as the member of the owner family. My interpretation of this case is that, based on his superior ability as a manager, Koyata was well-suited for the position. There were hardly any other examples similar to Koyata's case. Iwasaki Hisaya, who was the head of the main family and the president of the holding company, entrusted direction of Mitsubishi to Koyata.

This type of family intervention and control can be observed in the Meiji period, as can leadership disputes between managers and the family, although gradually the role of managers became established.[4] Until the leadership of the 'salaried managers' in the subsidiary companies and also in the main office or holding company was established in the 1910s, various organisational regulations that defined the relationship between the family and the holding company, such as the Family Constitution, were established. The capacity for family intervention was reduced.[5] In the case of Mitsui, the low pay-out ratio was based on family regulations; no more than 20 per cent of net profits, after various deductions to the reserve fund, were to be paid to family members. Each *zaibatsu* converted its separate business divisions into subsidiary companies. With each such change in the structure of the business organisation, the distance between the family and the business increased. The holding company became a neutral zone for the co-ordination of the family and management's interests.

However, despite the establishment of such regulations and organisation, the family retained the authority to make major changes in the overall business. Even holding company managers could not completely stifle the family's voice. A clear indication of this voice was the organisational reform in Mitsui at the beginning of the 1940s. The family needed funds for payment of inheritance taxes. Several measures were considered, among which was the acquisition or absorption of the parent company, Mitsui Gomei into Mitsui Bussan, a subsidiary company. Despite management's opposition to the organisational confusion that this acquisition would create, the family imposed the change as a means squeezing the capital and the inheritance tax payment. Decisions should be judged by their appropriateness from a perspective of administrative rationale. However, in this case, the problem arose from the family's financial circumstances, not from a dispute over the nature of the business. Because of this, 'salaried managers' could not resist the forceful demands of investors. It was not until the dissolution of the *zaibatsu* after the Second World War II that the families lost their power.

The Relationship between Holding Companies and Subsidiary Companies

The founding of holding company was based on the process of joint stock company formation of diversified business offices. The increasing centralisation of management power in the holding companies reduced the room for intervention by the family in each individual company's office. This brought about the decentralisation of authority and responsibility to *zaibatsu*-affiliated enterprises, that is to say the growth of 'salaried managers' within each enterprise.

However, at the same time, the rise of a *konzern*-like organisation in which ownership was concentrated raised the problem of how much authority, from the organisational standpoint of the *zaibatsu*, should be entrusted to the subsidiary company and how much should be held by the head office. In the establishment of a *konzern*-like organisation that had the opportunity for the centralisation of authority and at the same time decentralisation, neither dimension became predominant. On the one hand, the organisational strength of the *konzern* was its ability to unite the diversified businesses into a larger business group. From the perspective of managerial techniques, the establishment of a holding company system was judged to be highly rational, because the resulting organisational structure encouraged a decentralisation that was effective for the development of multiple businesses.[6]

With regards to this development of decentralization and the role played by the holding company, four points need to be made. Firstly, it was the holding companies that recruited the talented personnel that would become future executive candidates. The *zaibatsu* maintained the fundamental role of deploying talented employees on a centralised basis. Among traditional business families such as Mitsui and Sumitomo, it was the role of the current head of the family to recruit a talented employee, to appoint him as manager (*banto*), and finally to entrust him with full decision-making power.[7] In turn, the salaried managers of the *zaibatsu*, as employees of the family, displayed an attitude of being a servant. At first glance, this type of relation appears curious and far from rational. However, as investor or owner, the family knew well that family members did not have enough knowledge and experience to control the full breadth of their business. To entrust it to an employed manager was an approach dictated by traditional wisdom. All the family had to do was to control the moral hazard of managers, that is the failure to draw out his best efforts. The discipline of the master-servant relationship can be viewed as logical from a governance point of view.

Secondly, the supply of investment capital had the same characteristics associated with the exclusive ownership exercised by *zaibatsu*. While exclusive ownership gave absolute authority to the holding company office over the subsidiary company, the subsidiary company charged the head office with the general responsibility of providing the necessary capital. From the perspective of the subsidiary company, the main office or holding company was an absolutely stable shareholder. As this office was a shareholder that did not demand high dividends, the managers of subsidiary companies enjoyed a high level of freedom with an abundance of internal capital reserves. In the case of an insufficient internal capital reserve, all they had to do was to persuade the holding company to raise additional funds from the internal or external capital markets. In general, in order to obtain capital smoothly through the stock market, dividend pay-outs were increased, as a signal to the stock market, and stock prices rose accordingly. However, the managers of subsidiary companies within the *zaibatsu* did not need to worry about such matters. Free from financial responsibility, managers concentrated on their own firm's affairs, and this firm-based experience became the soil that nurtured managers and their objectives.

Table 4.4 Budgetary Control by Japanese Big Businesses, 1936

Organization

	Manufacturing	Others	Total
Number of Firms Establishing Budgetary Committees	56	59	115
Number of Firms Reforming Budgetary Control	162	159	321
Total	218	218	436

Frequency of Budget Committee Meetings

Once a week or twice a month	3	0	3
Monthly	17	9	26
Few times a half year	6	4	10
Once a half year	5	12	17
Once a year	2	2	4
Others	4	4	8

Nature of Budgetary Control

	Cos.	Period of Budgets (months)					
		12	6	3	2	1	Others
Sales	119	31	66	1	0	8	13
Sales Costs	102	29	54	0	0	9	10
Management Costs	109	30	60	0	0	10	9
Production Volumes	123	31	63	1	0	12	16
Production Costs	118	27	61	1	0	13	16
Capital Expenditure	60	20	26	0	0	5	9
Cash	92	21	40	0	1	10	20
Profit and Loss	111	31	63	0	0	4	13
Assets and Liabilities	41	10	27	0	0	1	3

Thirdly, the role played by the holding company was the monitoring of its subsidiary companies' operations. With respect to monitoring, it is important to look at the size of holding companies. Generally, the number of personnel at the holding company was few. This fact is often evoked to demonstrate the absence of control. During the 1920s, the number of Mitsui Gomei's personnel ranged between 110-150. In the case of Mitsubishi, the number of personnel at the main office was 82 in 1917 and 175 in 1928. At Sumitomo, the figure was between 70 and 80. Based on these facts, it is difficult to imagine that the head office exercised strategic management, or strongly unified the subsidiary companies. Plainly, the head office was unable to exert much influence on management. However, the number was sufficient to sustain its monitoring system. As research related to budgetary control in that period has pointed out, the concrete means were in force by which the holding company was constantly monitoring the subsidiary companies' situation.[8] Table 4.4 shows the number of firms that adopted budgetary control and supervising committees. More than 70 per cent of big firms adopted budgetary control, and one third founded a committee to examine and to supervise budgets, which included the various types seen in Table 4.4. According to this research, Mitsubishi Mining submitted documents demonstrating detailed budgetary control to its parent company on a monthly, biannual and annual basis. In the case of Sumitomo, the 13 documents comprising the 'Accounting Estimate Report' and the 'Results Report' provided the means to monitor each business sector on a monthly and annual basis.[9]

Governance through budgetary control was implemented at the beginning of each accounting period, in which sales, costs per unit, and other data were detailed, and subject to the main office's assessment and approval. Achieved results were compared to target levels. This type of quantitative performance evaluation by the holding company did not require as much staff as one may think. Indeed, the frequent submission of reports under the budgetary control system tended to create a deep, interlocked relationship between the holding company and its subsidiaries. This type of monitoring, together with the type of personnel management described above, was an effective means of extracting the best efforts from managers of subsidiary companies.

Fourthly, there exist conflicting opinions as to whether or not the holding company participated in the decision-making and managerial strategy of the subsidiary company. For example, Asajima Shoichi emphasises the strong unifying authority of the main office and the characteristic of centralized power in the *zaibatsu* in his study of rules and regulations prescribing the relation between holding and subsidiary companies. On the other hand, Hashimoto Juroh indicates the necessity of looking at the real implementation of these rules. He argues that almost full decentralisation had occurred.[10]

This paper proposes an eclectic and unsurprising answer to this question, by citing a number of cases.

1. Expansion towards the trading business planned by Sumitomo during the First World War was not realized because of the opposition of the General Manger, Suzuki Masaya.

2. The entry into the rayon industry planned by Mitsui Bussan in the 1920s through the establishment of Toyo Rayon was curtailed, and negotiations with Mitsui Gomei took over two years.

3. When Mitsui Mining branched out into the synthetic dye industry, the new firm accepted the technological choice indicated by Mitsui Gomei.

4. Sumitomo Fertilizer tried to expand into the ammonium sulphate industry, hoping in 1928 to exploit new technology. However, the plan was revised according to the wishes of the holding company. The executive director who was responsible for the introduction of the technology was blamed for his 'arbitrary action', and he was released from his position.

5. Tokyo Maritime, a Mitsubishi affiliate, attempted to branch out into the fire insurance business during the First World War by purchasing Meiji Fire. This was opposed to the policy of Mitsubishi Ltd towards the maritime insurance business and the newly-established Mitsubishi Marine Insurance.

6. Mitsubishi Trading in 1924 transferred its sales rights back to Mitsubishi Mining, which had fallen into commercial difficulties.

7. In the case of Sumitomo, it branched into the aluminum and life insurance businesses, and under the leadership of the main office the purchase of Japan Dye Company occurred.

8. In 1934, Mitsubishi Shipping amalgamated with Mitsubishi Aircraft, and established Mitsubishi Heavy Industries. This was based on the initiative of Iwasaki Koyata and the Mitsubishi holding company.

In business history, only cases of conflict tend to remain in the records. In many instances, these records confirm the ability of the parent company as the shareholder to intervene in the subsidiary company's decision-making. Concerning cases one to four inclusive, the subsidiary company's plan was not realized because of the opposition of the holding company, and revision became necessary. Numbers five and six were cases where the parent company harmonized the conflict between subsidiary companies, and, in numbers seven and eight, the holding company kept the initiative to establish new subsidiary companies. Of course, there is no doubt that the cases where plans of the subsidiary company were approved without problem in comparison were incomparably higher.

In numbers one to six, the subject of the plans was a subsidiary company, and, apart from the amalgamation of Mitsui Bussan and Mitsui Gomei in 1940, there are no known examples where subsidiary companies resisted the plans of the holding company. It cannot be denied that basic administrative decision-making and plans were more suitably located at the subsidiary companies, which were closer to the concrete business issues. The process of decentralization as emphasized by Hashimoto Juroh was fairly advanced, and the participation of the holding company of the *zaibatsu* was limited.

However, as well as the process of monitoring, the holding company provided the conditions that enabled subsidiary companies to express opinions. In this case, the conflict was a difference in the judgment of the salaried managers at the holding company and those at the subsidiary company. It goes without saying that the difference in judgment revolved around the risk associated with new businesses. Concerning approval gained for the down-scaling of plans, as in numbers two and four, the opinion of the subsidiary company was respected, and opposition developed around the supply of necessary capital. Based on the principle of exclusive ownership, the holding company bore the responsibility of supplying funds, as, similarly, the family bore responsibility to the holding company. In order to fulfill this role, the holding company of the *zaibatsu* sold in the market part of their own stockholdings and gained a premium. Also, the holding company relaxed the principle of exclusive ownership, and opened the stock of subsidiary companies to the public. Regarding branching out into the life insurance business, as in number seven, and the establishment of Mitsubishi Heavy Industry, in number eight, we can see that the holding company tried to strengthen its own financial base.

Since the holding company had the responsibility and the authority of supplying capital, such conflicts cannot be viewed as examples of intervention in subsidiary company management. Accepting the premise that there was a division of responsibility between the subsidiary company, which drafted and implemented plans of operation, and the holding company, which supplied required funds for these plans, then a fair number of the conflicts between holding company and subsidiary company can be explained.

Despite the fact that the family and holding companies had a strong voice based on exclusive ownership, the subsidiary company maintained a high degree of freedom with respect to business management. Of course, reports to the main office on operations were frequently requested, and detailed information was handed over. This frequency was much higher than that of the average joint stock company's disclosure of information to stock market investors. However, this relationship, when compared with portfolio management that relies on stock market information, reduced the necessity to pay attention to short-term stock price fluctuations and the dividend rates that influence these prices. Because of a base of absolutely stable stockholders, which relieved market pressure and provided greater freedom, there was a greater chance that the managers of *zaibatsu* subsidiary companies could rationally draft operation plans from a long-term perspective.

Finally, concerning the corporate governance of subsidiary companies, let us turn to the question of what kind of organizational problems existed. There was the possibility that cartels and other trade associations had a strong influence on the decision-making of subsidiary companies during this period. Anti-monopoly law did not exist, and, in Japan before 1945, cartels were formed in many business sectors. For example, in case number six, it is said that the recovery of its sales rights made it possible for Mitsubishi Mining to obtain greater profits in addition to joining the copper cartel. Up to that time, Mitsubishi Trading had the sales right and participated in the cartel's price agreements.

However, when this cartel implemented an agreed production cutback, it was impossible for Mitsubishi Trading to join the new agreements without the concurrence of Mitsubishi Mining. The issue of which subsidiary company would represent Mitsubishi in this cartel was problematic. Consequently, Mitsubishi Goshi, the holding company of Mitsubishi *zaibatsu*, decided that Mitsubishi Mining, having recovered its sales rights, would carry the burden of the production cutback.

In case of the copper cartel, there is one more interesting example to be offered. Up until the period of the Showa economic crisis, Sumitomo Beshi Mine was an outsider to this cartel alliance, but Sumitomo Electric Wire was able to draw it into the alliance. Sumitomo Electric Wire was a member of the copper-purchasing cartel that had a harmonious relationship with the copper-producing cartel. Using its connections, the producer's cartel asked Sumitomo Electric Wire to persuade Sumitomo main office, and succeeded at gaining the agreement of Sumitomo Beshi Mine, which had resisted becoming an insider.

The reason for the resistance of managers at Sumitomo Beshi Mine was that, because of the cartel agreement, there was a possibility of losing administrative autonomy. In this case, and that of number six, the holding company determined the coordination of interests among subsidiary companies. This shows that the voice of the holding company was to a certain degree manifested in the harmonization of interests between subsidiary companies.

At the same time, where trade organizations existed, the management of the subsidiary companies was not free from outside intervention. Important problems at the level of management strategy concerning prices, production volumes, and investment in equipment were decisively influenced by cartel agreements. This influence might be exerted on subsidiary companies outside of the cartel through the interest harmonization of the *zaibatsu* holding company. Any discussion related to corporate governance cannot ignore trade associations as a stakeholder.

Conclusion

Firstly, the *zaibatsu* holding company and its organisational structure were a system of negotiation between family and managers, which avoided unwelcome intervention by the family. From the viewpoint of rational decision-making, this choice of organisational structure was a critical success factor for the development of the *zaibatsu*.

Secondly, the pyramidal management structure constituted a formal management hierarchy, but, looking at the functional relationship between holding company and its subsidiaries, the *zaibatsu* developed a horizontal division of responsibility between the holding company and its subsidiaries. By monitoring subsidiaries through budget control and the allocation of managerial human resources, the holding company could obtain the operational information necessary for informed negotiations with the subsidiary.

Seeking a rational management structure, the *zaibatsu* sought to entrust the direction of the holding company and each business division's management to a group of salaried managers with accumulated relevant experience. The family had only a very limited voice with respect to the main office, and gradually the family members became 'rentiers'. The holding company, on the other hand, while maintaining its distance from the family, supervised by means of reports from the subsidiary companies. As investors responsible for the supply of capital, the main office also sought to revise the plans of the subsidiary company in times of need. However, the managers of subsidiary companies became increasingly independent in their recruitment of future managers, and increased the scope of their contribution to the development of the business.

Through the family and the holding company, the *zaibatsu* acquired the organisational characteristics of an exclusive investment relationship. This characteristic of *zaibatsu* corporate governance reveals the underlying organisational structure of the Japanese economy before the Second World War. If this view of corporate governance is accepted, one can say that financial markets did not govern the holding company's relationship with its subsidiaries. The history of *zaibatsu* holding companies shows the possibility of non-market-based governance; that is a corporate governance free from stock market evaluations, and able to provide an efficient structure for advancing the development of the overall enterprise.

Notes

1   H.Takeda, 'The Structure of the Corporate Economy and *Zaibatsu* during Inter-war Period', in T.Yui & E.Daito (ed.), *Japanese Business History*, vol.3, Tokyo (1995). On the *zaibatsu*, also see H.Takeda, '*Zaibatsu*', in K.Oishi (ed.), *The History of Japanese Imperialism*, vol.1, (1985); H.Takeda, 'The Monopolistic Structure and Big Business', in K.Oishi (ed.), *The History of Japanese Imperialism*, vol.2 (1987); H.Takeda and A.Okochi (eds), *The Business System in the Formative Years of Big Business in Japan and Great Britain* (1993).

2   Mitsui Hachiroemon Takamine, *Biography of Mitsui Hachiroemon Takamine* (1988), p.342. See also H.Matsumoto, *Historical Studies on the Mitsui Zaibatsu* (1979).

3   H.Morikawa, *Zaibatsu* (1992), p.219.

4   H.Morikawa, *Studies in the Business History of the Zaibatsu* (1980).

5   Takeda, 'Monopolistic Structure and Big Business'; H.Takeda, *The Business Groups and Japanese Economic Development* (1992). See also H.Takeda, 'The *Zaibatsu* in wartime and its dissolution after the Second World War', in K.Oishi (ed.), *The History of Japanese Imperialism*, vol.3 (1994).

6   Takeda, 'Monopolistic Structure and Big Business.

7   H.Takeda, *The Era of the Zaibatsu* (1995).

8   Y.Hasegawa, *Research on Budgetary Control in Japanese Firm* (1936).

9   S.Asajima, *The Business History of the Sumitomo Zaibatsu during the Interwar Period* (1983).
10 S.Asajima, *Comparative Studies on Zaibatsu Financial Structure* (1986).

Chapter 5

Corporate Governance in British Insurance: How the Phoenix Lost Norwich Union and Lived to Regret London Guarantee and Accident

Clive Trebilcock

Introduction

In insurance dealings, corporate governance is a pressing issue, and it has always been so. All businesses are required to behave properly, and corporate governance equates to proper behaviour in several dimensions: a rational organisation of business; financial probity in the conduct of business; a due regard for shareholder (and here also policyholder) interest; a suitable balance between executive power and collective Board responsibility, or even a suitable balance of knowledge, since directors are not always kept as informed as they should be.

What is taken to be proper behaviour can, of course, be defined, often in the direction of increasing strictness, by law. These requirements are common to most businesses. But insurance has a special duty of care, because it is selling protection against the major threats in life, including fire, illness, damage, old age and death. It has a special duty to balance shareholder interest (or profit) against policyholder interest (remunerative products and prompt payment of claims). And when the office is a mutual association that does not have shareholders, and where the policyholders are the major stakeholders, their interest has to be balanced against that of the venture as a business. In all cases, the investment side of the insurance operation must be handled with prudence, so that there are sufficient assets - and especially sufficient reserves - to meet all claims including disaster claims. Because of the nature of the protection offered, policyholders with insurance companies are stakeholders in a particularly sharply-defined sense. The recent mis-selling of investment plans and personal pensions in Britain provide well-known instances in which that stake has been abused. Here, parts of the industry were more concerned with developing new products than in making them safe for consumers. The need to launch new products creates one kind of pressure upon proper behaviour.

Another follows from the stresses and strains that inevitably attend major acquisitions or demergers amongst insurance companies. Phoenix Assurance was one of the top six British offices for much of the 20th Century, and traded as an independent insurer from 1782 until 1984. At the heart of its modern history stands an incident in which the forces unleashed by a chain of acquisitions - notably that of London Guarantee and Accident in 1922 - and a crucial demerger put a special strain upon its corporate governance. This incident affected not just the Phoenix, but the development of the entire UK insurance industry. There is the problem, of course, as to what was *misgovernance* by the standards of the time. However, some of these events - those perpetrated by London Guarantee - were misgovernance by the standard of any time.

The story contains: an early, indeed precocious, divisionalisation on the organisational front at Phoenix; a startling lack of financial probity and total disregard for shareholder interest at LGA; and, in the following cases at Phoenix, a curious rejection by management of a prototype exercise in 'due diligence'; a Board unwilling to challenge its executive, and a dominant chief executive who was reluctant to surrender the reins, even when he became chairman.

There are two aspects of this chief executive that make general points worth picking up at the outset. Firstly, Gerald Ryan was a legend in the early 20th Century British insurance industry, the most able actuary of his time, the doyen of a difficult skill. He possessed a status within the business world of his generation comparable, say, to that of a Beeching, Harvey-Jones or Weinstock within their generations. Attaching to such figures is a problem that needs more analysis: the matter of managerial charisma or reputation. Nick Tiratsoo has rightly drawn attention to the almost magical status accredited to apparently successful CEOs, but this gives some of them the magical capability to make truly stupendous mistakes.[1]

Secondly, Ryan, like Beardmore in Robert Fitzgerald's paper, was successful in a particular market format. It would take ingenuity to make a mess of his business in the expanding armaments markets of the pre-1914 era (although Armstrongs managed it). But it was not the ageing of the first-generation weaponry specialists at Vickers, nor the innate over-confidence of Beardmore that caused problems for defence contracting in the 1920s; it was the turnaround in the market for arms.[2] The management problem in the defence sector after 1920 is not comparable to the management problem of the arms industry in the 1900s. Similarly, Ryan made his reputation as a takeover king in the favourable conditions of the 1900s, and did not read the more complex circumstances of the 1920s at all correctly. Like Beardmore, Ryan was trained to go, and he did not know when to stop.

From the Single Line to the Composite Insurance Office

Between 1870 and 1914, Phoenix moved towards becoming a genuine multi-national corporation. At home, around the turn of the century, adjustments to enterprise and structure were required. Much of the enterprise was shaped by the company's 'Second Founder', Gerald Hemington Ryan.[3] The adjustment in structure ran towards the multi-divisional 'composite' office, which dominated the insurance markets of the twentieth century.

By the early 1900s, the rationale for the older type of specialized, single-purpose insurance company was less firm than it had been. As company reserves grew to plutocratic proportions, the insistence of prudent founders of the insurance business that different lines of business should be protected by distinct and separate allocations of investment reserves lost some of its force.[4] Similarly, the underwriting market became more complex, containing by the 1900s accident, travel, burglary and industrial insurances, as well as the venerable staples of fire, life and marine. There was less reason for retaining the separation of function that had served well when the whole of the business had been devoted to cover of buildings, lives and ships. The new lines blurred the old distinctions.

Alert insurance men began to argue that the way to boost premiums was to offer all the industry's 'commodities' across a single 'counter'. Then, one could draw life or accident or, later, pension business from one's fire risks; home protection policies from life risks; marine business from industrial business, and so on. Typically, a manufacturer seeking fire cover might also be sold accident cover for his workshops, and group insurance for his workforce. By July 1907, even *The Times* was using a fashionable analogy to describe the change: 'Insurance offices are rapidly losing those specialist features which at one period were carried to excess and are becoming stores at whose counters all kinds of insurance are retailed.'[5] As the underwriting processes became more diversified, it made good sense to reflect that diversification within the structure of insurance companies.

It is arguable also that, with the transition from the single product office of the nineteenth century to the composite office of the early twentieth, the insurance business produced a pioneering form of the multi-divisional corporate structure subsequently adopted by many of the largest manufacturing concerns. To be sure, the idea in insurance was to sell a wide range of insurance products through a single marketing organization. But, behind the single marketing organization, were a number of specialist 'divisions' - life, fire, accident, marine, and later aviation - each with its own expertise and 'technology'. As in many other industries, the pressure towards product diversification was the shaping influence behind the divisional system.[6] Phoenix felt its way towards these insights in the first years of the century. In this process, it had one true guide. On 1 January 1908, Gerald Ryan became General Manager, and continued in the post of Chief Executive until 1920; he then became chairman of the company, and served an active term in this role until 1931; even after retiring from the chair, he remained on the board until his death in 1937.

For 30 years, Ryan dominated the Phoenix. He was one of the major influences upon its development in the twentieth century, and perhaps the strongest influence of all. Between 1907-22, Ryan transformed an office which had prided itself on its specialization in fire business into a complex underwriting organization able to offer a full service across the life, accident, marine and fire markets. He did so primarily by buying capacity: the period 1907-22 saw a string of acquisitions by

Phoenix. Starting relatively modestly with the full absorption of the Pelican and British Empire, its sister life office, in 1908, the Phoenix's successful shopping list went on to incorporate the Law Life Assurance in 1910; the Union Marine Insurance in 1911; the Northern Maritime Insurance in 1917; and its most ambitious purchases, Norwich Union Fire in 1919, and London Guarantee and Accident in 1922.[7]

Scale and Scope and Insurance

The most imposing recent analysis of the modern business corporation, laid out in Chandler's epic two volumes, *Strategy and Structure* and *Scale and Scope*, argues that the hallmark of 20th century big business is the appearance of a central and specialized executive staff.[8] As this central command structure develops, the firm divides into separate departments, each of which is answerable to the headquarters cadre. Such business organizations first developed in the US in the years before 1914. In the inter-war years, the global contraction of trade encouraged a further development: large enterprises split into distinct divisions, and created branch organizations for handling overseas markets, the whole array again reporting back to and being directed by the executive core. This distinctively modern version of big business was centred upon manufacturing industry. Its 'classic' location was the US, but Germany had created a similar (if less competitive) apparatus of large-scale business organizations over the same time period. On the other hand, Britain, encumbered by an inheritance of small, family-based enterprises, was slow to effect the transition to Chandler's ideal business type. Although market and technological pressures are allowed a place in this development, the premium influence is reckoned to be the business leadership: the strategic choices that mould the new business form are taken by the captains of the executive cadre.

Do the Phoenix reforms of the 1900s, therefore, cast Ryan as a classic Chandlerian hero, and Phoenix as a specimen from a mesolithic stage of pre-Chandlerian divisionalisation? Certainly, Ryan created a multi-divisional structure, with a multi-national spread, a branch system of organization, and a central executive group. But the width of genuine choice he exercised may be open to doubt. And, by Chandler's standards, he is oddly located in both time - before 1914 - and place - the UK.

Indeed, the applicability of Chandler's formula to large business organizations in the services sector may be questioned. There are few attempts in his work to fit the master-pattern to the service sector in any country. Yet, in Britain, the multi-divisional composite insurance company, with multi-national spread, was in full cry well before 1914. However inclined British manufacturing may have been towards unsuitably old-fashioned forms of family-based organization, this had never been an option for insurance ventures. Scale and scope had been an imperative here from the start. If the myriad risks in a given field of insurance were to be covered effectively, a certain mass of resources was essential: this could come from a sizeable group of rich capitalists, a more sizeable group of partners in a given profession (such as Phoenix's founding sugar-refiners), or an even more sizeable group of the less rich (such as house-owners) clubbing together to find mutual relief from threat.

So the insurance sector does not make a suitable landscape for Chandler's strictures upon British enterprise. But had its divisionalized and multi-national expression of scale progressed so far by 1914 that it may be reckoned to have stolen a march on Chandler's exemplars in American manufacturing? And, if so, why? Certainly, it does not seem to have been as a result of dashing business leadership by Ryan and his peers. Rather, they were carried along by peculiarities of market, costs and 'technology'. Insurance customers increasingly wished to cover their different types of risk - against fire, death, injury, burglary, and so on - in a reduced number of transactions. Convenience for the insured was to acquire the various types of product from the same insurer. High levels of competition and rising costs also made it economical for the insurer to group the different insurance lines within the same administrative structure. This was a classic, if early, instance of organizational change driven by transaction costs. 'The modern corporation', according to Oliver Williamson, 'is mainly to be understood as the product of a series of organizational innovations that have had the purpose and effect of economising transaction costs'.[9]

Yet the 'technology' of the different lines of insurance did not cohere especially well; there was no strong 'production' logic which pointed in the direction of the composite form. Fire, life, marine, and, more recently, accident insurance had developed, down to the 1900s, largely within different, specialized firms, and had created very distinct insurance practices and processes - in an industrial sense, quite *different* technologies. This is scarcely surprising since the tasks of insuring a ship's cargo, a domestic house or a human life involve quite different issues of title, risk appraisal and probability management. Viewed as products, as Supple points out, these different items have 'little more in common than, say, the respective purchases of clothing, furniture, gardening implements and food'.[10] This suggests a technological reason for the containment of management within the division and for the kind of residual divisional independence that Fitzgerald also reports.[11]

The institutional systems and skills built up to deal with these problems had not developed convergently. Therefore, if the different insurance technologies were brought under the same roof, there was effectively little choice but to organize them within a divisional *structure*: the divisions of fire, life, marine, accident did not have to be designed; they were ready-made. Here, the divisional layout is not the choice of the corporate strategist; it is presented to the corporate strategist by pre-existing markets; and then forced upon him by demanding clients and escalating costs.

Ryan and his contemporaries read the inscription that these market forces left on the underwriting wall. It indicated not only that they should grow by diversification, but also how they should grow. The method was to be by external means - that is, the acquisition of new companies - rather than by internal means -

that is, the development of new departments. Given that the technologies and skills of the various fields of insurance were so different, it made more sense to pursue them by purchase than by the re-education of existing staff. Of course, this was particularly true when 'new-type' insurance products, such as personal accident, employers' liability or, later, motor insurance were concerned. Phoenix, under Ryan, was to use the external method.[12] The companies which did so, including the Royal and the Commercial Union, were to achieve greater success in building multi-division composites than offices like the Royal Exchange Assurance and the Alliance, which attempted to amass new capacity by the internal method.[13] However, a strategy of divisionalization through acquisition required special care in the corporate governance of the acquisition process.

Phoenix in Search of Accident

Ryan in 1907 brought off his first really major insurance merger, the fusion between the old sister companies Phoenix and Pelican, which had transacted fire and life business in familial harmony since the late eighteenth century. They had shareholders and directors in common, and, for decades, they lived across the road from one another in Lombard Street. The merger, which took effect from early 1908, may have obeyed the composite logic of the time, but it was found fairly predictable by the financially streetwise of the day, although they did spare a moment to wonder why the richer Pelican was climbing into the nest with the more dangerous Phoenix. They might have wondered less if they had known that Ryan's plan actually called for a *three-way* merger, which was intended to include an accident company. It was his first mistake in corporate strategy to let his choice fall upon London Guarantee and Accident. He missed LGA in 1907. It was his second major mistake in corporate strategy to keep his eye fixed on LGA, and to return to this bone fifteen years later. And it was a major failure in corporate governance that allowed him to do so. The cost to Phoenix was to be the loss of the far more valuable Norwich Union Fire, which Phoenix had acquired by 1920. If Phoenix and NUF had stayed together, the story of British insurance would have been different, and indeed Phoenix may not have belied its name and perished in 1984. For the demise of the Phoenix had much to do with its inability to achieve any further major merger in its next sixty years of life. The acquisition of LGA was a glaring example of the high cost of misplaced corporate memory.

The Workmen's Compensation Act of 1906 had dramatised the new market opportunity for workplace insurance, and Phoenix responded by writing its first accident policies in January 1907. It also kept a weather eye on the activities of the other veteran offices: the Royal Exchange had first broached the accident market in 1898, and joined the Accident Offices Association in 1904, while the Sun set up a specialized Accident Department in 1907.[14] However, by 1907, Ryan and his colleagues at Phoenix calculated that they needed additional capacity and expertise in the field, if they were to match the diversification policies of their peers. This was an attempt to procure an accident business *larger* than any that Phoenix and Pelican could support, so diversifying by the external route.

For its part, the target company, the LGA, felt itself to be in a vulnerable position. As a specialist accident company, it had suffered a paradoxical blow at the hands of the Workmen's Compensation Act. In consequence of this legislation, the LGA Directors informed their shareholders that 'most of the leading Fire Insurance Companies are now undertaking Personal Accident, Workmen's Compensation and Burglary Insurance. They no doubt will be formidable competitors'.[15] Doubtless, they also had in mind the parlous state of the market in the US, where much of their business was, then as later. Their first thought for a remedy was a direct return of service: instead of waiting to be assaulted by incoming fire offices, they would attack by entering the fire market on their own account. However, shareholder unrest both on this issue and on the failure of the dividend to rise spoiled the volley.

In March 1907, shareholders representing about one third of LGA equity protested at the design of the balance sheet: 'It is, as it always is, excellent, but it is set out in such a way as to prevent the majority of shareholders from understanding it properly'. What they were being prevented from understanding was that, if the Board were allowed to go into fire risks as well as accident risks, how much *more*, asked the rebels, would they consider it prudent to salt away in reserves? The outlook for the dividend was not deemed to be bright. The obfuscation was a small point of pre-1914 corporate governance, but one which was typical of LGA and of endurance long beyond 1914.

Answerability to stakeholders was not a prominent feature of LGA. In 1907, however, the shareholder propaganda was effective; it forced the LGA directors to seek an alternative method of protecting their business. Again, they adopted a direct tactic: a frontal approach to a fire office, which, by merger, would 'keep their business together'.[16] The initiative was taken when LGA put this proposition to Phoenix in May or early June 1907. With great swiftness, a provisional agreement was beaten out, and signed, by mid-July. Just before this, on 29 June, A. R. Kirby of LGA wrote to Ryan, 'I would join on reputation and your published figures. One reason (is) that I believe the Combined Company will be able within a reasonable period, to be able to double the business we have now. But I have to convince others', though he added, scarcely reassuringly, 'I return your letter to enable you to have a copy made. I am sorry to say I never keep a copy of any letter I write, with the result that I never write if I can help it'.[17]

Despite Kirby's sales talk, however, doubts were beginning to spring in Lombard Street. Although LGA's US profits had risen between 1903-06, the current year, with securities depreciating in New York and London, promised to be a miserable one. And Phoenix, of course, had just taken the hammering of a lifetime in America, in consequence of the Great Earthquake at San Francisco in 1906. A company which depended as heavily as did LGA on the US market would not have been at its most alluring in 1907. But even more damning was a legal query, which had surfaced by early July. Doubt had arisen as to whether any successor company to LGA would be empowered to retain the benefit of its American accident trade. The prospect of LGA with its American portfolio was bad enough. But the prospect of LGA without its American portfolio was not worthy of attention from Phoenix and Pelican. Between 15-17 July, they terminated negotiations with LGA. In the longer perspective, the flirtation with LGA was a fateful one for the Phoenix. The company's - or Ryan's - ambitions for an accident acquisition became unhealthily concentrated on LGA. The flirtation became a fixation. Phoenix returned to it in the 1920s, when it would have done better to remember its doubts about the relationship between the LGA and the USA.

The Bird Takes the Norwich Union

In its quest for further corporate growth in the inter-war years, Phoenix participated in one of the oddest incidents in modern insurance history. For the veteran insurer acquired two major offices, one each in the fire and accident sectors, within five years of the Armistice, and lost one of them within six. The offices acquired were the Norwich Union Fire and the London Guarantee and Accident. The office sold on was the Norwich Union Fire. Ryan, it transpired, could make mistakes. And they followed, much like Beardmore's, from an inability to make the transition from the markets of the 1900s to those of the 1920s.

In 1914, and still in 1918, Phoenix compared poorly with the other great composites in two areas of insurance activity. These were the fire market - ironically, for this was the Phoenix's birthplace - and the accident market. If Ryan's strategy of advance by acquisition was to be sustained, these were the natural target zones for the next offensive. But, of course, offensives of a different sort had occupied the hearts, minds and energies of the nation between 1914 and 1918. It is striking that, in the immediate aftermath of the First World War, Phoenix's appetite for acquisition was sustained virtually irrespective of economic conditions; there was no sign of any abatement from pre-war levels. On the contrary, two of Ryan's most ambitious coups were tried during this period, one in 1919, the other in 1922. In general economic terms, it is perhaps easier to understand the first than the second.

For the economic phase that followed the Armistice did deliver the re-stocking boom which all good capitalists had been anticipating ever since the war began. Investment levels were high, and there was much speculative activity in the promotion and amalgamation of companies; shipping and cotton textile firms were prominent in the sharper aspects of this activity. But financial and insurance ventures did not escape attention. Ryan observed in January 1920 that 'during the last few months, the market for insurance shares has become active and speculative and...(has) forced prices up to a very high level'.[18] The market peaked in October-November 1919. The expansionary optimism of this period encouraged many schemes of corporate reconstruction.

Large insurers had been as encouraged as any, the Royal Insurance and the London and Lancashire prominent among them: the former had purchased a sizeable interest in the Liverpool and London and Globe at the end of October 1919, and the London and Lancashire had absorbed the Law Union and Rock at around the same time. But then the managers of the Norwich Union had themselves shown more initiative than merely noting the trend among their competitors.

Late in 1919, R. Y. Sketch, General Manager of Norwich Union Fire, put a proposal to Ryan which the Phoenix General Manager found highly congenial: it concerned a plan for the fusion of the two old offices - Phoenix had 137 years, Norwich Union 122 - on equal terms.[19] Norwich Union, a rich and successful but deeply provincial office, was probably looking for better defences in a confusing post-war world of rising competition and intensifying amalgamation. There are suggestions also that Sketch wished to give his stalwart East Anglian veteran a little of the metropolitan gloss displayed by Ryan's Phoenix. And it is unlikely that Sketch, anymore than Ryan in his British Empire days, missed the potential advantage to be had as the conductor of a larger band.

Indeed, there are some hints of head-hunting in Ryan's handling of Norwich Union and Sketch. In 1919, Ryan was 58, had achieved all that he might reasonably have expected, and was looking forward to a lighter non-executive role. His appointment as chairman of Phoenix was announced on 28 November 1919 - inaugurating an era for the company quite as distinct as 'the inter-war years' were for the economy as a whole - and Phoenix needed a general manager. There was no obvious candidate within the Phoenix. It is surely significant that, upon completion of the Phoenix-NUF agreement, a senior colleague telegrammed his congratulations to Ryan: 'Scheme *and man* are all that could be desired.'[20] For Phoenix, Sketch's appearance in 1920 seemed providential: he provided the succession to Ryan, following him as general manager in 1920-35, managing director 1935-40, and chairman 1940-48.

Nevertheless, Ryan did not go after Norwich Union simply to get Sketch. There was much emphasis on the naturalness of a marriage between two veterans in difficult times. Ryan described the notion as 'an ideal one...cementing the alliance of two old friends', while *The Times* agreed that 'the offices have long worked very harmoniously together'.[21] Similarly, a Special Committee of the Phoenix board, briefed to consider the proposal, were told that it was 'a transaction of the first magnitude with... an old-established institution transacting business all over the world on much the same lines as the Phoenix'.[22]

But there was more to it than that: in the welter of speculative amalgamation after the war, *both* Phoenix and Norwich Union Fire were potential targets for the biggest predators, and particularly for the two which furthest outstripped Phoenix in premium income, the Royal and the Commercial Union. Ryan was well aware that Phoenix and Norwich Union shared an interest in keeping themselves off the menu of these offices. Nor did it escape him that the two companies shared more than a similarity of styles and strategies. Their equality was also of the plutocratic variety, for each of them could dispose of some £2m in free assets. The accretion of financial power that this represented to Phoenix - and the debilitating loss, should it be misplaced - was awesome. Ryan was duly impressed. Nevertheless, he found other arguments to assist his directors. On 8 December 1919, he listed these for the Special Committee. In the fire market, Phoenix would 'acquire a very large accession of profitable business of all classes in all parts of the world'. Indeed, since the NUF between 1913-19 took over 70 per cent of its premium income from the foreign sector, it would powerfully reinforce Phoenix's great historical specialism as an exporter (see Table 5.1).

Table 5.1 Norwich Union Fire, Foreign Earnings, 1913-19

Year	Total NUF Premiums £	Foreign Premiums as % of Total	Foreign Losses as % of Total	NUF Foreign Premiums £	Phoenix Foreign Premiums £
1913	1,187,670	73.3	57.6	870,582	2,311,516
1915	1,188,767	70.6	50.7	838,858	2,464,438
1917	1,365,245	73.7	47.9	1,006,319	2,835,101
1919	1,921,292	71.6	43,2	1,375,299	3,075,337

Sources: NUF Fire Manager's Account Book; Phoenix Foreign Agents Book.

Within the UK, the company's position would also be greatly strengthened, 'especially in places and districts where the Phoenix is not at present strong'. So, if Phoenix's City lore would add polish to NU, the Norwich office's provincial power would create a balancing asset for Phoenix. Then, somewhat disingenuously, Ryan added:

> Incidentally also, the Phoenix will obtain a means of starting an Accident business in the United States by reason of the other company having machinery and funds available there for the purpose. For a long time we have desired to enter the American field for casualty business, but it would require transmission of funds to America in order to put up the necessary capital and reserves and this is quite impracticable in the present state of the exchange.[23]

NUF possessed a sizeable accident account, and, given Ryan's strategy of diversification by acquisition - given, especially, his failure to acquire an accident company in 1908 - it is difficult to see this factor as merely 'incidental' to the negotiations of 1919-20. Nor, surely, was it fortuitous that Sketch by training was an accident specialist. Indeed, accident business, and, most unfortunately,

American accident business, was to remain central to Ryan's thinking throughout the 1920s. It was a powerful influence on Phoenix's appetite for NUF, even to the point perhaps of compulsive eating.

The first attempt to satisfy the craving was an oddly ingenious scheme for integration on entirely equal terms. The notion was to create a third insurance venture, a holding company to be called the British Empire Insurance Co., which would control *both* Phoenix and Norwich Union. Ryan was to be Chairman of all three companies, Sketch the General Manager of all three, and the Board of the holding company to be composed of six directors apiece from the London and Norwich offices. Ryan emphasised that 'One policy would be pursued throughout the three companies, the control being unified by the common Chairman and General Manager. Thus the business of the two companies could be worked together with very great advantage in many directions'.[24] The combined capital of the three units would be £2.9m and the total funds an impressive £21.9m. Shareholding in the superstructure company was to be exactly split between Phoenix and Norwich Union Fire and - in a stipulation that was to prove fatal - it was to be purchased at the ruling share price of the other company. That is, NUF would buy its half-share of the holding company equity at the current Phoenix share price, and *vice versa*.

Neither office wished to pass out of existence or become the subsidiary of the other. The British Empire device protected this desire for autonomy beautifully, leaving the two original companies, names and styles intact. Moreover, it defended a flank vital to NUF: its special relationship with Norwich Union Life. Originally, in 1808, the life office had been an off-shoot of the fire office, which was then itself a mutual office. However, in 1821, NUF became a proprietary company, while NUL stayed a mutual. Subsequently, the two Norwich offices developed as separate ventures in capital and organization. Nevertheless, over many decades, they maintained a close collaboration, sharing directors and agencies, handing on business and enjoying high reputation within their home city. In its relations with other companies, NUF could not afford to compromise the Norwich identity, sacrifice its own name, or divert business from NUL; within the local economy, the consequences would have been dire. However, a joint interest in the British Empire Insurance would have enlarged the scope of NUF's operations without risking any of these outcomes.

It is not surprising, then, that Sketch found the British Empire proposal 'the one that appeals to us, in fact it is the only one to concentrate on'.[25] It fitted the Norwich calculus. But it also fitted the Ryan composite strategy. He reflected upon the neatness with which the NUF project conformed with the current flow in the multiple insurance market:

> The present feature of insurance business is the movement in the direction of large combines which constitute a very powerful rivalry to those undertakings which maintain an isolated existence. The

scheme...provides a means of defending the interest of two of the oldest companies while fully preserving their separate identities.[26]

Ryan had in mind growth, competition, defence, and, of course, accident. Yet, despite the rapid construction of an accord between Ryan and Sketch, and despite the obviously warm personal relations between the two men, reinforced by Sketch's trips from Norwich to Ryan's conveniently situated mansion at Hintlesham Hall, the proposal was not accorded an equally swift or rapturous reception by the Phoenix Board. The fall in insurance company shares in late 1919 did not help, for, in a bear market, it would be more difficult to promote the equities of a new holding company than those of two old dependables. But these were not the only worries over shares. Sharp eyes detected evidence of over-eagerness in the financial arrangements especially. Critics pointed out the flaw in the proposed scheme for the purchase of joint shares in the holding company: the NUF shares stood at £90, the Phoenix shares at only £15. If Phoenix were required to buy its half of the equity at £90 per share, and NUF its half at £15 per share, the London company would end up £2.2 million out of pocket, to the profit of the Norwich office. Yet the Phoenix opposition stressed 'our free capital is at least £1m, not to say £2m, bigger than the Norwich Union. Our premium income is bigger. Our profits are bigger'.[27]

The only inference to be drawn from Ryan's apparent willingness to accept such financial sacrifice is that he was desperate to have NUF in the Phoenix fold. Certainly, his regard for the sharp price, so evident in his pre-war acquisitions, is notably absent here. So too is his ability to carry the Board. Although the introductory stages of the negotiations had been carried out with Ryan's customary secrecy - his directors had no inkling before early December - the Phoenix Board, when they did find out, declined to let him have his way at this price. Another way had to be found.

The second way was found with enormous speed. The coffin nails were hammered into the holding company scheme on 6 December 1919. On the same day, Sketch and Ryan met again at Hintlesham. Their discussion produced the framework for a full fusion between the two companies; the formal notes of these talks are virtually a draft of the final agreement between Phoenix and NUF. When Ryan told the Special Committee about the NUF proposal on 8 December, it was the fusion scheme that he put before them. Also, on 8 December, the NUF Board agreed to receive an offer couched in these terms and to recommend it to their shareholders.[28] Two days later, the scheme was approved by the full Phoenix Board, and the press announcements went out on 12 December. The memorandum of agreement was signed on 12 January 1920, although the arrangement was actually to run from the first day of the new year. Final confirmation was achieved on 18 February 1920. Ryan clearly was in a hurry.

However, the scheme was executed with much of Ryan's old panache. Its general design retained many of the guiding principles of the British Empire device. As *The Times* realized, the intention was 'a real fusion...not a mere absorption...(but) a new career of the closest joint working'.[29] As before, each company was to pursue business under its own name, its own organization, and its own Board. The individuality of each office was to be emphasized, the whole 'gaining advantage from joining with the other'. Capital in the new venture was again to be held equally by Phoenix and NUF shareholders. The same power structure as envisaged in the British Empire scheme was to be retained, since the Chairman of Phoenix (Ryan) was to become the Chairman of both Boards, while the General Manager of NUF (Sketch) was to become General Manager of both units within the fused company. There was to be an exchange of directors with five NUF directors joining the Phoenix Board, and five Phoenix men sitting on the Norwich Board. At this point, the question of travelling and hotel expenses for the Norwich directors caused some consternation, but it was decided that the larger good justified the costly shuttle between East Anglia and the City.

Perhaps most important was the renewed - indeed strengthened - concern about Norwich Union Life. With NUF effectively absorbed by Phoenix - whatever the disclaimers - this was obviously a sharper worry than that raised by the proposal to incorporate NUF within the British Empire scheme. So the safeguards were stringent. The longstanding community of interest between NUF and NUL had to be protected.[30] Thus, Phoenix was not to compete in the life market with NUL, and NUF was not to pass life business to Phoenix. Here a major principle of the fusion and of all Ryan's acquisitions, the generation of non-fire diversification, was abrogated in favour of NUL. Sketch was very exercised that his back should be protected in Norwich: 'Our income here is a very, substantial, profitable one and anything that safeguards this should be done. Our competitors here will not be slow to try and foster the idea that we are no longer *the* local choice.'[31] Proper handling of NUL was indispensable to remaining the local hero.

At the end of it all, Phoenix emerged with a total nominal capital of £3.7, divided into three different types of ordinary share. By the end of March 1920, Phoenix had acquired 95 per cent of NUF capital. Effectively, Phoenix secured NUF for a 30 per cent premium. The joint market capitalization of the two companies on the eve of the fusion was £10.3 million. NUF's share of this was £3.96 million.[32] But Phoenix paid half of the joint sum to get NUF into the fusion, or £5.15 million; hence the premium. The Royal had paid a 30 per cent premium to take Liverpool and London and Globe at the top of the market in 1919. The London & Lancs paid a more modest 27 per cent to get the Law Union in 1919. It was the premium paid in a *falling* market, rather than the recent track record in asking prices, which singled out the Phoenix-NUF deal.

Some Phoenix observers believed that the Norwich shareholders had been 'uncommon well treated'.[33] Others were more forthright: the *Evening Standard* reported that 'Evidently some shareholders of the Phoenix Assurance fail to enthuse over the absorption of the Norwich Union...(feeling) that the Norwich Union has had the best of the bargain'.[34] One Phoenix director, R.K. Hodgson, recovering from his annual attack of influenza, warned Ryan in only semi-jocular style that he could only 'hope yet to face our infuriated shareholders.'[35] Over-eagerness seemed once more to be expressing itself in the form of an improbable financial largesse.

Nevertheless, Ryan sailed on. He attended his first Board meeting in Norwich on 29 December 1919, and was 'highly gratified at the kindness of my reception'.[36] This was scarcely surprising: in Norwich, Ryan was regarded as a metropolitan Merlin, the underwriting equivalent of the man who had discovered the philosopher's stone. When addressing his first joint shareholders' meeting as Chairman at the end of January 1920, he stressed the familiar themes, 'a natural development of an old alliance'; 'the greater powers of defence against competition'; and, certainly, not least in his mind, 'the co-operation of two powerful companies (which) will open up a wider field of enterprise in that important part of the world.'[37] By the last he meant, of course, the United States.

However, even amidst this optimistic and congratulatory review, he did find it necessary to concede that 'a few unfavourable comments have reached the Board, based upon the view that the terms are too liberal to the Norwich Union shareholders'. But he defied their mathematical logic, and, concentrating upon the future gains to capacity, ended with his own rousing approach to the figures. 'If I had not great respect for the laws of arithmetic, I should say that, in this case, 2 and 2 do not make 4 but 5 or a higher number.'[38] Yet there were some who muttered that this was precisely the kind of arithmetic that he must have applied to the NUF share values.

The Phoenix-NUF fusion has some of the old Ryan magic. It was done with great speed, yet across an enormous sweep of detail. His control of the detail was formidable, as was the ability to re-work it to create within days an alternative to the failed British Empire proposal. As before, he prided himself, justifiably, upon the standard of negotiations conducted 'in the most amicable and harmonious spirit'.[39] He was right too about the boost to capacity. Total Phoenix premium income more than doubled between the earning years 1919-20. Fire and marine earnings rose by similar amounts (128.4 and 117.4 per cent respectively), while accident earnings, reflecting significantly on Ryan's priorities, rocketed by 852.8 per cent. Life income provided something of a control, since NUF could not transact this type of business: it rose by 2.1 per cent only. Taken all round, Phoenix was about twice as big at the end of 1920, as it had been towards the end of 1919.

There are perhaps three pauses for thought. The negotiations were marked by a kind of financial over-optimism, even a type of rashness, that was new in Ryan's handling of major acquisitions. NUF was clearly worth having, but it would have been more reassuring had Ryan sought to have it at a keener price. A second doubt follows from the first: despite the ready acceptance of a high price for NUF, the negotiations considered few *other* aspects of the deal than the financial. There was a little, but not much, discussion between Ryan and Sketch on the business implications of the fusion, and even less upon its possible administrative repercussions. This preoccupation with financial assets and relative disregard for business and administrative content are common danger signs in mergers and acquisitions: here, it carried some penalty in regard to Phoenix's fusion with NUF, but was to prove positively lethal in regard to the next item on Ryan's shopping list, London Guarantee and Accident. Lastly, there is a serious reservation concerning Phoenix's growing preoccupation with accident business, and particularly American accident business. Again, this was a feature which proved reasonably safe in the NUF fusion, but enormously destructive in the takeover of LGA.

Nevertheless, an optimistic reading would concentrate on what NUF brought to Phoenix. By 1925, Phoenix would have been a great deal poorer if it had *not* possessed NUF. Indeed, it would have been poorer to the tune of about £2,228,260 or 41.5 per cent of its fire account, by about £2,152,705 or 35.2 per cent of its accident account, and by about £506,995 or 48.7 per cent of its marine account. Altogether, in 1925, Phoenix would have been a smaller operation by some 30 per cent had it not possessed NUF. We know these counterfactual proportions so exactly, because, unfortunately, by 1925, they were not counterfactual at all. By 1925, an optimistic reading was not possible, because Phoenix no longer possessed NUF, and *was* poorer by exactly these amounts and proportions. The reason was that Ryan's final acquisition - LGA - went so badly wrong that his successful penultimate acquisition - NUF - had to be sold to cover the cost of the damage.

An American Accident in London

The acquisition of London Guarantee and Accident in 1922 was one of the worst things that happened to the Phoenix in the 20th century. In the short term, it was a financial disaster. Before long, it became a corporate disaster, involving the loss of Norwich Union Fire. Responsibility is difficult to allocate. Ryan, though a non-executive Chairman, was much involved in the deal and many of his long-running interests were centrally in play. The power, range and vivacity of his Chairman's Reports in the early 1920s establish beyond doubt that Ryan remained a central power in the Phoenix's affairs.[40] Sketch, though very proficient in the subsequent damage control, displayed a good-natured innocence in the earlier financial negotiations, together with a deference to Ryan, which sometimes beggars belief. The affair raises unusual questions of corporate governance, due diligence, and executive control.

Ryan had tried to buy London Guarantee once before, in 1907; but then LGA had priced itself out of the deal. Also, Ryan had at that time been properly wary of the gains to be had from the American market; and it may be that he would have done better to maintain this wariness. He had wanted an accident company in 1907. And, in 1922, Phoenix, though it had Norwich Union Fire, and its accident capacity, still lacked a specialist accident company. Yet to go back to the same accident specialist in 1922 could argue for a certain lack of imagination. Why should diversification into accident equate to diversification into LGA? At this point, Phoenix seems rather to have been running on rails.

The explanation for this lies in a peculiar saga that centres on the years 1912-22. Of course, the LGA of early 1922 was a very different company from the LGA of 1907. Its total premium income had risen from £0.4 million to £5.1 million, over three-quarters of it drawn from the US at each point. However, by 1922, it also took business from 18 other countries. It had enjoyed particularly rapid income growth during the war period, and, in the immediate aftermath, especially in US general accident business. But these major increases in scale did not depend on accident or America alone. In 1909, the company had diversified into UK and European fire insurance, in 1915 into marine, and in 1919 into life. From 1920, it added the American fire trade of the North Empire Insurance Co. of Canada, and, from 1921, most of the equity of the important United Firemen's Insurance Co. of Philadelphia. London Guarantee's authorised capital had remained at £250,000 since the company's inception in 1869, but was increased to £375,000 in 1920, 52 per cent paid up. Total assets had soared from their pre-war levels, from £1.0m in 1911 to £6.25m in 1920.

Undoubtedly, LGA had become a much bigger, and, apparently, richer prize, and one which had gone through its own process of evolution towards the composite form in the 1900s and 1910s. By 1920, its total income flow of over £5.1m was considerable, even by Phoenix standards (£9.9m). But it was LGA's accident business that remained the lure for Phoenix. Around 1909, LGA's accident account had dwarfed Phoenix's own by a factor of 10, but by 1919 the disparity had worsened to a factor of 17. This was before Phoenix got its talons into the accident income of NUF, but, even after it had done so, LGA retained a superiority of better than two-to-one, with total accident receipts in 1921 of £3.5m against the Phoenix-NUF figure of £1.7m. If the Phoenix in 1921 was roughly twice as large as the LGA in terms of total earnings, the LGA's accident account remained double the size of Phoenix's own, despite the latter's best efforts and a major amalgamation.

The position of LGA in the American accident market looked similarly impressive.[41] In 1920, it took $14m in US accident premiums, making it the third largest UK operator in this business after the Employers' Liability and Ocean Accident.[42] It seemed that the enlarged LGA offered Ryan what he had wanted since the early 1900s, the possibility of becoming an outstanding force in the accident market. LGA had size, rich assets, useful subsidiaries and geographical spread. But LGA was a company of appearances, and many realities were much less appealing. Profitability was one reality: there were difficulties from the 1900s, and they did not diminish with time. Even in 1906, the US had yielded a gross profit on premium income of 9 per cent - against 10 per cent for the UK, 20 for Canada, and 30 for Australia - and LGA was devoted to the American business. Results for the company's net underwriting surplus for 1913-18 were even more worrying (see Table 5.2); the average trading surplus for all departments over this period was a paltry 1.89 per cent on net premiums.

During the negotiations between Phoenix and LGA in 1921, Sketch was in possession of figures that gave a scarcely more impressive result of 2.76 per cent for the years 1916-20.[43] If LGA's American business grew strongly during the war, so did LGA's American losses: exceptionally heavy claims on liability business extinguished all profit from that department between 1912-16.

Consequently, at no point in the pre-war years, or down to 1920, was there much left over for the proprietors. LGA suffered much shareholder discontent on this score: the passing of the dividend in 1912 and the meagre distributions of profit in subsequent years produced sheaves of angry letters. And comment was not restricted only to insiders: as early as 1915, a senior Phoenix official had detected that LGA's 'trading profit is…a dangerously narrow percentage of premiums', and he concluded, prophetically, 'it is not a figure that would justify anyone in forming very optimistic views for the future'.[44]

Table 5.2   Net Underwriting Profits of London Guarantee & Accident as a Percentage of Net Premiums, 1913-20

	General Business	Accident	All Business
1913	1.6	2.4	1.3
1914	0.8	0.3	0.9
1915	1.1	0.3	0.9
1916	1.1	0.3	1.3
1917	1.8	4.4	2.1
1918	3.1	2.8	3.0
1919	-	-	8.4
1920	-	-	0.8

Sources: Phoenix Translation of LGA Accounts, 1913-18; Sketch Memorandum on LGA for 1919-20, 20 October 1921.

However, it was not simply the profit record that ran up warning signals over LGA. It was also the treatment meted out to insurance reserve funds, largely as a result of poor profitability. This danger flag first fluttered in 1912, but it was to fly continuously for the best part of the next two decades. Reserves against three dangers of the trade, unearned premiums, unexpired risks, and claims, were to be the heart of the LGA crisis for Phoenix. In 1912, LGA suffered an appalling year: the *Titanic* sank, the US authorities demanded bigger insurance deposits, and US employers' liability claims were punitive in the extreme. Shares halved and the dividend evaporated. Under such withering fire, LGA turned to accounting devices that were either unfamiliar by British standards, or unhealthy by any standards.

By the 1910s, British and American practice for dealing with one aspect of insurance reserves - the reserve against unearned premiums - already differed. All insurers of the modern era require a reserve against the portion of premiums that the client has paid or contracted to pay, but for which the risk has still some time to run at the normal balance sheet date. The British approach of the 1910s - and it remained the British approach until the 1960s - was to establish an across-the-board reserve of 40 per cent of gross premiums written. The American system was to gear the reserve *pro rata*, on a monthly basis, and on each contract, to the proportion of the gross premium written but not earned.[45] Since the effect of this is to include in the unwritten premium reserve an element representing expenses, which in reality have already been paid in acquiring the business, the outcome is to create a portion of 'artificial equity' in the reserve. This could amount to perhaps as much as 30-35 per cent of the fund. This more 'scientific' method can generate considerable financial strength for the insurer, as long as premiums are rising well.[46]

For LGA, however, there is surely significance in the fact that it first turned to this method in its *annus horribilis* of 1912. Presumably, the attraction was that, instead of any given percentage of total premiums written being drafted straight to the reserves, smaller allocations could be made *pro rata*; thus, quite modest sums could be presented as secure percentage reserves.[47] This *was* American practice, and, subsequently, British practice. So, there was some force in the complaint of LGA's Chairman, A.W. Tait, in his Report for 1914, that 'unjust criticism' had been levelled against his company, simply because it did not calculate its unearned premium reserve against total premiums written.

The snag was, of course, that the vast majority of British insurers remained puzzled by the 'American' method, if they thought about it at all, for a further half-century. So, it was natural that, between 1912-14, eyebrows should be raised. A pair of these belonged to an active and well-informed shareholder, who, in commenting on the 1913 results, complained to LGA's General Manager: 'I cannot find any improvement on those for 1912, and I fear that you have not earned any dividend...*The provision for unearned premiums...points to increasing weakness - indeed this is so serious that it calls for some explanation now.*'[48] Of course, he may also have detected that a whiff of implausibility attached to Tait.

In respect to the unearned premium reserve, LGA could cite American practice. It is far more difficult to defend the company's habits in regard to the reserve against unexpired risks. Phoenix had formally converted in 1917 to the convention that the unexpired risk reserve should be set at 40 per cent of premiums written. LGA's reserve hovered around this level in 1908 and 1909, but fell to 29.3 per cent by 1913; and was still below the convention in 1920. No comparative test afforded Tait any defence. Certainly, no redefinition of practice could make LGA's tactics look respectable by the standards of its British peers (see Table 5.3).[49]

At the least, Tait's defence of LGA's reserve policies was disingenuous. He must have known perfectly well the financial reasons which had pushed the company into these policies. In fact, LGA's dividend in 1911 had been maintained only be financing it from the reserves. This took the real unexpired risk reserve down to 36.1 per cent. Then, the 1912 results produced, but only to the discerning eye, a trading loss of £96,797. By 1913, there was a tremendous crash in the real reserve to 29.3 per cent. It was caused by a further trading loss of £30,000, but this did not show in the books at all; instead, these displayed a surplus of over £18,000.

The reason they did so was that £48,738 had been pillaged from the reserve in order to prettify the Profit and Loss account.

Financial tactics of this kind might, most generously, be described as audacious, and did not go unremarked, even in 1912. The *Financial News* commented that 'the progressive policy favoured of late years by the directors has led to a large increase in business', but concluded, rather mildly, that 'the quality of the business has suffered'.[50] The underlying reality was that a mixture of statistical manipulation and reference to American practice and selective representation if not outright misrepresentation of profits and reserves became the distinctive house style of the LGA, and remained well in place into the early 1920s. Many were confused by it.

Table 5.3 Reserves against Unexpired Risks as Percentage of General Premiums, Seven Companies, 1902-20

	1902	1912	1920
Century	-	138.0	49.0
Commercial Union	85.1	43.1	48.3
Employers Liability	-	-	40.0
Guardian	46.6	43.3	48.5
Ocean	31.3	36.3	58.0
Royal	40.8	40.0	40.0
LGA	58.5	37.4	37.1

Phoenix could surely not have been among them. For, by an extraordinary connection, the harshly critical shareholder of 1912 was provided with information by a particularly discerning eye that had followed the strange highlights through the LGA accounts. And the eye belonged to a Phoenix man. Indeed, this is the sole reason that we have such exact knowledge of LGA's unusual past, prior to the Phoenix takeover. In 1910, the shareholder, J.H. Coles, worried by LGA's performance, approached Ryan for advice. Always interested himself in LGA's performance, Ryan set Phoenix's best actuarial brain, the Life Manager, A. T. Winter upon the LGA accounts. Winter reported upon them continuously, for both Coles and Ryan, from 1910 until 1917. This was an extraordinary opportunity for the exercise of an early form of 'due diligence', and one vouchsafed to few predators of the 1910s or 1920s. If any office was in a position to judge the possible shortcomings of LGA, it was Phoenix.

Winter certainly found plenty of them. He picked up the initial fall in the reserve against unearned premiums almost immediately, in March 1911. To begin with, he thought that it might be due to variations in the average renewal dates, but warned: 'If, however, this is not so, and it is a weakness in the Reserve, it is, of course, a very important feature of the accounts.'[51] Winter, naturally, was applying British conventions. The 1913 balance sheet left him in less doubt; there he found clear manipulation of the unexpired risk reserve: 'The serious feature of the Accounts is the large fall in the percentage of Premiums reserved for unexpired risks.'[52] He put the reduction at no less than £80,000. And, one year later, it was Winter who judged that LGA profit was 'a dangerously narrow percentage of premiums'.[53] The 1915 account he thought to be 'very poor', and its successor of 1916 only 'slightly more satisfactory'.[54]

Most important, Winter knew beyond a shadow of a doubt that LGA was in the habit of doctoring the reserves in order to conceal current trading losses. Not only the losses but the way of presenting them should surely have warned Phoenix off, especially as the company was in the remarkable position of being able to scrutinise both as they were perpetrated. Through Winter's assessments, Phoenix had carried out a very passable contemporary equivalent of due diligence. It is astonishing, in these circumstances, that Phoenix should have retained its buying interest in LGA. One has to struggle for explanations. Possibly the argument was that Phoenix at least knew LGA better than it could know any other accident company. This knowledge may have convinced Ryan and Sketch that they could reform LGA and clear a good profit. They may have embarked upon this course, only to be blocked by increasingly adverse US markets or unrevealed weaknesses in LGA. If Ryan had been carried along by the general burst of market speculation in 1919, this could scarcely have been true in the very different circumstances of 1922. More likely, perhaps, is the possibility that Ryan and Sketch simply believed the reassurances of the LGA team. The Phoenix men had the correct doubts and these were robustly 'corrected' by Tait and his colleagues; impressed by this forcefulness, Ryan and Sketch failed to detect that there was still more to doubt.

Consistent with this last position is a preoccupation of Sketch's, which is the most frequent refrain in the documents. It is his desire to obtain the *interest* earnings of LGA. He had noticed that LGA drew on very little of these earnings to pay its dividend. The remaining large margin of interest could be brought into the Phoenix accounts to strengthen its dividend-paying position. This was particularly attractive since the fusion with NUF had been conducted entirely through an exchange of shares, and, in consequence, Phoenix was somewhat less well placed than before in meeting dividend obligations from interest earnings. If the interest earnings of LGA could be captured, any strain could be eased and any risk of reducing the dividend escaped.[55] Sketch later recorded this as the 'main object' of the LGA purchase.[56] This potential investment advantage and matter of financial 'face' seems to have bulked larger in Sketch's mind than it should have done. Here Phoenix repeated the error of 1919; but the attribution of greater weight to investment assets than to business content, which had looked dangerous in the NUF acquisition, proved deadly in the presence of LGA.

In contrast, the attractions to LGA of a buy-out from Phoenix are all too obvious. The American market was not running smoothly, and there were signs that it would become rougher still. There were reserve problems. There was a profit problem. Trading profit in 1920 and 1921 was still only fractionally above two per cent of total net premiums and that total in 1921 was 11.2 per cent down on the

1920 figure. And there was a debt problem. LGA had never been flush with funds, but its resort to temporary loans increased massively after 1918 (see Table 5.4). The main reason for this illiquidity, before the onset of the American problems, was LGA's singularly ill-judged expansion of marine business from 1917, at a time when the shrewd operators, Phoenix among them, were cutting back. But at the end of 1921, LGA was having to consider increasing its borrowing powers up to the full amount of its authorised capital, and this was carried out in 1922. But the debt was still rising during the period of the takeover negotiations: by June 1922, it had reached an accumulated total of £368,000, only £6,000 short of the new limit, and more heavy payments on the marine account were imminent. LGA had every reason for presenting itself seductively to Phoenix.

Table 5.4 LGA: Total Temporary Loans Incurred Per Annum (Gross of Repayments, £)

1912	63,000	1916	17,000	1920	231,000
1913	17,200	1917	10,000	1921	970,000
1914	0	1918	31,000	1922	437,000
1915	3,000	1919	94,000		

Source: LGA Minute Books.

So, for a complex of reasons, Phoenix and LGA were once again negotiating by August 1921. These negotiations were very private, and the press which reported fully on Phoenix's eventual acquisition of LGA in mid-May 1922 never got wind of these talks. They were restricted, very much in the Ryan style, to a cast of six: for the Phoenix side, Ryan, Sketch, and Southam, the Accident Manager of NUF; and for LGA, the Chairman, A.W. Tait, the General Manager, H.C. Thiselton, and Ryan's contact on the LGA Board, Whittall. True to form, at no time in 1921 did Ryan even tell his Deputy Chairman what was afoot. It may not be irrelevant to the character, nor to the outcome of these talks, that Tait, who held 24 industrial directorships, fell foul of a public scandal in 1925. He was moved to resign from many boards, including the chairmanship of the British Aluminium Company, and the Phoenix seat which he had gained through the LGA takeover. Tait was a highly-placed accountant, partner in Messrs George A. Touche & Co., reconstructor of companies, and one of the influences behind the formation in 1916 of the Federation of British Industries.[57] Yet, early in 1925, it was revealed in the High Court that the British Trusts Association Ltd, of which Tait was also Chairman, was Trustee for the debenture holders of the Magadi Soda company, a company under offer from Brunner Mond. The Association was deemed to have failed to defend the interests of these debenture holders or even to answer properly their inquiries concerning the bid, while itself purchasing the debentures at knockdown prices. In a scathing summing up, Mr. Justice Eve revealed a clear abuse of powers and found the action of the trustees in 'the deliberate concealment of matters vitally affecting the value of the beneficiary's interest...unsavoury and discreditable'. Tait was deeply implicated, and was judged to be in 'grave dereliction of duty'.[58] In view of the difficulties caused to Phoenix by the LGA acquisition, the conjunction is at least unfortunate.

Unfortunate, too, was the fact that the secrecy of the Phoenix-LGA talks eliminated from the early discussions the man who knew most about LGA's closets, A.T. Winter. This was a barely credible omission on Ryan's part. He possessed an excellent source of intelligence; but he discounted it. Nevertheless, even without Winter's guidance, Phoenix gave little sign of over-keenness in 1921. Southam's eye was no less sharp than Winter's, and it spotted trouble. This time it lay in a third area of reserves. Southam thought that LGA's American figures 'have been to some extent "doctored" in the General Balance Sheet, especially as regard Claims Reserves'.[59] He judged that these were £110,000 short of a safe figure.[60] Alongside the doubts provoked by LGA's handling of its reserves, Phoenix also began to suspect that the accident men were again tending to overprice themselves. By August 1921, they were asking two Phoenix shares for one LGA share, whereas the most Ryan was prepared to offer was three Phoenix for two LGA. After two months of talking around these numbers, Ryan was all for withdrawing 'with a bow and an apology'.[61]

However, LGA was not prepared to give up so easily, and, towards the end of October, Thiselton came back with a very hard sell: that 'the Accounts as published did not disclose the full strength of the company...the business was capable of producing a greater profit than their past record would appear to justify'.[62] Sketch was actually satisfied 'that there were undisclosed assets for a substantial amount'; but it does not seem to have crossed his mind that there might also be more undisclosed liabilities.[63] Nevertheless, for all their energetic puffing, LGA was not disposed to move on their price, and, by December 1921, the negotiations were effectively stalled. Ominously, however, Sketch let slip how impressed he was with Thiselton's 'thorough grasp...of the American position', and Tait returned from America in December 'full of enthusiasm as to the future prospects for their business over there'.[64] Clearly, the Phoenix men were still vulnerable to the siren call of the transatlantic market.

This impressionability surfaced again, when negotiations restarted in earnest in Spring 1922. The critical talks took place in Tait's quarters at Touche's, and were concluded very rapidly between 5-17 May. It is unclear why the process should have recommenced so abruptly, and concluded so quickly. Conceivably, publication of LGA's results for 1921 provided the trigger, but, with premium income down by over 11 per cent, it could not have been because they were especially good. Nevertheless, to the historian's eye, these 1921 accounts are, unintentionally, highly revealing in regard to LGA's methods of thought and presentation. They are spectacularly unhelpful. Premium receipts of a few hundreds or thousands of pounds are cited for UK business in the sectors of Accident, Employers' Liability and Fire. By contrast, the anonymous heading 'Other Classes' is attributed over £3m worth of income; almost all of this was unspecified American income. The accompanying note merely says: 'In this account is included the Workmen's Compensation and Employers' Liability business in the United States, which has shown satisfactory results.' This formula, used yearly, in fair weather and foul, concealed, on this occasion, a loss ratio in excess of 60 per cent. Naturally, Phoenix had the means of obtaining better information than LGA's luckless shareholders. But, even so, the bland distortion of these public documents is instructive.

From the LGA's viewpoint, it was very likely an element that *was* on display - the reduction in premium income - which produced a greater willingness to accept a keener bid price. And a further privately conceded element - a loss of LGA home business of £90,000 - would have reinforced this effect. Sketch knew about this loss, but was glad to accept that it was 'due to high expenses incurred in maintaining their home organization in competition with the large composite companies', a feature which, of course, would disappear once LGA was itself part of a large composite company. From the Phoenix viewpoint, there may well have been relief that the figures were not worse. The American results were undeniably poor, but this merely provoked the major misjudgement from Ryan that they constituted 'a mere incident, only a bad start'.[65] Indifferent results were greeted with an outbreak of optimism in the Phoenix camp.

But the rapidity with which optimism was expressed in action did not lead to a lack of care. After all, Phoenix had been asking careful questions about LGA for some 15 years, and they were not about to stop. As late as 3 May 1922, R.K. Hodgson, circling for the umpteenth time the problem that Winter had first identified a decade earlier, calculated that a full reserve for unexpired risk would have reduced the profit shown in the LGA account for 1920 by £51,877, and that shown in the 1921 account by £115,425. On 9 May, Sketch was still asking for 'proper evidence' as to the way the reserves were calculated in the accounts. Phoenix scarcely jumped with its eyes shut.

And it jumped at a convincing price, certainly less lavish than that offered to NUF. Ryan shrewdly recommended negotiations on 5 May with a bid that was defined by Phoenix at the outset as a maximum; if LGA would not accept it, there would be no more talking. This offer was one Phoenix share for one LGA share; plus the issue of £1 million worth of Phoenix debentures. Each LGA share, then selling at £10 5s, would receive one Phoenix share with a current market worth of £11, and £8 in debentures. This total bid price of £19 appeared a good deal lower than the £22 (two-for-one) insisted upon by LGA in 1921, but somewhat up on the £16 10s (three-for-two) offered by Phoenix at that time. A more sombre reading of its prospects by LGA may have underlain the 1922 price.[66]

The new Phoenix shares and debentures would require servicing in dividend and interest to the tune of £125,000. But this would leave, to Phoenix's credit, £71,000 in free interest on LGA assets and the whole of the LGA trading profit. Superficially, this looked a much tighter deal than the NUF fusion. But, of course, much depended on what the trading profit actually was and how much of it, under proper management, would need to be dedicated to the reserves. Nevertheless, in 1922, it looked as if Phoenix had laboured effectively to strike a good price.

Once the outline of an acceptable financial deal was fixed, and only then, did Ryan and Sketch draw their directors into their confidence. A Special Committee of the Phoenix Board, comprising ten directors, met to consider the matter on 10 and 11 May. These meetings immediately provided Ryan with some justification for his insistence upon secrecy: on 11 May, the LGA share stood at £10 10s; on 13 May, it topped £16, and Thiselton had to circularise shareholders telling them not to sell. Despite the leaks, however, the Committee addressed the right points. Correctly, it approved the financial details of the bid. Concern was voiced about uncertain conditions of trading and fierce official regulations in the USA. It was met by reassurances from Ryan and Southam that the powers of individual states in the USA rendered remote the prospect of any uniformly adverse regulation. Wary on this point, the meeting on 10 May, nevertheless, expressed itself generally content, and did not raise the issue of the reserves.[67]

The next day, however, with Tait, Thiselton and Heron from LGA in attendance, the wider forum did address this problem. It is scarcely surprising that the question of insurance reserves should have been in the minds even of contemporaries, who had not studied the accounts of LGA in depth. A major insurance scandal early in 1922, the collapse of the large reinsurer, City Equitable, had dramatised this issue among many. As scandals go, this one had everything to frighten the insurance man.

City Equitable had been a cautious, modest affair before 1914, but had expanded greatly during wartime, and turned to highly speculative investment from 1916; it was over-committed to marine business when others were pulling back, and over-exposed to equities when markets were on the turn. Its speculation included insider dealing by at least one director. Two board members were charged with malfeasance, another with conspiracy, and the Chairman - who was sufficiently conventional to flee the country when twigged - with fraud. The collapse of City Equitable shares late in January 1922 exerted downward pressure on all insurance shares in the following month.[68] Re-insurance reserves became a matter of rapt scrutiny for many underwriters. Phoenix directors, encountering the LGA proposition in May, had thus only recently experienced sharp confrontation with the question of the reserve level maintained by a specialist insurer expanded by war and inclined to speculative practices. If, by any remote chance, they had missed the parallel, the fact that Sketch served on the committee of inspection for the City Equitable fiasco must have forced it home. The insurance business was unusually sensitive to the matter of reserves in the spring of 1922, and Phoenix was more sensitised than most.

So, the Phoenix Special Committee came to the matter of reserves with something like a head of steam behind them. The LGA representatives handled this phase brilliantly. At a preliminary meeting between Ryan, Sketch, Tait and Thiselton on 9 May, Thiselton had made the major tactical move, disarming much criticism, by suggesting that 'he would be prepared to touch on all the weak spots he could think of in the Accounts so that there should be no necessity for long and detailed investigation'.[69] This deliberate stroke of self-revelation was very effective. When the LGA men encountered the inevitable questions about their level of reserves on 11 May, they replied sturdily that they observed strictly the 40 per cent requirement on short-term policies, but adopted lower standards on annual or more-than-annual policies.[70] Thiselton and Tait gave further assurances that the American reserves were sufficient to cover outstanding claims, and Sketch, apparently disarmed by Thiselton's baring of the LGA soul two days previously, proclaimed himself satisfied! Again, one can only wonder if Sketch's financial acumen was equal to his talents in other fields.[71]

Infected by the general enthusiasm, Southam decided that the amount of £1.7m set aside by LGA for outstanding losses was adequate. Extraordinarily, Winter, who *was* present at this meeting, was restricted to commenting on the worth of LGA's Stock Exchange investments; he found these adequate too. Veteran Phoenix director, Lord George Hamilton decided that Tait and Thiselton were splendid fellows, and Sketch contributed the valuation that the final stages of negotiation had 'increased our confidence in the other side - they certainly seem good people'.[72] By this point, the Phoenix leadership seems to have been lulled, most skilfully, into a romantic sense of reassurance. On the 17 May, the Provisional Agreement was confirmed.

It is worth noting that the press also applauded. The *Liverpool Post* thought that Phoenix had struck 'a good bargain in acquiring the London Guarantee on these terms', and even the *Financial Times* thought that 'the price now to be paid is by no means excessive'. Even more to the point, it judged this price had been achieved by LGA, having been 'very closely scrutinised, not only by the Phoenix, but by independent experts of acknowledged standing'.[73] The *Policyholder* saw a fair exchange: LGA received a greatly-increased capital value for its shares, an enhanced dividend, and 'partnership in one of the oldest, strongest and most progressive composite offices'; while Phoenix acquired 'one of the pioneers of accident business', and thus 'a very strong position in the American accident world'.[74] The emphasis chosen by the journalists was very much that Phoenix had at last bought in a major accident capability.

Interestingly, the Phoenix management was not so confident on all fronts. It maintained a firm and successful pose in regard to its own directors. And the press did it proud. But it expected trouble from its shareholders, most notably at the Extraordinary General Meeting arranged for 7 June 1922. In anticipation of this, the executive prepared a draft of the awkward questions shareholders might ask. These are very revealing. The list included: 'Have you satisfied yourself that the £700,000 reserved for the purpose is amply sufficient to meet liabilities on reinsurance treaties in view of the recent scandals?', and 'Does not the "arrears" position of the LGA compare unfavourably with that of the Phoenix?' Perhaps most tellingly of all, the executive imagined the Chairman being asked 'Is it wise to take over a business on these terms, largely comprising American casualty premiums which adverse legislation may prejudicially affect at any time?'.

Unfortunately, for the historical record, the prospective answers to these searching questions were not filled in. The questions turned out to be almost uncannily prescient of impending danger. Fortunately for the executive, however, the shareholders proved more peaceable than had been feared, and the most difficult questions were never put. The extraordinary meeting went off smoothly, with the Phoenix shareholders ratifying the agreement on 7 June. Now all that remained was to count the real cost.

This became apparent only gradually. But the damage was spread over a remarkably broad front. Phoenix encountered financial trouble from LGA in no less than four main areas: reserves, premium growth, American premises, and company debt. The first inklings were produced by the task of conciliating LGA accounts with the Phoenix accounts. This operation revealed that the issue of the suspect reserves had deserved every doubt that had been levelled at it. By late 1925, Phoenix was at last sure of this. Southam, the Accident Manager, who visited America at least yearly during the 1920s, in an attempt to pick up the pieces of the LGA operation there, reported home his definitive conclusion from the site of the crisis: 'After exhaustive examination, I concluded the reserves set up for outstanding compensation and liability claims...were insufficient.'[75]

But suspicion had been hardening from as early as August 1922, merely weeks after the agreement was finalised. On 29 August, Dr Heron, Secretary of LGA, wrote for Sketch a memorandum on 'The Hidden Liabilities and Assets of the London Guarantee'. This followed from Thiselton's clams during the negotiations concerning undisclosed assets. Poor Heron - until 1915 an academic statistician of some standing - now had to own up that these assets of £173,291 were composed largely of allowances for reserves that had not been used in past years. But, much worse, he had also to show how the current reserves stood. The 37 per cent reserve for unexpired risks shown in the 1921 account turns out to have been produced by an 'arbitrary transfer' from the General Claims Reserve. Before this robbing of Peter to pay Paul, LGA's real reserve against unexpired risks was only 30.6 per cent. Even Heron had the grace to concede that this was 'window dressing'. Phoenix's leaders began to realise the cost of filling the window: in 1922, the price of establishing full 40 per cent reserves at LGA would have been £355,423.[76]

Then, in 1924, the US Government did precisely what Sketch and Southam had calculated it was unlikely to do: introduced an across-the-board stipulation affecting all insurers. It required them forthwith to increase their level of reserves against outstanding claims. This, of course, hit LGA in one of its most vulnerable areas. The Commissioner of Insurance for Boston, Massachusetts, showed that on 31 December 1923 the American branch of LGA suffered from a deficiency between its specific and its statutory reserves of over $2m. Phoenix's share in rectifying the shortfall cost the company £181,521. At the same time, Sketch decided that the lingering affliction of the unexpired risk reserve had best receive treatment. A transition to a full 40 per cent in one dose was ruled out as too expensive for 1924. So the palliative of 33.3 per cent was adopted. But even this cost £320,000.[77]

However, it was just as well that Phoenix applied the medicine, even if the relief was only partial. For, as Sketch found on his own visit to USA in 1925, the American authorities had no love for LGA: the New York Superintendent of Insurance emphasised to him that 'the leading American and British casualty companies doing the same volume of business as LGA have *much more substantial surplus and capital than LGA*'. All that Sketch could say was that the Phoenix staff were working assiduously 'to repair the errors under the old regime'.[78] To begin with, Phoenix took the cost of the repairs fairly nonchalantly. They were, said Sketch, 'merely transfers from one hidden reserve to another (and)…will greatly improve the appearance of the accounts without weakening the reserves'.[79] But, within months, he was singing a different tune, stressing 'the tightness in regard to liquid assets that has arisen from the necessity of such large deposits abroad'.[80] Every suspicion that Phoenix had nurtured about the LGA reserves was well-founded; every reassurance from LGA had been baseless. On his 1925 visit, Sketch found, somewhat belatedly, that LGA was a byword for reckless growth, and, in New York, 'the most dangerous of any business in the States' had pursued a policy of 'unbridled expansion'.[81] Phoenix had been taken for a ride.

The upshot was that Phoenix had to embark upon its historic transatlantic remedy, 'purification of the books'. This shedding of the worst risks cut LGA's American premiums by 30 per cent between 1922-28 and by 50 per cent between 1922-24. American profits went the same way: down. After ostensibly averaging, over the five years down to 1920, a profit on American liability business of $660,000 per year, the LGA account fell into the red in 1921, and stayed there for many years.

In 1926, the combined Accident Account of Phoenix and LGA in the USA recorded a loss of £275,000 on a premium income of some £4m. At this time, the loss ratio for this class of business in the USA was 67 per cent, while the matching figure for the UK market was 54.4 per cent. The worst hit sector was the largest transacted by LGA, Workmen's Compensation insurance, which suffered astronomical loss ratios throughout the 1920s and into the mid-1930s. Southam's verdict for 1926 - that 'we have to face the fact that the trading results of the past two or three years have been disastrous' - could have been repeated in many of these years.[82] Of course, it was not difficult to lose money on accident insurance in the America of the depression decade. Indeed, of the 60 casualty companies operating in New York, 41 suffered serious financial losses during the 1920s. But the state of the market alone does not explain the state of LGA before 1929. Nor was it simply bad luck or bad judgement that put Phoenix into this market at such a time. The true state of LGA was revealed by a report from the USA, which was not formally discussed by the Board.

In June 1926, Sketch sent B.H. Davis to conduct an undercover scrutiny of all Phoenix's operations in the US. It lasted until November, and Davis kept a meticulous day-by-day diary of the astonishing malpractices that he found. On the 'administrative shambles' at LGA, he is scathing:

The impression I got...was that in the past the whole organisation was hopeless and that even now the leaks in the sieve are not all discovered and stopped up, the office wants reorganising almost throughout.[83]

Clearly, part of LGA's problem was rotten management. So, why did Phoenix buy an inefficient, inept and disorganized accident insurer, just as it moved into a phase of severe losses?

Neither luck nor judgement had much to do with this; but information did. The full implications of LGA's marine losses were not revealed to Phoenix. There was endless obfuscation on the matter of reserves. Moreover, the LGA management must have known, during the negotiations of 1922, that their results for 1921 were going to be bad; but they did not tell Phoenix. Not until Heron's memorandum for Sketch in August 1922 was there a hint that the final account 'may show a loss', and that by that time LGA was in deep trouble.[84] Its senior officials had known for months that they faced major losses. All that they did not know was precisely how major. Left to its own devices, it must be doubted whether LGA could have survived the period 1922-29. The Davis diary reveals that the LGA managers shared these doubts: it records the views of one who 'does not know how the company held together'.[85] The answer, of course, is that they persuaded Phoenix to take them over. But one of the reasons that Phoenix bought such a 'pig in a poke' is that the 'pig' was busily manufacturing its own 'silk purses' throughout the talks. Or, put another way, it was hinting at hidden assets, while concealing hidden liabilities.

The real cost of acquiring LGA, when repairs to its reserves, adjustments to its debt funding, and rectification for its appalling US real estate speculations are all taken into account, was probably around £1.4 million, and that is on top of the purchase price. It is impossible to suppress the suspicion that elements of bad judgement were present in Phoenix's acquisition of LGA: that senior management had wanted an accident company for too long, and, by the 1920s, were over-anxious to acquire one. Perhaps they suffered also from an expectation lag; their expectations took over-long to adjust to the new circumstances of the post-war markets. Certainly, Ryan misread completely LGA's results for 1921: they were not merely 'a bad start'; instead, the Workmen's Compensation market did not settle for another 14 years. And Sketch in 1925 rather pathetically emphasised Phoenix's original motivation, its current disappointment, and its still inaccurate anticipation: 'We look forward to a return to that prosperity in the casualty business which made the purchase of LGA a desirable transaction for the Phoenix'.[86] Phoenix had to wait a long time for this outcome. It seems clear that Phoenix's appetite for LGA's interest earnings was seriously misplaced. Insurance acquisitions which go wrong often prove to have been pursued on the grounds of 'good investment return'; concern for the composition of the insurance business itself is neglected in the quest for the financial 'crock of gold'.

On the other hand, if Phoenix had been given accurate information in 1921, Ryan and Sketch no doubt would have adjusted their expectations and refrained from entanglement. They were prevented from escaping the effects of a threatening chronology largely because they were misled. But, on yet another hand, if they were misled, they also had sufficient information of their own to detect the deception. Due diligence had given it to them - in theory. History is not short of leaders who prefer to disregard the intelligence they actually have in their possession.

The LGA affair is an immensely complex problem. Probably, it is fairest to say that the result was determined by an interaction of unfortunate timing, miscalculation and misrepresentation. Undoubtedly, it was Ryan's worst takeover, and it proved bad for his heart. He was ill for much of 1926, took leave from the Chairmanship in the winter, and was not fit enough to return until May 1927. The LGA fiasco and Ryan's failing strength combine to convey the impression that a distinct era was coming to an end.

A Loss of Substance: The Sale of Norwich Union Fire

Phoenix fused with Norwich Union Fire in 1919, and de-coupled in 1925. The first action was willed, the second was forced. Whilst it included NUF, Phoenix ranked third among the UK composite offices with £12.9m in premiums. Without NUF, by the end of 1925, Phoenix still ranked third, but with the reduced premium income of £9.0m. However, for the future, the loss was incalculable. One can only speculate on the possible standing of the Phoenix in the post-1945 insurance market, had it been able to hold on to the growth capacity of the Norwich office.

Table 5.5 Premium Income and Reserve Funds, Top Seven Offices, 1923

	Premium Income	Reserves	%
Royal	20,952,159	21,430,959	102.3
Commercial Union	14,556,101	13,377,141	91.9
Phoenix	12,893,100	7,727,250	60.0
London & Lancs	5,769,875	6,886,881	119.4
North British	5,499,605	6,425,436	117.0
Employers Liability	5,022,103	4,605,094	91.7
Northern	5,019,218	5,758,298	114.9

Notes: Reserves equals capital and free reserves; premium excludes life premiums.

The compulsion which forced Phoenix to surrender NUF was LGA. The cost of that acquisition had weakened the Bird. Before long, this showed in its own level of reserves. By 1923, the ratio of reserves to total premiums was significantly below the level considered wise by the senior offices; in fact, the proportion was hardly more than half that of the best-protected office, the London & Lancashire (see Table 5.5). Somewhat disingenuously, Sketch gave as the reason for this uncharacteristic weakness 'the necessary strengthening of our American reserves during the last ten years which has left our General Funds with a very small margin of liquid securities in other countries, particularly at home'.[87] No doubt, reserves had been a problem in the US for a decade, but the real issue was two years old rather than ten. Nevertheless, whatever the time-span, such a disparity was clearly dangerous and could not be allowed to persist.

But how to eradicate it? An obvious, if drastic, ploy would be to sell the company which had done most damage to the reserves. But to shed in 1924 or 1925 a company purchased in 1922 would have had catastrophic effects on public confidence in Phoenix, as well as imposing a severe financial loss upon the transaction. And there was the problem of finding a buyer: if Phoenix did not want LGA, who else would? This sequence of thought prompted the notion of realising capital by selling Phoenix's shares in NUF. But here too there was a dilemma. How could the need for the sale be presented? Phoenix could scarcely announce that it needed to sell NUF shares in order to cover the financial crisis caused by its acquisition of LGA. Such a revelation would also wreck confidence in Phoenix. The only way of justifying a sale would be by receiving a bid for NUF that was simply too good to refuse. But how could such a bid be provoked? Phoenix could scarcely invite offers. And, even if it could, its need for a high price would surely deter buyers. A low price would attract them. But it would not solve the reserve problem; it would not justify the sale to shareholders or directors; and it would again damage confidence in the vendors. The only feature of the sale that was clear was that at least one potential buyer existed. There was no problem about who might want NUF, if Phoenix did not want it: its old partner in Norwich, Norwich Union Life ought to want it. So the crucial issue was to persuade Norwich Union Life to offer exactly the sort of price which would allow Phoenix to raise the wind on its NUF shares without loss of face. Still better if this contrived bid from NUL could be presented as an independent offer inspired from Norwich.

If this could be carried off, it would stand as a brilliant stroke of damage control; but it was a very tall order indeed. An attempt was made in 1924, but this foundered. However, by further cajolement, a cheaper price, and more than a little luck, NUL was induced in June 1925 to make a bid for NUF. By 26 June, this had become a formal offer. The Phoenix Board accepted the offer on 30 June. Shareholders of Phoenix and NUF were circularised on 7 July. The sale was completed on 15 July. So, Phoenix moved from a rationalisation strategy that included NUF to a sale strategy, which completed the shedding of NUF in less than a calendar month.

For Sketch, the NUL initiative was a godsend. The rationalisation strategy aimed at an improvement in corporate governance through a tidier divisionalisation of the corporate morass produced by the double acquisition. Although it had been seriously pursued, the worsening news from LGA had raised problems which threatened to outrun this form of defence. In such circumstances, the revived prospects of a beneficial sale could 'put the Phoenix in a magnificent position financially...enabling us to meet any difficulties without recourse to the drastic steps that we should otherwise have had to take'.[88] The stroke which put Phoenix in a 'magnificent position financially' was the bid by NUL for the NUF shares, priced at £6.5m, to be paid in gilts. It represented a premium of 23 per cent on the market value of the NUF shares. The transaction would bring an immediate increase in Phoenix's free assets of £4.5m.

We know exactly how the money from the NUF sale was used. Of the £4.5m available, £1.2m was set against existing liabilities, with £0.35m apiece going to the particularly troubled areas of the marine funds and the outstanding claims reserve. A further £1.8m went to creating 'free reserves' for contingencies. Over half a million of this went to a dividend reserve to improve Phoenix's ability to pay dividends out of interest earnings, a point on which Sketch was sensitive. And the strengthening of contingency reserves freed the existing Inner Reserve to become an Investment Reserve, a particularly valuable defence in the tumultuous markets of the inter-war years.[89] It is also clear that these contingency funds were used early in 1926 to finance directly an injection of nearly £0.3m into the LGA Reserve for Outstanding Claims.[90] Finally, the balance of £1.5m represented a genuine addition to capital reserves. Important and topical defences were shored up here.

Allowed access to some if not to the most central issues of the deal, the press commentators were mostly - though not uniformly - kind to the Phoenix initiative. The *Financial Times* stressed the constraints placed upon Phoenix by the NUL-NUF link, and the composite's inability to exploit the potential life assurance capacity of NUF. It concluded that 'the Norwich Union Life will be in a better position to get the utmost value out of the Norwich Union Fire than the Phoenix could ever hope to secure'. And it understood that one prime result of the sale was that Phoenix's 'ratio of reserves to premium income will far exceed that of any of the other giants of the insurance world'. Nevertheless, the paper still considered that Phoenix and NUF should separate at all: 'An Insurance Sensation...one of the most important and most interesting transactions that have ever taken place in the history of British Insurance.'[91]

Sketch was well aware that 'the disposal of any portion of our business might be regarded as a retrograde step'.[92] He consoled himself with two counter-points. One was the vast accession to reserves created by the sale. Undoubtedly, this provided a clean and swift answer to a lately revealed and rapidly worsening financial crisis without drastic surgery upon Phoenix's internal organs. The other was the fulfilment of the original intention behind the fusion plans of 1919-20: both Phoenix and NUF had been protected from takeover, and were now safe from it. However, there were other implications.

The purchase of LGA and sale of NUF constitute one of the fateful moments in the life of 20th century Phoenix. These transactions had a more potent effect upon the company than the San Francisco earthquake of 1906, and are perhaps properly comparable only with the acquisition of a 22 per cent stake in Phoenix by the giant

American insurer, Continental of New York, in 1964. Ironically, both the NUF sale and the Continental purchase were dramatic, rapid and apparently incisive reactions to shortages of financial resources. For the sale of NUF did not solve Phoenix's asset problem finally. By the 1960s, in a time of international expansion, Phoenix was again short of substance, most severely within the UK base. The injection of American-owned equity in 1964 was intended to remedy this.

But the loss of NUF surely closed an option and its absence had a bearing upon Phoenix's problems in the 1960s. For, if Phoenix and NUF had been able to expand together, one of Phoenix's worst post-war problems might have been reduced substantially: the lack of scale within the home market, and the inability to establish a convincing link with another large-scale UK operator. Sketch sold in the 1920s the sort of connection Phoenix needed in the 1950s and 1960s.[93] Lack of assets in the 1960s drew Phoenix towards the American investment power of Continental. And that American connection made it more difficult for the Bird to attract any other major UK company into its nest. It was not the sale of NUF which started this sequence. It was rather the purchase of LGA and entanglement with a more sinister American connection. There are excuses for Sketch. Phoenix had been duped. It was under pressure in violently precarious markets. In 1925, its financial circumstances were revealed to be worse even than feared. Extremely difficult negotiations offered the chance of a swift cure. Sketch made his very substantial best of a bad job. As damage control, it was brilliant. But the damage began with LGA. That acquisition has a lot to answer for.

Conclusion

This is a story about ambition, power, egos and bad information in the context where corporate governance is put under most strain - the context of an acquisition, merger or takeover. It demonstrates four lessons:

> That corporate memory can exert a deleterious effect on acquisition strategy. Phoenix and Ryan should not have returned in 1922 to their 1907 plans for an accident takeover. Even more so, they should not have returned to LGA.

> That an early exercise in 'due diligence' was properly applied to the LGA acquisition, but was effectively discounted by Ryan's long-term ambitions and deployment of executive power. Under more modern circumstances, it would be unthinkable - one may hope - that critical analysis of the kind carried out by A.T. Winter should be set aside by senior management.

> That the takeover of a badly managed target company can force major managerial rationalisation on the predator company - here,

Sketch's attempted divisionalisation of the clumsy leviathan produced by the Phoenix-NUF-LGA merger.

That the enforced sale of a valued subsidiary can entail long-term structural distortion for the parent company, and impose penalties decades after the event.

The incidents described above compose, of course, only a case study in the economic history of corporate governance. But this case affected the development of a major multinational corporation, and an entire sector of the UK financial services business. It describes a pivotal moment in the history of British insurance. And some of the leading insurance men of the day made an unmitigated hash of it.

Notes

I am grateful to the Royal & Sun Alliance Insurance Group for the support and access which made this research possible.

1   See chapter 9.
2   C.Trebilcock, *The Vickers Brothers; Armament and Enterprise, 1854-1914* (1977). See also chapter 3.
3   From 1911, Sir Gerald Ryan; and he was further created a Baronet in 1919.
4   This was true in regard to most classes of business, but not in regard to life assurance. That class could be offered across the composite counter, but separate funds would always be required to secure it.
5   *The Times*, 11 July 1907.
6   This idea developed from a discussion forming part of a conference on the theme, 'Organisational Change in the Corporate Economy', held at the University of East Anglia in September 1987. I am grateful, in particular, to Oliver Westall and the late Professor Donald Coleman for sparking these thoughts.
7   This left Norwich Union Life as a separate and independent venture. Norwich Union Fire was sold back to Norwich Union Life in 1925. This was an astonishing, lost opportunity, forced upon Phoenix by the unwise acquisition of LGA.
8   A.D.Chandler, *Strategy and Structure* (1962); *Scale and Scope: Dynamics of Industrial Capitalism* (1990).
9   O.E.Williamson, 'The Modern Corporation; Origins, Evolution, Attributes', *Journal of Economic Literature* (December, 1981), p.1537.
10 B.E.Supple, 'Insurance in British History', in O. Westall (ed.), *The Historian and the Business of Insurance* (1984).
11 See chapter 3.
12 See C.Trebilcock, *Phoenix Assurance and the History of British Insurance, Vol.II: The Era of the Insurance Giants, 1870-1984* (1998), ch.5.
13 T.Yoneyama, 'The Rise of the Large-scale Composite Insurance Company in the UK, *Kyoto Sangyo University Economic and Business Review*, 20 (1993), pp.11-14.
14 B.E.Supple, *The Royal Exchange Assurance, 1720-1970* (1970), pp.262ff; P.G.M.Dickson, *The Sun Insurance Office, 1710-1960* (1960), p.194.
15 LGA Circular to Shareholders, 8 March 1907.

16 Pelican and British Empire, Confidential Memorandum, 14 June 1907.
17 Phoenix Guardbook, B4/40, Directors' Correspondence, Kirby to Ryan, 29 June 1907.
18 Chairman's Speech to Phoenix Extraordinary General Meeting, 20 January 1920. This was his first address to shareholders as Chairman.
19 Sketch may have been encouraged in this direction. Habitually, Ryan put his better ideas into the minds of others, and then welcomed them when they returned homewards.
20 Allen to Ryan, 9 December 1919.
21 Ryan to Sketch, 12 December 1919; *The Times*, 18 December 1919.
22 Phoenix Special Committee, 8 December 1919.
23 Ryan to Phoenix Special Committee, 8 December 1919.
24 Ryan to Phoenix Special Committee, 8 December 1919.
25 Sketch to Ryan, 26 November 1919.
26 Ryan to Sketch, 4 December 1919.
27 Tryon to Ryan, 6 December 1919.
28 NUF Private Minute Book, 8 December 1919.
29 *The Times*, 18 December 1919.
30 It had been codified by an important agreement of January 1908.
31 Sketch to Ryan, 19 December 1919. Emphasis in original.
32 NUF's pre-fusion market worth was 44,000 x £90 shares, or £3.96m; Phoenix's was 422,875 x £15, or £6.34m.
33 Lescher to Ryan, 9 December 1919.
34 *Evening Standard*, 31 December 1919.
35 Hodgson to Ryan, 27 January 1920.
36 Ryan to Sketch, 1 January 1920.
37 Chairman's Speech, 28 January 1920.
38 Chairman's Speech, 28 January 1920.
39 Chairman's Speech, 28 January 1920.
40 See Trebilcock, *Phoenix Assurance, Vol.II*, ch.8
41 The US usage is, of course, 'casualty', in place of accident, but, with UK companies writing US accident business, matters become confusing. It seems best to retain 'accident' as the standard form.
42 Memorandum of R.Y. Sketch on London Guarantee & Accident, 27 October 1921.
43 Memorandum of R.Y. Sketch on London Guarantee & Accident, 27 October 1921.
44 Memorandum, A.T. Winter, Phoenix Life Manager to General Manager, 15 May 1915.
45 More recent practice is to revise the reserve on a daily basis.
46 And as long as the anticipated loss ratio used in calculating the original rate for the insurance is not exceeded. Of course, if gross written premiums begin to fall, the boot is on the other foot.
47 This requires the manipulation of the start, or renewal, dates of contracts.
48 J.H. Coles to H.C. Thiselton, 30 September 1912.
49 Technically, LGA's levels of claims reserves *could* have been sufficient had the anticipated loss ratio remained low (say below 30 per cent). But this was rarely the case for US accident business 1910-41.
50 *Financial News*, 30 September 1912.
51 Winter to Ryan, 15 March 1911.
52 Winter to Ryan, 27 March 1914.
53 Winter to Ryan, 15 April 1915'.
54 Winter to Ryan, 20 April 1916; 17 April 1917.
55 Phoenix was very successful in maintaining dividend payments during the 1920s.
56 Sketch to Walters, 23 October 1920.

57 See R.P.T. Davenport-Hines, *Dudley Docker, The Life and Times of a Trade Warrior* (1984), p.108.
58 *The Times*, 13 February 1925; *Daily Mail*, 14 February 1925.
59 Southam to Sketch, 3 August 1921.
60 Southam, Memorandum on Company X, 5 August 1921.
61 Ryan to Whittall, 10 October 1921.
62 Sketch, Memorandum, 27 October 1921.
63 Sketch, Memorandum, 27 October 1921. This was a major error. LGA was showing 'savings' on its US reserves.
64 Sketch to Thiselton, 27 October 1921; Sketch to Ryan, 28 December 1921.
65 Phoenix Special Committee Minutes, p.18, 10 May 1922; Ryan's notes on Agenda for meeting of offices of G.Touche & Co., 9 May 1922.
66 The LGA Minute Books are studiously quiet on the details of the negotiations.
67 Phoenix Special Committee Minutes, pp.17-20; 10 May 1922.
68 *Financial News*, 4 April 1922; *Statist*, 28 January, 4 and 11 February 1922.
69 Sketch, Notes on Interviews, 10 May 1922.
70 Modern practice would ask for a *larger* premium reserve on annual policies than on lesser periods, as, in the latter case, there is greater likelihood that the premium would be fully 'earned' by the accounting date.
71 Administration, underwriting and the management of honest people.
72 Phoenix Special Committee Minutes, pp.20-22; Sketch to Walter, 16 May 1922.
73 *Liverpool Post*, 18 May 1922; *Financial Times*, 18 May 1922.
74 *Policyholder*, 24 May 1922.
75 Accident Manager's Report on Visit to USA, submitted to Phoenix Board, 9 Dec 1925.
76 Heron to Sketch, 'Memorandum on Hidden Liabilities and Assets of the London Guarantee', 29 August 1922.
77 Phoenix Special Committee Minutes, pp.55-6; 18 March 1925.
78 General Managers' Report on Visit to USA, submitted to Phoenix Board 25 November 1925. My emphasis.
79 Phoenix Special Committee Minutes, p.56, 18 March 1925.
80 Phoenix Special Committee Minutes, p.66, 18 June 1925.
81 General Manager's Report on Visit to USA, 1925.
82 General Manager's Report on Visit to USA, Southam to Berger, 25 November 1926.
83 B.H.Davis, American Diary, pp.55&79, 2&7 August 1926.
84 Heron to Sketch, 29 August 1922.
85 Davis, American Diary, p.171; 14 September 1926.
86 General Manager's Visit to USA, 1925.
87 R.Y.Sketch, Private Memorandum on the Norwich Union Fire and Life Offices, 22 July 1924.
88 Sketch to Beresford, 9 July 1925.
89 Phoenix Directors' Special Committee Minutes, p.83; 5 December 1925.
90 Phoenix Directors' Minutes, 24 March 1926.
91 *Financial Times*, 8 July 1925.
92 Sketch, Memorandum for Phoenix Directors, 27 June 1925.
93 Although, of course, NUF's accident business in the USA probably would have brought its own problems.

Chapter 6

Japanese Corporate Governance in the Major Life Assurance Companies: an Historical Perspective

Takau Yoneyama

Introduction

To understand the industrial structure of the Japanese insurance business, we cannot ignore the role of government. The insurance business, as well as banking and securities, is under a comprehensive regulatory authority. In Japan, all insurance companies, as specified under the Insurance Business Law, have conducted operations under the supervision of the Ministry of Finance (MOF) since 1941.[1] Generally, regulations have been stronger than in other industries, and stricter than in the pre-war period.[2] Whenever discussing the corporate governance of life assurance, we should consider the role of the governmental authority and its high-ranking officials.[3] Life assurance companies in the pre-war period enjoyed a free-hand over their life funds. Life assurance companies in the post-war period had to obey guidelines on investments, as stipulated by the authorities.

Since profits from securities should be transferred into a reserve fund, life assurance companies selected so-called 'gentle' investment policies, which preferred long-term capital gains to short-term dealing.[4] Moreover, the anti-monopoly law prohibited holding companies.[5] So, life assurance companies never saw the exertion of stockholder power in the post-war period, and large life companies did not operate as typical examples of stakeholding in post-war Japan.[6] This paper will focus on internal corporate governance style rather than corporate behaviour as a stakeholder. The aims of this paper are to discuss when and under what process Japanese corporate governance style emerged in the life assurance business, and to understand its distinctive features from historical perspective.

Emergence of Japanese Corporate Governance Style

Contrasts between the Pre-War and the Post-War Period

The post-war industrial structure of life assurance is clearly different from the pre-war one. The major differences are to be found in governmental authority and policy; price formation; the different structures of the life assurance markets; the contrast in the distribution of profits; and, lastly, the inter-corporate relationship between life assurance companies and major banks and other members of the *keiretsu* (and, formerly, *zaibatsu*). These differences reveal a change in culture, life style and economic conditions, and brought contrasts in enterprise strategy and sales channels. Let us explain the above differences in detail.

Firstly, we should concentrate on the change of authority. The first governmental authority supervising the insurance business was the Ministry of Agriculture and Commerce.[7] When the Ministry of Commerce and Industry separated from this body in 1925, it took over regulation of the insurance business. The MCI became the Ministry of International Trade and Industry (MITI) after the Second World War. It is, however, well known that the authority overseeing the insurance business is the Ministry of Finance (MOF) in post-war Japan. This responsibility was transferred to the MOF during the war economy. The government recognised the importance of huge life assurance funds as an indispensable source of money for the issue and absorption of government bonds.[8] There was also a change of regulations. Ministry (or Bureau) of Commerce and Industry officials would visit an insurance company with a poor reputation to inspect the management and its financial condition. If they found mismanagement, or financial weakness, the authority made a recommendation of improvement to the company. In the worst cases, the authority took administrative measures.[9] The MOF's form of regulation stands in contrast. The authority forced all life assurance companies to present fundamental information on finance and management in the same format. Ministry officials supervised companies by using this information, and seldom undertook direct inspection. The essential element of MOF regulation is to collect complete information on business expenses, and to impose restrictions on the company's budget. As a result, life assurance companies refrained from overspending in pursuit of reckless sales competition.

In understanding both Ministries' policies, we should pay attention to the historical backgrounds. The difference did not occur merely because of contrasting bureaucratic characteristics. In the pre-war and war periods, life assurance companies adopted their premium rates on different actuarial bases, using different interest rate assumptions, as well as differing mortality tables. It was hardly possible for the former authority to collect comparable information on the business expenses of all companies. The MOF developed the standardisation of life assurance products during the war economy.[10]

Secondly, price formation was quite different. In the pre-war period, the industry evolved dual price competition. Companies could issue life products freely according to both benefits and price of the product, while life salesmen also developed almost illegal sales techniques, like premium rebates and the use of secret, cheaper premium tables.[11] In the post-war period, price competition was maintained through uniform premiums and a regulative law on sales activities.[12]

Thirdly, there were differences in market structure.[13] It was easier to set up a life assurance company in the pre-war period than after the Second World War. The number of life assurance companies grew until the early 1920s, and was as many as 50 companies at its peak. Once an economic slump happened in 1927, weaker companies suffered financial troubles. The major task of the authority changed from supervision and inspection into promoting and restructuring weak companies. The prolonged painful aftermath and war economy accelerated rationalisation of the industry. The number of life assurance firms fell to 20 by 1945. After the Second World War, until 1975, the MOF did not give a business licence to any company other than the 20 already established, when the first foreign-affiliated life assurance company was founded.[14] Eight foreign-affiliated life companies followed between 1979 and 1995. Under the new insurance business law of 1996, the authority could allow parent life or non-life companies to form subsidiary life or non-life companies. As a result, 11 subsidiary life companies were formed by parent non-life insurance companies, and the total number of life assurance companies incorporated in Japan increased to 43.[15] Although the post-war concentration of enterprises was generally higher than pre-war, the big five life assurance companies in the 1920s had much stronger powers of action than the top seven in the post-war life market.[16]

Fourthly, there is a clear contrast in the appropriation of surplus. We cannot understand the difference without recognising the change in business organisation. Although two mutual life companies, Chiyoda and Dai-ichi, began to rival the established big three in the late 1920s, major players in the pre-war life market were joint-stock companies. In the post-war years, all major life assurance businesses are mutual companies. It is natural that this development would have an effect on the appropriation of surplus. Top managers did not neglect shareholders in the pre-war period, and shareholders affected a wide range of management activities. For example, after the resignation of Kataoka, the president of Nippon Life, who decided to devote himself to national politics in 1919, his post was vacant until 1928, when Kataoka sold many of his shares.[17] The long vacancy can be explained by the fact that this big shareholder hoped to return to the business. There was, furthermore, shareholder pressure to increase dividends, and we can find cases of hostile acquisition, which could never have occurred in the post-war insurance market.[18]

Shareholders disappeared from life assurance companies after the Second World War. Almost all life assurance companies converted into mutual life companies between 1947-1948.[19] As a result, the role of shareholders in the internal corporate governance of major life assurance companies was completely swept away. We can see simultaneous changes in the top management of many life assurance companies. For example, Naruse, president of Nippon life, resigned in December 1946, and chief officials were ousted from office in the same year through pressure from the salaried employees union.[20] In most life assurance companies, a change in management and generation occurred, and the power of the salaried employees was largely strengthened.

The different ways of appropriating surplus have a connection with the conversion of business organisation and change in top management. The pre-war top managers had to consider the dividends of shareholders as well as policyholders, so that they had fewer incentives to increase internal reserves. The post-war top managers only thought about policyholders' dividends. Their loyalty or identification with the company clearly strengthened, because they were internally-promoted salaried managers. They had an incentive to accumulate internal reserves.

Fifthly, and lastly, the inter-corporate relationships of the life assurance business changed. In contrast to non-life insurance, companies did not have strong connections with the *zaibatsu*, even in the pre-war period. Of the four big *zaibatsu*, only Mitsubishi was linked to a major life assurance business, Meiji Life. Three *zaibatsu* had some connection with small life assurance companies. A founder of the Yasuda *zaibatsu* was one of the key figures in the early business of Kyosai Life, which kept strong links with Yasuda, and it was renamed Yasuda Life in 1929. But Kyosai Life was far from a major company, although it grew rapidly after 1929. Both the Sumitomo and Mitsui *zaibatsu* were latecomers to the life business. Both acquired small or weaker life assurance companies in the late 1920s. Of the five big life companies, only the Meiji *zaibatsu* was prominent. Others amongst the big five, like Nippon and Dai-ichi, did not belong to major business groups.

However, the relation between banks and life assurance companies was not neglected. For example, as Yamaguchi Bank influenced Nippon Life, some contemporary journals regarded Nippon Life as a member of the Yamaguchi *zaibatsu*.[21] Whatever the definition of *zaibatsu*, it is not difficult to imagine that the relation between banks and life companies was stronger than in the post-war period, when all major life assurance companies, including *zaibatsu*-related companies, converted into mutual organizations. Therefore, internal corporate management could not be monitored by outside shareholders. As a result, banks or corporate groups could not influence the internal corporate governance of major life assurance companies after the Second World War.

There are two important historical conditions that promoted these contrasts. One is the change in governmental administration during the war economy. Another is the financial, managerial and business troubles of the reconstruction period. Historical perspective is necessary, therefore, if we are to understand the Japanese corporate governance style.

Changes during the War Economy, 1936-1945

The war economy was a turning point in the life assurance business. The most outstanding event was the transfer in governmental authority.[22] The first and most important reason for this change was the government's intention to take control of the huge life funds. As these funds grew rapidly in 1920s, life assurance companies became the focus of public attention. The MOF hoped life assurance companies might buy more national bonds, even in the years before the needs of the war economy. When conflict erupted, it became necessary to make use of life funds to provide rising expenditure without stoking inflation. The MOF asked the Ministry of Commerce and Industry to force life assurance companies into action, but the effect was limited. Life companies hesitated to buy because expected returns were too low. The MOF wanted directly to control the holding of war bonds in life funds. Another reason was that the Ministry of Commerce and Industry had to concentrate on the maintenance and distribution of limited resources and materials, as the war continued. It became difficult to supervise the insurance industry.

Ultimately, administrative jurisdictions were modified. Bureaucrats had traditionally been conscious of territory, but the *kakushin kanryo* or 'new-type innovative bureaucrats' abandoned old customs in pursuit of *shin keizai taisei* or the 'new, controlled economic system'. Their influence grew within the government. Shinsuke Kishi, one of the most influential *kakushin kanryo*, was influential in this transformation at the critical phase.[23] Once the insurance business was completely supervised by the MOF, in 1941, control became more strict, and the authority forced the insurance industry to implement a rationalisation and reorganisation plan. However, the change of governmental authority did not lead directly to the transformation of the life insurance system, which occurred gradually under the war economy. It is noteworthy that the standardisation and unification of life products developed, keeping pace with maturing war regulations.

In fact, standardisation and unification had strong connections with the increasing need for national bonds. The large issue of war bonds tended to suppress market interest rates, and life assurance companies were worried about their life products, as premiums were calculated on previously higher expected interest. Actually, some companies found themselves in serious financial difficulties. Under the strong leadership of the authority, all companies let the expected interest rate decrease at the same time. This was a bargaining point for increasing the holding of national bonds. What is more, when the war intensified, the unified insurance conditions began to rationalize the life assurance industry as a whole. Incidentally, although these trends towards unification were more important for shaping the Japanese life assurance system than the change of the governmental authority, the trends were not complete during the time of the war economy, but under the special conditions of the reconstruction period.

Transformation during the Reconstruction Period, 1945-1957

Defeat in 1945 left life assurance companies with three predicaments. These were financial difficulties, management troubles, and business or selling problems. Each life assurance company overcame these predicaments in its own way during the reconstruction period, so making a foundation for business growth from 1957. Finding a way out of financial difficulties was the most urgent problem of life assurance companies just after the war. Since a large part of their assets consisted of bonds and loans to war-related industries, the life industry's assets suddenly deteriorated. Of course, such difficulties occurred within financial institutions generally. The government enacted the Financial Institutions Accounting

Emergency Measure Act and the Financial Institutions Reorganisation and Readjustment Act in 1946.[24] The point of both laws was as follows. They separated a company's assets as listed in the old and weaker accounts from those on new and healthy accounts. Business was continued on the new accounts, and companies tried to clear bad debts on the old. Accordingly, once the old accounts had been cleared, both accounts were merged. Moreover, life insurance policies of more than 10,000 yen had been suspended on old accounts.

Life assurance companies tried to clear bad debts under MOF guidance, but they could not clear them all by the deadline of March 1948, when they would in theory be able to close the old accounts, and borrow a low interest loan from the state.[25] As a result, the government decided to enact a new law for troubled insurance companies, and the companies established adjustment accounts.[26] Large sum life contracts of more than 10,000 yen were suspended again, while the government loan was repaid. All life assurance companies having an adjustment account re-paid the government by 1956, and closed their adjustment accounts between December 1956 and March 1957. Economic recovery from war damages was said to complete by 1955, when GNP reached the standard of the peak in the pre-war economy. But the revival of the life assurance business fell behind the Japanese economy as a whole by about two years.

Next, there were serious employee disputes in some life assurance companies. In the reconstruction period, the outflow of able persons from life assurance companies was a critical problem. Some companies faced serious managerial difficulties, although this problem was not more critical than the financial difficulties. Yet pre-war managers had almost disappeared from top management in life assurance companies, because of resignations. Therefore, the newly-elected top managers could make decisions without considering old-style approaches. It is also important that new top managers had experience of co-operating with ministry officials for the reconstruction of the life assurance industry. We can regard labour disputes in life assurance as a salaried employees' movement. For example, the main figures were section chiefs in the Nippon Life union, and sales persons seldom belonged to the union. The labour disputes were a movement for 'managerial democracy'.[27] Management had substantial responsibility for each company's reconstruction plan. Life assurance companies responded to the shortage of talented persons by co-operating with ministry officials and the 'OB' or 'old boys' network of governmental officials.[28] This co-operation greatly influenced the making of Japanese corporate governance style. While life assurance sales rapidly improved from 1955, companies could not recruit adequate sales staff, and the employment of a female corps began. Female door-to-door sales persons, consequently, became the most distinctive feature of the Japanese life assurance business.[29]

Regarding the third predicament, the sale of life products was not possible just after the war. No consumers would buy them while lacking in food. When contracts of more than 10,000 yen were halted, consumers' confidence in life assurance was completely ruined. Furthermore, consumers recognised that life assurance was useless during the post-war hyperinflation. Managers who replaced the pre-war leaders did not sit idle. According to historical evidence from Nippon Life, the executives in 1947 convened all local branch managers at Nanzenji Temple, Kyoto, the US not having bombed the ancient capital, for the purpose of discussing the selling of life products. The important aspects of selling life products in the reconstruction period are as follows. First, they stated that the insurer should be a new company, separated from the old one with its weaker assets. To help them in this, it was wise to convert the joint stock firm into a mutual organisation. The conversion would impress on consumers that the new mutual life company had severed its connections with older, weaker assets. This is the reason why Nippon Life hurried in its organisational conversion in 1947. Second, since a lot of life contracts offered meaningless sums due to post-war inflation, sales persons would persuade customers to convert to new contracts. Third, the demand in farming areas was not exhausted. Some companies had tried to establish ties with the Agricultural Co-operative Union, but this sales strategy lost its affect after the Union undertook a mutual aid project.

Each life assurance company tried to overcome these predicaments in its own way, and the future growth of a life assurance company heavily depended upon changes during the reconstruction period.[30] And it is important to recognise that the co-operation between businessman and bureaucrat had never been closer. All life assurance companies faced financial difficulties, management troubles, and sales problems. Given the shortage of managerial resources, co-operation was a key element for the overcoming of problems. In a national economy with limited resources and materials, the post-war government managed to promote the efficient distribution of goods, and encouraged better economic performance. In the process of recovery, bureaucrats learnt that the war control system was useful for conquering contemporary economic difficulties. The insurance industry, therefore, cooperated strongly with ministry officials. The life assurance business, regarded as important by the MOF, enjoyed governmental support for its recovery, and competition under regulation is a feature of the Japanese life assurance system.

The Establishment of Japanese Corporate Governance Style

The Distinctive Features of Corporate Governance in Major Life Assurance Companies

The following four points list the distinctive features of corporate governance in the Japanese life assurance industry.

> There are no shareholders. The general meetings of policyholders replaced those of shareholders, but cannot act as a full check on the corporate management.

The functions and responsibilities of the CEO or top executive are comparatively limited.[31]

Salaried employees are an important stakeholder. They supplement the role of the CEO, who is, in other words, their representative or the most successful amongst them.[32]

Ministry of Finance authority has exerted monitoring functions. The role of policyholders is supplemented by this external check.

Most life assurance companies converted into mutual life assurance companies without shareholders. Although there were a small number of joint-stock companies, they did not have much influence in the business as a whole. The final decision-making body of a mutual company is the general meeting of policyholders. That is to say, policyholders are thought to be equal to the shareholders of a joint-stock company. It is, however, impossible to check management through the representatives of policyholders, because they lack knowledge of management.

This inability necessarily intensifies the powers of the CEO, as in the Anglo-American corporate governance style. However, the hegemony of the top executive in Japanese life businesses did not grow. To understand why, we need to understand the functions of top management in the major assurance companies. Roughly speaking, top executives did not make strategic decisions in the years 1957-1996. In the post-war life assurance system, regulation and supervision restrained their role. They acted as arbitrators or co-ordinators of executives and would-be executives, who were all the internally promoted employees. It is interesting that these top executives have hardly ever resigned as a result of external pressure. This is because they shared so much power and responsibility with other executives and would-be executives that, with their support, they have been in post for comparatively long periods.[33]

Such a system indicates the different style of corporate governance between the United States and Japan. The change of CEO, or top executive, was not a response to market forces or an attempt to improve efficiency, by using the mechanisms of corporate governance. Instead, it is important to consider the logic of internal promotion and informal competition amongst employees.[34] Most top managers in pre-war Japan were promoted and recruited from inside the company. That is to say, they were all salaried employees at first. The major life assurance companies did not invite top managers from outside, partly because there was no market for managers, and partly because of the different promotion logic and top management functions compared to the United States. Turnover amongst these salaried employees remains extraordinarily low. They demonstrate loyalty to the company, as important stakeholders, and their salary is comparatively high.

The regulation and supervision of the ministry prevented the corporate dictatorship of management. It is important, also, that the authority considered the efficiency of the industry as a whole. The comprehensive supervision and rigid regulation of business expenditures replaced the US-style corporate mechanisms for improving efficiency. Furthermore, ministry officials were not merely supervisors but stakeholders. As they devoted themselves to building up the post-war life assurance system, they became committed to the system. High-ranked government officials generally had a strong mission and sense of national service, but enjoyed, nonetheless, the benefits of their efforts. Once the life assurance system demonstrated a good overall performance, they had the possibility of becoming *amakudari*. There are many highly ranked posts for OB officials in both governmental and business-affiliated organisations, so institutionalizing Ministry officials as stakeholders in the life assurance business. These characteristics formed the background of governmental regulations and the nature of competition in the industry.

MOF Regulation, Competition and Price Mechanisms

Some of the most distinctive features of the post-war life assurance system are the uniform price system and the protection of smaller life assurance companies. Life premium rates moved towards unification in the war economy, but became fixed in the reconstruction period. The ability to increase life premium rates was the key means of overcoming the financial difficulties of the companies just after the war. The government was determined to increase the premiums of life products contracted from April 1946 onwards. It recommended that companies use a 'standard premium rate', but it was not forced on all companies. Soon after that measure, life assurance companies faced financial difficulties again, so a 'provisional premium rate', the 'standard premium rate' plus 3 yen, was applied from November 1946 with the agreement of all life assurance companies. Then, the MOF permitted life companies to apply the new 'provisional premium rate' to life products contracted before November 1946, by means of a special administrative measure. All companies could utilize the government's rescue measures. The 'provisional premium rate' was a temporary one, but the MOF did not want to give companies a free hand. The chief of the Ministry's Bank Bureau gave official notice to life assurance companies on January 1949: 'If a company offers different rates for life endowments, it will not benefit from retroactive measures'.[35] In other words, if a company decided it own premium rate, it gave up the special privilege of applying the 'provisional premium rate' to its past life contracts. As a result, no company selected to act unilaterally. The unification of the life premium rate as a temporary measure turned into an established system.

The life premium rate gradually fell until 1990, partly because of the downward trend in mortality, and partly because of improved business expenditures and costs. Applications from the more efficient companies to reduce premiums were not accepted immediately by the Ministry, until either the less efficient were able to match the new proposals, or were in a position to improve their efficiency in response to rate changes. Price regulation could be used, therefore, as a means of improving the efficiency of the industry generally. As the more efficient were often operating at premiums that they could afford to reduce, and as rates were fixed between the more efficient, they accumulated reserves for the benefit of their policyholders, funds that might not have been available under free competition. Smaller life assurance companies and their policyholders gained from the regulatory protection against financial difficulties.[36] The price system and the protection of smaller companies were two sides of same system.[37]

The MOF strengthened the regulation of business expenditures and formed the industry's price system during the reconstruction period.[38] The aim of regulation was to restrain wasteful expenditure and cut-throat sales competition, so promoting efficiency rather than market mechanisms. The authority restrained efficient companies from disposing of their surpluses at their discretion, creating a healthy system for policyholders, and directing resources towards consumer benefits. It assumed the role of consumer 'protector'. Moreover, by concentrating supervision, monitoring costs were reduced, and governmental regulation did not always contradict efficiency and consumer welfare in the post-war Japanese life assurance system.

Table 6.1 Disposal of Rents by Major Life Assurance Companies

A. Investment in Competitive Capabilities
        A-1 Expansion of Outfield Sales Force
        A-2 R&D in Life Assurance Products
        A-3 Investment in IT
        A-4 Improved Consumer Service
B. Investment in Strategic Competitiveness
        B-1 Investment in Support for Strategic Decision-Making
        B-2 Lobbying on the Legal Environment and Regulation
        B-3 Discovery and Solving of Organizational Problems
C. Employee Salaries
        C-1 Improvement of Salary System
        C-2 Enhancement of Fringe Benefits
D. Executive Salaries and Rewards
        D-1 Improvement of Executive Salaries and Rewards
E. Policyholder Dividends
        E-1 Increased Dividends and Issue of Additional Dividends

The Logic of Competition and the Application of Rents

Regulation did not neglect the efficiency of the industry as a whole, and the authority did not totally reduce competition. As we have seen, price competition was strictly prohibited in the post-war life assurance system. As a result, businesses turned to non-price competition. If we divide the non-price competition into strategic and functional competition, life assurance companies focused on functional competition. The scramble for new life contracts was very severe. Since the price of life products was uniform, and the solvency of the company was guaranteed by governmental supervision, consumers generally did not have to research the cost of life products. Instead, personal service, relationships or friendships were the most important motivations for purchase decisions. Japanese life assurance companies intensified sales competition by sheer force of numbers.

So, most life assurance companies rapidly increased the number of female sales persons from 1955. The high rate of economic growth had tightened the male labour market. The turnover of female sales persons was so high that companies also continued to recruit. But, although they continuously quit, and took the customer connections they had formed, operations could remain profitable so long as wages were low enough to balance initial costs. As a result, the female sales corps became the most important and typical sales channel of the Japanese life assurance system. Yet the strategy of force of numbers did become costly. The average wage of female sales personnel approached the standard of other industries. By 1988, many small companies had abandoned the system.[39] Why, therefore, were major life companies able to maintain such a costly sales channel?

Where and how did efficient companies invest or dispose of the rents generated by the controlled price mechanism? As seen in Table 6.1, the policyholder's dividends (E) were equalized by implicit agreement among the life assurance companies, and the major concerns paid more money to policyholders than the smaller companies. Executive salaries and rewards (D) were not such an important proportion of expenditure, far less than US top management salaries and rewards, because of the more limited role of top management in Japan. We have no details on employee salaries (C), but it is said that the salaries and fringe benefits of major life firms are amongst the highest for financial institutions, themselves better than other industries. It is generally said that the wage levels of the top companies clearly differ from the smaller ones, so that the major companies used rents to improve salaries and benefits. Next, regarding investments as a means of competition, we can differentiate between functional and strategic investments. Major life assurance companies were unwilling to make investments in pursuit of strategic competition (B), because strategic decision-making was strictly limited by the regulatory regime. Although lobbying (B-2) was inevitable, it was generally achieved via a trade association like the Life Insurance Association of Japan, not by the individual company. Therefore, rents were not used for competition, but for co-operation. A scramble for new contracts did develop, and life assurance companies made these activities an important area of investment. Research and development (A-2) was not so important to major life concerns, because new products were not favoured by the authorities, although the attitude of the smaller life businesses was different. The most important expenditure is the sales force (A-1), and major life concerns invested a large proportion of their rents in order to increase their market shares. Only major life companies kept a large corps of female sales persons, and they had strong financial and commercial reasons for establishing a 'unique' sales channel.[40]

Corporate Goals and Salaried Employees

Top managers have always emphasised the number of insurance contracts more than the annual premium income in their business results during the post-war period. For instance, a report presented to a meeting of managing directors in the 1970s, focused on sales trends, analysing business performance by growth rates of insurance levels for each product from the previous year. Life premium income was only mentioned in the last part of the report, in order to account for income versus expenditure. This attitude suggests that growing market share could bring profits to a company, and that profits were the results of the growing rents produced by the regulatory system. Yet it also shows that incentives to increase annual profits were very weak, because there were no shareholders, very limited competition, and no check from policyholders. Why did top managers regard insurance sales as the most important criterion? Incidentally, as opposed to common products, life products have long duration, and Japan did not have the investment-oriented life product, such as the unit-link type in the UK, until October 1986. Therefore, the level of insurance in force could guarantee the company's future longevity.

As we have seen, the core of salaried employees retained a strong influence on internal corporate governance in major life assurance companies. Within the Japanese employment system, internal labour markets were dominant, and an employee who took up other employment was generally disadvantaged. The core of salaried employees was strongly interested in the company's longevity, as well as improvements in salary. If we consider the final corporate goal as the maximisation of long-term salaries for the core of salaried employees, it is easy to understand the top managers' preference for insurance sales levels. The corporate behaviour of major life assurance depends upon an internal corporate governance, where the core of salaried employees holds a stake in their company. Subject to strict regulation from ministry officials, employees are conscious of their stake in the longevity of the whole post-war life insurance system.

Conclusion: Japanese Life Assurance and Corporate Governance

We cannot compare parts of the Japanese corporate monitoring system with the United States, because the aggregation of complementary attributes differs in both cases. Moreover, the corporate system in Japanese life assurance is a sub-system of the whole economic system, the financial system, and the employment system. Since we cannot usefully discuss characteristics of Japanese corporate governance in isolation, historical perspectives help us to understand the inter-connections. This paper, therefore, has explained when and how the post-war life assurance system emerged, and what its distinctive features were.

We can find differences in life assurance from the general Japanese corporate governance style. It is said that two pivotal elements in the Japanese system of corporate governance are the roles played by 'main' banks and parent firms, and the high degree of interlocking shareholdings.[41] However, these two elements did not operate in the life assurance system. Instead, governmental regulation had a significant role in monitoring corporate management, and the core of salaried employees executed a form of internal corporate check. Both the external and internal check systems worked well in certain institutional and economic conditions, and the post-war life assurance system achieved long stability and high efficiency.[42] Although two general elements in Japanese corporate governance were less important, we can see common features between major life assurance and big business in other industries. It is common that the core of salaried employees held stakes in their companies, and the executives and would-be executives shared top management functions with one another. They monitored corporate management, and executed internal corporate governance. If cooperation occurred smoothly, and if the monitoring was effective, then the company had strong integrity. But, now, cooperation tends to cover faults in the securities business, and monitoring is breaking down in many Japanese big businesses.

In conclusion, this paper reviews the merits and demerits of the Japanese corporate monitoring system in life assurance. In Anglo-American structures, corporate management is monitored by shareholders *ex ante*, and, when it is shown as inefficient, it is checked via the capital market *ex post*. In the Japanese life assurance system, ministry officials, instead of shareholders and the capital market, monitored all corporate management, checking by inspection if necessary. High-ranked ministry officials, conscious of national interests, deliberately instituted a regulated life assurance system for the purpose of promoting efficiency and supporting market stability. The system made savings on the monitoring and disclosure costs that would be borne by policyholders.

In the United States, the CEO has so much influence on corporate performance and its growth that the person is given large powers and responsibilities for corporate management. But top executives in Japanese major life assurance had limited powers for strategic decision-making because of the regulatory regime. The core of salaried employees shared with top managers the task of corporate management. This established an internal checking system in the post-war period. Top executives were expected to behave as integrators and co-ordinators, and acted as figureheads for the corporation. The system operated effectively, because strategic decisions were not important under the post-war life assurance system. But under the 'big bang' of financial reform, and the trend towards global standards in financial market rules, top management functions are becoming far more critical.

Notes

1   Mutual aid projects, and postal life and pension plans other than life assurance company issues came under the Insurance Business Law. The former refers to cooperatives or

unions that people from specific work sites or geographical areas joined. The cooperatives provided mutual aid that ensured the welfare of members. They provided benefits related to death, accident, sickness, injury, and so on. There are many mutual aid organisations in Japan, including *zenkyoren*, established under the Agricultural Co-operative Law, and *zenrosai*, established under the Law for Consumer Cooperatives. The latter was provided by the government via post offices. Postal life assurance was introduced in 1916, after studying closely the failures of the postal life assurance project in the UK. At first, it offered only small sums without medical examination. Postal insurance and life assurance were complements of each other before the war. The governmental authorities for such projects were different. While the Ministry of Agriculture and Forestry supervised *zenkyoren*, *zenrosai* came under the Ministry of Commerce and Trade. The postal life and pension plan was a governmental service under the Ministry of Post and Telecommunications.

2   The periods in this paper are divided as follows: pre-war (before 1931), the war (1931-1945), the reconstruction period (1946-1957), and post-war (1957-1990). If this paper states 'the war economy', it means the period between 1937-45.

3   Former ministry officials who form the core of the OB network are important too. The role is referred the following paper: U.Schaede, 'Understanding Corporate Governance in Japan: Do Classical Concepts Apply?', *Industrial and Corporate Change* (1994), pp.317-319.

4   This is a legal reserve as prescribed in Article 86 of the previously-mentioned Insurance Business Law, which was replaced by a new one from April 1996. 'It was originally established to protect the income and expenses of a company from the influence of accidental profits and losses caused by the buying and selling or valuation of assets. Hence, profits were allocated to this reserve, and losses were made up by withdrawals from it. With permission from the Ministry of Finance, profits may be used for other purposes, either wholly or in part.' See Nippon Life, *The 100-Year History of Nippon Life: Its Growth and Socioeconomic Setting 1889-1989* (1991).

5   The holding company form will be available to finance companies, following the 'big bang' financial reform. Even a mutual life company will be able to form a holding company as a subsidiary after Autumn 1998. See 'The Lifting of Life Assurance's Holding Company Ban after Next Autumn', *Nihonkeizai Shinbun* (*Japan Economic Newspaper*), 20 October 1997.

6   Life assurance companies regard sales-oriented investments as important, because they hope to obtain large sales from the growing market for group life assurance schemes. But investment policy is gradually changing due to the experience of the bubble economy and its prolonged and painful aftermath.

7   The Bureau of Commerce and Industry took responsibility for insurance regulations.

8   See T.Yoneyama, *Sengo Seimei Hoken Sisutemu no Henkaku* (*The Transformation of the Life Assurance System*) (1997), pp.27-36.

9   It was not easy for the authority to have enough staff with whom to inspect all companies, according to a newspaper article. See 'The Regulation of Life Assurance Companies', *Tokyo Asahi Shinbun* (*Tokyo Asahi Newspaper*), 2 September 1922.

10 It is remarkable that the MOF researched all life assurance companies on their expense structures just after the war. The information was used when the MOF developed regulations in the reconstruction and pre-war periods. See *Showa Seimei Hoken Shiryo* (*Life Assurance Business Materials*), vol. 5, pp.268-273.

11 It is too simple to say that the pre-war economy was market-oriented or Anglo-Saxon in style, and that the post-war economy was regulation-oriented or Japanese in style. Although the pre-war economy looked Anglo-Saxon, the essence was not so. For example, price competition in life products did not develop with real market disciplines.

Life companies could contract life assurance by making use of incomprehensible products. Competition could not develop without a proper disclosure system.

12 The law concerning the control of insurance soliciting was enacted in 1948. 'It is aimed at protecting the interests of policyholders and promoting the healthy development of the insurance industry. It concerns insurance soliciting in both the life insurance and the property casualty insurance industry.' See Nippon Life, *The 100-Year History of Nippon Life*, p.347. Illegal sales techniques nearly disappeared in the post-war life market, although sales persons often gave small gifts to customers at their own expense.

13 See Y.Tsutsui, et al., 'The Japanese Life Insurance Industry in the Inter-War Period', *Proceedings of the First International Conference of Business History of Insurance, Kyoto* (February 1996); T.Iguchi, *Gendai Hokengyo no Sangyo Soshiki (The Industrial Structure of Contemporary Insurance Business)* (1996).

14 The Seibu Allstate Life Insurance Company was established by means of joining the Seibu Retailing Group and Allstate Insurance of Sears Roeback. The American Family Life Assurance Company had already obtained a licence for selling life products in Japan in 1974. AFLAC had not, however, established its affiliated company.

15 These are the figures for July 1997. The figure includes the newly-established foreign-affiliated companies like Zurich and Scandia, and not Nissan Life, which ended its business in April 1997.

16 The top 5 in the 1920s were Nippon Life, Meiji Life, Teikoku Life (renamed Asahi Life after 1945), Dai-ichi Life, and Chiyoda Life. The top 7 are Nippon, Dai-ichi, Sumitomo, Meiji, Asahi, Yasuda, and Mitsui.

17 Nippon Life, *The 100-Year History of Nippon Life*, pp.89-92.

18 Osaka Life, under a reckless manager, launched some hostile acquisitions for many larger companies in the early 1900s. See I.Ogawa, 'Osaka Seimei no Seiho Nottori to Nihon Seimei no Taiou' ('The Hostile Acquisition Activities of Osaka Life and the Countermeasures of Nippon Life'), *Hokengaku Zasshi (Journal of Insurance Science)* (1987), no.516.

19 Out of all 20 companies, 14 made the conversion into mutual life companies. Three comparatively small companies (Heiwa Life, Nihon Dantai Life and Taisho Life) did not convert. Three mutual life companies (Dai-ichi, Chiyoda, and Fukoku Life) continued.

20 The leaders were section chiefs, and the labour dispute at Nippon Life was 'a typical dispute of the salaried people class'. See *Mainichi Shinbun (Mainichi Newspaper)*, 5 April 1946); *Shin Osaka Shinbun (New Osaka Newspaper)*, 9 April 1946.

21 Whether Nippon Life belonged to Yamaguchi zaibatsu or not depends upon definition. While the influence of the Yamaguchi bank was strong, it did not act as a 'main bank'.

22 T.Yoneyama, *Sengo Seimei Hoken Sisutemu no Henkaku (The Transformation of the Life Assurance System)* (1997), pp.27-38.

23 He was the Minister of Commerce and Industry when the transfer was completed. He was found guilty of war crimes just after the war. After release from prison, he became the 56th Prime Minister in 1957.

24 No. 6, 15 August 1946; No. 39, 30 October 1946.

25 Specialised life companies like Nippon Dantai and Kyoei could clear bad debts by themselves.

26 Financial Institutions Reorganisation and Readjustment Amendment Act (No. 184, 21 July 1948).

27 This movement was not unusual at this time. For example, Banjo Otuka, an original member of *Keizai Doyu Kai* (Japan Association of Corporate Executives), emphasised the participation of salaried employees in management decisions: B.Otuka, 'Keizai Minshuka to sono Gutaisaku' ('Economic Democracy and its Concrete Plan'), *Keieisha (Managers)*, April 1947.

28 This is the origin of amakudari ('descent from heaven' in Japanese myth), which means the appointment of a former official to an important post in a private company or a government-affiliated organisation.
29 See T.Yoneyama, 'Life Insurance in Post-War Japan: Competition under Governmental Regulation', *Proceedings of the Twelfth International Economic History Congress* (1998).
30 T.Yoneyama, 'The Industrial Organisation of Japanese Life Insurance: Historical Aspects', in T.Yuzawa (ed.), *Japanese Business Success: The Evolution of a Strategy* (1994), pp.172-174.
31 As the top management functions are generally limited in Japan, we should recognise that the meaning of CEO was different from that of the United States.
32 Most salaried employees, except 'outfield' sales persons, are would-be executives.
33 Top executives shared even their profits with executives and would-be executives. His salary was not far from the average of salaried employees.
34 This logic is similar to one amongst high-ranked government officials. See E.F.Vogel, *Japan as Number One: Lessons for America* (1979).
35 Official Notices, Bank Bureau, Ministry of Finance, No.178, 29 January 1949, in *Showa Seimei Hoken Shiryo (Life Assurance Business Materials)*, vol.5, pp.237-238.
36 To protect smaller companies, some special life products are not licensed to larger companies.
37 The MOF did not permit new entrants until a foreign-affiliated life assurance company received a licence in 1975. This was for the protection of smaller companies.
38 Official Notices, No.516. 19 April 1948, in *Showa Seimei Hoken Shiryo (Life Assurance Business Materials)*, vol.5, pp.271-272. See also *Hoken Mainichi Shinbun (Insurance Daily News)*, 26 April 1948, in *Showa Seimei Hoken Shiryo (Life Assurance Business Materials)*, vol.5, p.723.
39 T.Yoneyama, *Sengo Seimei Hoken Sisutemu no Henkaku (The Transformation of the Life Assurance System)* (1997), pp.69-73.
40 Yoneyama, *Sengo Seimei Hoken Sisutemu no Henkaku*, pp.69-73.
41 P.Sheard, 'Japanese Corporate Governance in Comparative Perspective', *Journal of Japanese Trade and Industry* (1988), no.1, p.9.
42 The Japanese post-war economic system is transforming, because of radical changes in institutional and economic conditions, which had previously supported the system. See T.Yoneyama, 'Évolution des assurance japonaises: l'improbable retour au modèle anglo-saxon', *Risque* (1977), no.31, pp.99-101.

Chapter 7

The Main Bank System and Corporate Governance in Post-War Japan

Chikage Hidaka and Takeo Kikkawa

Introduction

The year 1997 was one of the most alarming years in Japan's recent economic history. Following the failure of a major city bank, the Hokkaido Takushoku Bank, one of the four main securities houses, Yamaichi Securities Co., filed for bankruptcy. Naturally, this has heightened criticism concerning the stability of the Japanese financial system, and the major problem cited in particular has been the excess of bad debts held by many financial institutions. This accumulation of bad debt strongly suggests that the investigation capabilities of financial institutions in Japan are poor, and that their function as monitors is inadequate. However, this observation is in contrast to presently-accepted theories concerning the function of Japanese financial institutions. In the first part of this paper, we will provide a basic summary of the widely-held view of the Japanese main bank, and, in the second and third parts, we will present case studies on Japan's steel and petrochemical industries during the period of high economic growth. The aim is to use these case studies to gain a clearer picture of corporate governance and the post-war Japanese main bank system.

The Main Bank and Corporate Governance

The system of Japanese corporate governance is said to have changed greatly from the so-called classical governance structure of shareholder leadership prior to the Second World War. Okazaki's explanation of how the governance system evolved will now be outlined.[1] In prewar Japan, it was the industrialists who, as major stockholders, maintained a great deal of power and personal interest in the governance of large enterprises. The banks played a relatively small part in the financing of enterprises, so that they had a supporting role within a classical structure of shareholder governance. Employees, too, had little influence on corporate governance, as they generally remained only a short time with one enterprise. However, the wartime economy began with the Sino-Japanese War, and stockholder power was quickly restricted, as symbolized by the introduction of dividend control. The power of large shareholders and outside officials was greatly reduced in the corporate executive system, and internal promotion became more prevalent. With the aim of making up for the lack of physical capital, the government pressed for employee participation in management through the Industrial Patriotic Society. After shareholder power was curtailed, and stock markets altered, so hindering the supply of capital, the banks then acquired a more important position. The structural transformation brought about by wartime, namely the rise in the position of employees and the reduction of corporate control by stockholders, continued through the post-war reconstruction.

What kind of governance structure arose in the companies of post-war Japan? Aoki maintains that a governance system with the *main banks* as monitors was formed in post-war Japan.[2] 'Main bank' is originally a term used by practitioners in Japanese financial institutions and industrial firms. They call a particular bank the main bank when the firm obtains its largest share of borrowings from that institution. It also holds a certain amount of equity in the firm.

Then, why has the main bank come to play a central part in the corporate governance of post-war Japan? Aoki's reason is as follows.[3] With an increase in the insider authority of corporate management, it becomes easier for moral discrepancies to occur. So, a governance structure was created that linked the control of the company contingent to its financial condition, in order to provide employees with the incentives to work hard for increased production, while preventing moral discrepancies. For example, when production was high, and the financial conditions were favorable, remuneration was provided to the internal organization in the form of surplus claims that originally belonged to the shareholders. Conversely, when production was low, and the financial condition was poor, severe penalties were imposed, which included the break up of the corporate organization.

For the kind of governance contingent on the company's financial condition, the situation had to be watched closely, and it became necessary to have an entity monitoring corporate management authority. In post-war Japan, it was the firm's main bank that was in the best position for monitoring. Main banks had developed the ability for corporate governance through the dispatching of special managers under the Corporate Management Emergency Measures Law, as well as the dispatching of managerial officials for cooperative financing after the war. In post-war Japan, since there was a lack of human resources with the necessary specialized knowledge for corporate monitoring, it was significant that the three stages of corporate monitoring for investment projects were highly integrated to the firm's main bank. The three stages were: *ex ante* monitoring (assessment of the profitability of proposed projects); *interim* monitoring (checking the management situation after the funds had been committed, and, in particular, whether or not the investment capital was being used effectively); and *ex post* monitoring (the verification of performance outcome or the financial state of the firm). Having the largest share of short-term loans to the firm, and holding the major payment settlement account, the main bank could gather more information on the customer than other financial institutions. From the perspective of other interest parties, it was rational to depend on the main bank's monitoring, rather than developing their own monitoring capabilities. In his work, Aoki understands the corporate governance structure as the main bank monitoring of post-war Japanese companies. That structure encouraged hard work among the company's own employees, while also controlling the danger of insider control. Moreover, it was an effective system because it saved on monitoring costs.

After the War, the capital procurement of Japanese firms came to depend heavily on bank borrowing, and the relationship between financial institutions and firms became very close.[4] However, was the relationship constructed between firms and banks so ideal for the economy of post-war Japan? In order to answer this question, it is necessary to verify the relationship between firms and banks, by looking at the history of production among individual firms. This will be done, firstly, by investigating the steel industry, which was one of the industries developed by exceedingly large-scale capital investment in the high-growth era. We will also look at the resulting growth, which is held to be an effective benefit of the main bank system.

Capital Investment and Bank Monitoring in the Steel Industry

Capital Investment and Funds Raising

The basic development of capital investment in the steel industry will first be presented.[5] Substantial capital investment in the post-war Japanese steel industry began in 1951 with the industry's First Rationalization Programme. The Programme focused on bridging the large technological gap between the industry and international standards for steel rolling. Along with this came the important movement towards integrated manufacture. This development was announced when Kawasaki Steel, which, until then, had been one of the open-hearth furnace steel works, set up its first blast furnace. The Chiba Works, which Kawasaki Steel began constructing, was at that time an extremely large-scale, ocean-front steel works, and posed a threat to the already established three large blast furnace manufacturers, namely Yawata Steel, Fuji Steel, and Nippon Kokan (or NKK). It also served to encourage the other major open-hearth furnace companies - Sumitomo Metal Industries and Kobe Steel - to modernize with blast furnaces.

The Second Rationalization Programme, which began in the fiscal year 1956, reflected the stimulus provided by Kawasaki Steel, and the government announced its steel self-sufficiency policy as part of its new long-term economic plan of 1957. Influenced by specific targets for establishing ten blast furnace plants, the original three blast furnace companies along with the three former open-hearth manufacturers began competing through the construction of blast furnaces. Then, at the beginning of the 1960s, there was a remarkable increase in the demand for steel. Aided by the 'Income Doubling Plan', announced in November 1960, the construction of integrated steel plants by the six largest integrated firms gained momentum. Up until fiscal 1960, capital investment by all the companies was subject to proper regulation, based on industry-level rationalization planning, which was established by discussions between the Council for Industrial Rationalization and the Ministry of International Trade and Industry (MITI). However, from the 1960s onwards, capital investment developed without general long-term planning. The furious investment in equipment by all the companies was achieved without coordination between firms and the establishment of long-term plans. Opposition among firms was not eliminated by the various initiatives: by the 'Volunteer Round Table Conference', established to promote self-regulation at the end of 1959; by the 'Steel Equipment Regulation Research Committee', made up of the presidents of the six largest integrated firms, and begun in 1965; nor by the steel branch of the industrial construction organization that was the focus of equipment regulation after 1967.[6]

Table 7.1 Funds Raising by Japanese Steel Industry, 1951-70

100m Yen, Net Increase

	Stocks	Bonds	Domestic Loans	Foreign Loans	Subtotal Loans	Internal	Total
1951-55	178	232	353	61	414	456	1,280
1956-60	1,189	694	1,394	725	2,119	1,873	5,875
1961-65	2,941	855	3,310	192	3,502	3,620	10,918
1966-70	918	1,357	9,135	645	9,780	11,334	23,389

Percentages of Total Funds Raised

	Stocks	Bonds	Domestic Loans	Foreign Loans	Subtotal Loans	Internal	Total
1951-55	13.8	18.2	27.5	4.8	32.3	35.7	100.0
1956-60	20.3	11.8	23.7	12.3	36.0	31.9	100.0
1961-65	26.9	7.8	30.3	1.8	32.1	33.2	100.0
1966-70	3.9	5.8	39.1	2.8	41.8	48.5	100.0

The conditions for funds raising at this time are shown in Table 7.1, and the degree of reliance on borrowed money is consistently high. Looking at Table 7.2, during the First Rationalization Programme, the share of governmental financial institutions (the Japan Development Bank) is noteworthy, and, during the term of the Second Rationalization Programme, the amount of foreign investment (by the World Bank) is significant. Mutually beneficial relations with private financial institutions can be observed. However, after 1960, it is clear that the funds-raising system centred solely on private financial institutions. Relating to this, the number of banks doing business with the steel companies throughout the 1960s steadily increased.[7] In the case of Sumitomo Metal Industries, the number of domestic financial institutions providing long-term credit increased from 12 in 1963 to 30 by 1970, and, in the case of Kawasaki Steel, the number rose from 14 in 1963 to 26 by

1970. This trend continued even into the 1970s. The number of financial institutions doing business with Nippon Steel, which was 60 for long-term lending and 60 for short-term in 1970, had risen to 110 and 90 respectively by the end of the decade. From the viewpoint of corporate governance, there was growing investment in large-scale equipment and facilities, as well as an increase in the role of financial institutions as stakeholders in the steel industry.

Table 7.2 Funds Provided by Financial Institutions to Japanese Steel Industry, 1956-1970

100m Yen, Net Increase	1956	1960	1965	1970
Government				
JDB	-25	8	-10	2
NEF	-	3	-	18
Others	-	-	4	46
Subtotal	-25	11	-6	66
Private				
IBJ	22	62	132	292
LTCB	-3	47	78	206
Commercial Banks	-3	-6	45	480
Trust Banks	-3	125	267	705
Insurance Companies	1	100	173	879
Others	-26	10	1	362
Subtotal	-12	338	696	2,924
Foreign				
IBRD	27	137	-39	-
EIB	-	2	2	84
Others	-20	99	-80	-
Subtotal	7	238	-117	84
Total	-30	587	573	3,074

Notes: JDB means Japan Development Bank; NEF, The North East Finance of Japan; IBJ, Industrial Bank of Japan; LTCB, Long-Term Credit Bank; IBRD, International Bank for Reconstruction and Development; EIB, Export-Import Bank.

Monitoring by the World Bank

During this furious development of capital investment, what was the relationship between the stakeholders of the six largest integrated firms and their corporate management? The interesting aspect of this question is the relationship between the steel companies and the World Bank (the International Bank for Reconstruction and Development), which offered loans to the steel industry during the Second Rationalization Programme. The World Bank concluded a total of 11 loan contracts with all six blast-furnace companies between 1955-60.[8] Among these loans, a number of early loans in particular were exceedingly important as long-term capital, meaning 15 years, given the tight domestic capital market at the time. Cases include the second construction capital fund for Kawasaki Steels Chiba Works, and the construction fund for the first blast furnace at Sumitomos Wakayama plant. These loans not only made up 40-50 per cent of the total capital required for the projects, but they also served the purpose of inducing capital from private financial institutions, by increasing the credit worthiness of these companies. In that sense, it was the driving force of the Second Rationalization Programme.[9]

World Bank financing included 'regulations for very substantial financial improvement, different from the usual practice of Japanese financial institutions', according to the words of the Japan Development Bank.[10] That is to say, the World Bank sought a one-to-one debt-equity ratio for a specific term.[11] The World Bank knew that, if the steel companies could improve their financial condition, they would need more access to capital procurement on the overseas markets, particularly in New York.

However, the conditions imposed by the new stakeholder, the World Bank, were too stiff for the steel companies, which were trying to finance successive large-scale equipment projects with huge borrowings. The steel companies appealed to the World Bank, seeking a more preferable financial ratio. They applied through the Japan Development Bank, which had become the loan agent for the steel companies. The first application was made in December 1962, when the steel companies cited the serious recession. That year, demand subsided after the successive completion of new large-scale plants, and the prices of steel products fell to unprecedented levels. It reached the point where MITI began issuing administrative guidance for production curtailment measures. However, despite the stabilization of the weakening market, the steel companies were extremely strapped for capital.[12]

After the World Bank received the appeal from the steel companies, it dispatched a research delegation to Japan. Their findings were that, despite the severe depression, the management of steel firms was primarily concerned with market share maintenance and expansion, and even the domestic financial institutions approved of the corporate battle for market share. After having violated its loan agreement with the World Bank, Yawata Steel told the Bank: 'We will do EVERYTHING to maintain our share of the market'. Also, Fuji Bank, NKK's main bank, told officials: 'It might be true that construction of a new steel plant is too heavy a burden for our customer NKK, but we feel that we must give the company a fair chance to maintain their share of the market'.[13] The World Bank was worried about the excess capacity that might result from the intense struggle for market share, and advised the steel companies that the excess capacity would have a negative effect on sales prices, which, in turn, would affect earnings. Despite the warning, the companies replied that 'excess capacity is a normal feature of a growing economy'.[14]

This surprised the delegation, which reported that 'the Bank's viewpoint on sound financing has not been adopted by steel companies or the financial circles in Japan'.[15] Though the steel manufacturers seemed to be aware that shoring up equity capital would lead to financial improvement, this did not mean, however, they understood the importance of it. The Ministry of Finance as well as financial institutions expressed their intentions to the World Bank officials, supporting the strengthening of equity capital in the steel industry. However, they stated that 'the 50/50 rate is an international obligation which should be honoured in order to get future funds from the Bank for other investments, and to bolster Japan's international financial reputation'.[16]

In the end, the term for financial improvement was extended by three years until March 1967, as a result of negotiations. However, in September 1965, the steel companies again began negotiations to re-examine the financial improvement provision, and notably the March 1967 deadline.[17] The reason for these negotiations was officially disorder in the planning of new stock issuance, due to deterioration in the stock market. The real reason was that the steel companies did not want the World Bank to put a brake on their capital investment. The Japan Development Bank, which represented the steel companies in the negotiations, proposed that, from 31st March 1967, all companies would maintain their debt-equity ratio at a level no higher than 2:1.[18]

These negotiations were even fiercer than the previous ones. In the end, the World Bank ended their financial role in March 1967, just before the deadline. After that, it decided to give responsibility to the Japan Development Bank. This did not mean that the World Bank decided there was no need for financial improvement within the steel companies. The World Bank's decision was influenced by the observation that, even if they extended the deadline, the steel companies would just keep extending it. Also, the World Bank could not ignore the statement of the Japan Development Bank during the negotiations: 'The proposed 2:1 debt-equity ratio is nothing unusual in comparable Japanese large scale industries'.[19] In any case, the steel companies were freed from restrictions on their financial structures and from monitoring by the World Bank, following five years of negotiations. On receiving this decision, the Japan Development Bank harmonized the debt-equity ratio improvement targets at 2:1, and, furthermore, abolished the provision itself in 1970, when the loan repayment balance was minimized.[20]

At the same time, discussion arose over the proper financing methods of financial institutions in Japan. This was sparked by the 'World Bank Financing Reference', which was prepared by the MOF's Banking Bureau in September 1963. The report proposed 'the establishment of a series of lending procedures to be followed by bankers based on the financial ratios of borrowing enterprises. The proposal should correct the excessive corporate reliance on bank loans, and encourage corporations to improve their capital and financial structures, thereby strengthening their competitiveness in the international market'.[21] After this, the question became the subject of discussion for the Research Committee on Financial Systems (an MOF advisory body), and there was criticism of 'over-lending' by banks. This referred to insufficient consideration of corporate earnings in relation to capital investment, and to 'over-borrowing' by enterprises giving insufficient examination to production capacity and profitability after the building of new facilities in the struggle for market share.[22] But there were objections from the financial industry, saying that there were against 'such financial rules that would restrict the autonomy of individual companies'. Finally, in 1965, this debate died down without producing any specific regulations.[23]

Capital Investment and Management after 'Liberation' from the World Bank

Let us look at the management of steel companies after they were freed from monitoring by the World Bank. Among the six largest integrated companies, we will look at just those firms where steel production is a predominant part of their business structure, namely Kawasaki Steel, Sumitomo Metal Industries, and Nippon Steel, created by the 1970 merger between Yawata Steel and Fuji Steel. First, the example of crude steel production capacity and its impact on capital investment will be cited. Comparing the two years 1965 and 1975, production capacity increased from 4m to 15m tons for Kawasaki, 1.5m tons to 7m tons for Sumitomo, and, for Nippon Steel, it rose by about 400 per cent from 11m tons to 45 million tons. Nippon Steel's original 11m ton total had been composed of 7m from Yawata and 4m from Fuji.

Next, we will look at the transition in capital structure. Although the following does not correspond with the World Bank's definition of debt-equity ratios, the trend can be indicated. In the early 1960s, there was still the previously mentioned restriction of the World Bank, which placed debt-equity ratios at 1:1. The deadline for this arrangement was set at March 1964, but, after the negotiations, it was supposed to have been achieved by March 1967. However, as stated earlier, following the negotiations of March 1967, the restriction was withdrawn, and so the proportion of debt increased. Looking at these figures, it is plain that the steel companies did not take to heart the advice of their former stakeholder, the World Bank. The debt-equity ratio for Kawasaki Steel and Sumitomo Metal grew from approximately 6.5:3.5 in 1962 to 9:1 in 1976; at Nippon Steel, the figures were just over 8:1 in 1969 and just under 9:1 in 1977.[24] All these companies were, for the most part, able to achieve favorable sales increases: those at Kawasaki Steel and Sumitomo Metal increased some tenfold between 1962-76; those at Nippon Steel demonstrated a fourfold growth between 1969-77.[25] However, interest payments at Kawasaki Steel and Sumitomo Metal progressively increased throughout the 1960s, not surprisingly considering the greater debt-equity ratios. In the 1970s, however, interest payments at these firms and at Nippon Steel rose more steeply, just as net profits were falling sharply.[26]

From the above data, it seems that the steel companies, which were freed from monitoring by the World Bank, made expansion their primary management goal. In addition, the further increase in the degree of debt reliance, which had long been at a high level due to this expansion, indicates that every company gave precedence to expansion over the maintenance of financial stability at the level advocated by the World Bank. It, also, shows that financial institutions, including the main banks, supported the management of steel companies, which increased its heavy reliance on borrowed money.

Summary

As is proposed by Aoki, with regard to the steel industry during the period of high growth, private financial institutions and the main banks in particular created multi-faceted relationships with companies as lenders, shareholders, and bond trustee banks. These banks represent the largest influence on the corporate governance structure. So how did the 'main bank monitoring governance structure' interact with the management of steel companies, and where did it lead the management in result? As shown above, the World Bank became one of the important corporate stakeholders just as the competition for capital investment was really beginning in the steel industry. Moreover, the Bank was concerned about the weakening of management, due to over-competition for capital investment, and advised the steel companies to balance their capital investment planning by ensuring financial soundness as well. However, the companies preferred to rid themselves of this restraint, so that they would not fall behind their competitors in their investment, given the growth assumptions, and continued with their feverish capital investments. The domestic financial institutions, including the main banks, gave substantial support to the companies in the negotiations with the World Bank, and, after abolishing the World Bank's financial regulations, they became even bigger lenders. Due to robust capital investment, the steel companies increased their production capacity by great strides, and their sales increased as well.

Why did the main banks support the goal of corporate expansion? Here is one possible explanation. The interest rates of Japanese financial institutions were regulated by the Ministry of Finance, according to the Law on the Temporary Adjustment of Interest Rates of 1947. In order to maximize their earning opportunities in a regulated interest rate environment, bankers must capitalize on their lending capabilities to the fullest extent, which means increasing their customer deposit base. For bankers, the most effective means of achieving this goal would normally be to expand their network of branches. However, the MOF continued to impose stringent restrictions on the efforts of banks to increase the number of branches. It managed its policy in this regard mainly on the total balance of customer deposits held by banks. Given these circumstances, it was quite natural that bankers would try to increase loan balances with corporate borrowers, due to their higher potential as deposit funds, in order to increase the overall balance of deposits at existing branches. Consequently, it was in their best interest to assist companies in their efforts to make capital investments, which would in turn help to maximize sales revenues.[27] It may also be noted that, having a large financing role with corporations, they had a strong interest in expanding the scale of corporations.

Okazaki asserts that, in post-war Japan, a growth-promoting corporate governance structure, constituted of growth-oriented lifetime employees, and also growth-oriented financial institutions, was established.[28] However, we must be wary of the word 'growth', however favorable it may sound. In other words, in the case of the steel industry, the system achieved 'growth' in the sense of increased production. It does not mean growth in the sense that profit-generation capacity has been strengthened or increased. Within the theoretical framework of Aoki and Okazaki's main bank system, the main banks, being entrusted with the monitoring role by other financial institutions, evaluated the profitability of investment projects. They are said to have ensured that investments are carried out on the basis of sound financial conditions. However, is this deviance away from profitability for monitoring standards only true in the case of the steel industry?

Capital Investments in the Petrochemical Industry and Bank Monitoring

Capital Investment and Funds Raising

The emergence of the petrochemical industry in Japan can be dated in the years immediately after the Second World War. Looking at the ethylene-manufacturing field, which was the industry's key sector, there were three main capital investment booms from the middle of the 1950s until the early 1970s.[29] The initial boom arose from the First Petrochemical Domestic Production Plan, begun in July 1955. Between February 1958 and May 1959, four production centres for ethylene were created: Mitsui Petrochemical's Iwakuni plant with its annual capacity of 20,000 tons per year; Sumitomo Chemical Company's Niihama plant with a 12,000 ton capacity; Mitsubishi Petrochemical's Yokkaichi plant with 22,000 tons; and Nippon Petrochemical's Kawasaki plant with 25,000 tons. These firms that made up the vanguard of the emerging ethylene industry in Japan are called the 'First Four'.

The second boom came with the Second Petrochemical Domestic Production Plan initiated in December 1959. Between March 1962 and September 1964, there appeared five new ethylene production centres: Tonen Petrochemical at Kawasaki (40,000 tons); Daikyowa Petrochemical, Yokkaichi (41,300 tons); Maruzen Petrochemical, Chiba (44,000 tons); Kasei Mizushima; Mizushima (45,000 tons); and Idemitsu Petrochemical, Tokuyama (73,000 tons). The firms that entered the ethylene business after the First Four were called the 'Later Five'.

The third boom was due to the 300,000 annual ton ethylene production standard established in May 1967, as a countermeasure against the inevitable Capital Liberalization. Between March 1969 and April 1972, nine ethylene production centres with an annual production of 300,000 tons were set up one after the other, namely: Maruzen Petrochemical (Goi), Sumitomo Chiba Chemical (Chiba), Ukishima Petrochemical (Ukishima), Osaka Petrochemical (Senboku), Mizushima Ethylene (Mizushima), Mitsubishi Petrochemical (Kashima), Tonen Petrochemical (Kawasaki), Shin Daikyowa Petrochemical (Senboku), and Sanyo Ethylene (Mizushima). The creation of this annual production base of 300,000 tons was brought about by the decisions of the Petrochemical Cooperation Council, constituted by MITI, the industry, and third-party representatives. These stated that ethylene production would be based on clear plans for the production and sale of final products, and a large part of the raw material, naphtha, would be available by pipeline.[30]

Table 7.3 Funds Raised by the Japanese Petrochemical Industry, 1962-72

100m Yen, Net Increase	1962	1965	1970	1972
Total	424	1,016	2,427	1,455
Stocks	26	67	356	19
Bonds	3	32	22	35
Loans	234	522	1,329	145
Governmental	-3	37	91	14
JDB	-3	36	81	-
NEF	-	-1	-	-
Others	-	2	10	14
Private	183	474	1,282	180
IBJ	13	83	189	38
LCTB	16	63	102	36
Commercial Banks	53	34	222	-5
Trust Banks	43	170	279	57
Insurance Companies	29	49	276	57
Others	29	75	214	-3
Foreign	54	11	-43	-49
IBRD	-	-	-	-
EIB	-	13	-	-
Others	54	-2	-	-
Internal Funds	161	395	720	1,256
Depreciation	126	384	568	1,034
Other	35	11	152	222

Percentage of Total Funds	1962	1965	1970	1972
Total	100	100	100	100
Stocks	6	7	15	1
Bonds	1	3	1	2
Loans	55	51	55	11
Governmental	-1	4	5	1
JDB	-1	4	3	-
NEF	-	-	-	-
Others	-	-	2	1
Private	44	46	52	13
IBJ	3	8	8	3
LCTB	4	6	4	2
Commercial Banks	13	3	9	-
Trust Banks	10	17	11	4
Insurance Companies	7	5	11	4
Others	7	7	9	
Foreign	12	1	-2	-3
IBRD	-	-	-	-
EIB	-	1	-	-
Others	12	-	-	-
Internal Funds	38	39	29	86
Depreciation	30	38	23	71
Other	8	1	6	15

Source: *Yearbooks of the Petrochemical Industries.*

It was MITI that took the initiative in deciding to create an annual ethylene production standard of 300,000 tons. The Ministry strengthened the industry's international cost competitiveness by improving return ratios, lowering construction costs, and creating economies of scale, while simultaneously reducing excessive competition, limiting the number of investing companies, and increasing concentration. In the end, the former was achieved, while bringing about the exact opposite of the latter.

For the existing ethylene manufacturers, success depended on meeting an annual 300,000 tons. Therefore, the companies had survival strategies of successive joint or phased investments, such as the establishment of Ukishima Petrochemical jointly by Mitsui Petrochemical and Nippon Petrochemical; the phased investment in Sumitomo Chiba Petrochemical, Chiba, and Tonen Petrochemical, Kawasaki, by Sumitomo Chemical and Tonen Petrochemical; the establishment of Mizushima

Ethylene and Sanyo Ethylene by Mitsubishi Kasei and Asahi Kasei-Nippon Kogyo; and the establishment of Shin Daikyowa Petrochemical by Daikyowa Petrochemical and Toyo Soda.[31] The result was that all of the First Four as well as four of the Later Five, so not including Idemitsu Petrochemical, contributed to the achievement of the annual target. Moreover, there was also the example of Osaka Petrochemical, established in February 1965 by the joint investment of Mitsui Petrochemical, Toyo Koatsu and Kansai Petrochemical, which added to the 300,000 ton production project, as a newcomer to ethylene manufacturing.[32]

The feverish response of the petrochemical companies exceeded the projections of MITI. In 1967, when the standard was established, MITI anticipated the authorization of three or four of companies.[33] Finally however, between October 1967 and December 1969, nine companies received authorization. As previously mentioned, all the large-scale ethylene production facilities based on these plans began operation between 1969 and 1972. The investment for constructing large-scale facilities had a large influence on the Japanese petrochemical industry. The strengthening of international cost competitiveness was a reality, but the sudden expansion of production capacity generated a supply and demand gap, so competition amongst firms grew more intense. The latter point occurred in the area of induced products.[34] Ethylene was the most important product in the petrochemical industry, and the construction of ethylene plants was closely linked to the new construction of inducement product plants. Table 7.3 shows the funds raised for the Japanese petrochemical industry between 1962 and 1972. From the table, it is evident that the scale of capital investment in the industry increased substantially between 1968-71, when the construction boom for the 300,000 annual ton production capability ethylene plants was in effect.

According to Table 7.3, in the case of the petrochemical industry overall, the degree of loan reliance as the source of funds was even higher than in the steel industry. During 1962-65, and 1969-71, the contribution of loans was in net terms over 50 per cent. The weight of the private financial institutions was great compared to the contribution by governmental financial institutions. Most of the Japanese private financial institutions became important stakeholders in the petrochemical industry, as in the steel industry.

Since the petrochemical industry was called the 'star industry' of the rapid economic growth period, the Japanese banks at this time took an extremely positive stance toward the financing of the industry. For example, the Fuji Bank 'cooperated with large sums of capital' in the construction of two neighbouring ethylene production centres at Kawasaki for Nippon Petrochemical and Tonen Petrochemical.[35] At this point, the corporate history of the Fuji Bank states that, '[t]hough Kawasaki was the first to construct one of the two planned ethylene production centers, given the extremely rapid growth of the petrochemical industry, the inducement product manufacturers that had been supplied by Nippon Petrochemical began to welcome supply from both firms. So both ethylene centres were able to co-exist and prosper'.[36]

A Depressed Industry and Main Bank Monitoring

The co-existence and co-prosperity of two neighboring ethylene centres did not last for long. The petrochemical industry, which was the star of the high growth period, was rocked by the two oil shocks of the 1970s, and plunged into long-term structural depression. There were severe aspects of the depression in the Japanese petrochemical industry, largely unseen in other industries. Firstly, '[s]ince the petrochemical industries in the United States and Canada used mainly domestically produced natural gas, they did not suffer the effects of the jump in crude oil prices to the extent of Japan and Europe, where naphtha was the raw material'.[37] Secondly, unlike their counterparts in Europe, the Japanese petrochemical industry could not freely import naphtha at international prices, and were subject to the institutional restriction of purchasing the relatively expensive naphtha produced by the domestic oil refining industry.[38] Thirdly, there was an increase in the number of developing countries seeking to develop their own domestic petrochemical industries as national projects, before and after the oil crises, and this hampered exports of Japanese petrochemical products. Fourthly, as shown by the slowing demand for plastic products, the Japanese domestic, petrochemical products market had reached saturation. Fifthly, there was a remarkable increase in domestic production capacity, due to the large-scale investment of firms seeking to meet the 300,000 ton standard.

The first three reasons are closely related to the Oil Crises, and, in a certain sense, were due to forecasting difficulties. However, the fourth and fifth reasons were largely anticipated. Brushing these factors aside, the Japanese banks continued to finance large-scale ethylene plants, and they not appear to be monitoring profitability or attaching importance to financial standards. It was evident that the standards for monitoring by the main banks ignored profitability in the petrochemical industry, just as it did in the steel industry. Specific cases were: Mitsubishi Bank as the main bank for Mitsubishi Petrochemical, as well as for Mitsubishi Kasei; Mitsui Bank as the main bank for both Mitsui Petrochemical and Mitsui Toatsu, formed from the merger of Mitsui Chemical and Toyo Koatsu in 1968; the worsening friction between Mitsui Petrochemical and Mitsui Toatsu within the Mitsui group; or the friction between Mitsubishi Petrochemical and Mitsubishi Kasei within the Mitsubishi group, during the long structural depression of the petrochemical industry.[39]

The capital structure, sales, and net warnings against interest payments of Mitsubishi Petrochemical and Mitsui Petrochemical during the 1960s and 1970s reveal the problems. The debt ratio was exceedingly high for both companies, sales figures rose dramatically, and net earnings jumped up and down wildly, despite the fact that interest payments rose evenly. Sales at Mitsubishi Petrochemical grew almost tenfold between 1964-76, while those at Mitsui Petrochemical increased by a factor of approximately 3.5 between 1969-76. It should be pointed out that, before the oil crisis of 1970-72, the net earnings for both Mitsui Petrochemical (from late 1970 to early 1972) and Mitsubishi Petrochemical (from early 1971 to late 1972) fell sharply.[40] This is the effect of the fourth and fifth factors listed above. If the main banks had been monitoring the profitability of the oil firms, they would have implemented measures to counter these factors.

Summary

The accounting evidence on the management tendencies of major Japanese petrochemical manufacturers is basically consistent with the picture of the steel industry. Moreover, the funds raising situation during the rapid economic growth period for the petrochemical industry is largely in agreement with that of the steel industry. In other words, the same view given in the preceding section concerning the monitoring function of the main banks and the corporate governance of steel manufacturers can also be applied to the relationship between main banks and the petrochemical firms.

Conclusion

Aoki asserts that the Japanese post-war governance system, in which main banks monitor the corporate governance of enterprises, with its tendency to encourage the hard work of corporate employees, and limit the danger of insider control, reduced monitoring costs. The main point of this accepted viewpoint is that the main banks, which were responsible for monitoring on behalf of other financial institutions as well, evaluated the profitability of investment projects. However, during the period of high economic growth, when the Japanese main bank system is assumed to have had a very effective function, our case studies of the steel and petrochemical industries show that the assumption is questionable. There is a high possibility that the monitoring standards of the main banks were not focused on profitability. Even the 'growth-promoting corporate governance system' only promoted 'growth' in the limited sense of increasing the scale of production. This was not growth that strengthened or increased profitability. The implication is that there were problems that cannot be overlooked concerning the function of main bank monitoring, even in the high economic growth period.

This investigation has shown that the relations constructed between post-war Japanese banks and corporations were not always ideal for the economy as a whole. The view that the once-sound main bank system is no longer adequate cannot be accurate either. We can go so far as to say that the factors creating the current crisis in the financial system can be discovered over 40 years ago. The large-scale accumulation of bad debts in Japan is not just a temporary outcome of the bursting Bubble Economy. One cannot forget the important historical outcomes that sprang from post-war corporate banking relations themselves.

Notes

1   T.Okazaki, 'Nihon ni okeru Corporate Governance no Hatten' ('The Development of Corporate Governance in Japan'), in M.Aoki and R.Dore (eds.), *System to Siteno Nihon Kigyo (The Japanese Firm)* (1995).

2   On the main bank's definition, see M.Aoki, H.Patrick and P.Sheard, 'The Japanese Main Bank System: An Introductory Overview', in M.Aoki & H.Patrick (eds.), *The Japanese Main Bank System* (1994).

3   M.Aoki and I.Sekiguchi, 'Joutai Izon-gata Governance' ('The Contingent Governance Structure'); and M.Okuno and N.Hori, 'Gendai Nihon Keizai System no Rekishiteki Seisei' ('Historical Development of Modern Japanese Economic System'), in M.Aoki and M.Okuno (eds.), *Keizai System no Hikaku Seido Bunseki (Comparative Institutional Analysis: A New Approach to Economic Systems)* (1996). On the main bank's monitoring, see M.Aoki, 'Monitoring Characteristics of the Main Bank System: An Analytical and Development View', in Aoki & Patrick (eds), *Japanese Main Bank System.*

4   For example, see C.Hidaka, 'A Re-examination of Japan's Post-war Financing System', in E.Abe and T.Gourvish (eds.), *Japanese Success? British Failure? Comparisons in Business Performance since 1945* (1997).

5   For more details on the development of the steel industry, see C.Hidaka, 'Kigyo Kinyu' ('Industrial Finance'), in H.Takeda (ed.), *Nippon Sangyo Hatten no Dynamism (Historical Studies on the Competitive Advantages of Japanese Industries during the 20th Century)* (1995), pp.326-333.

6   See S.Yonekura, *The Japanese Iron and Steel Industry, 1850-1990* (1994), pp.232-234.

7   Annual Reports.

8   The total amount of the 11 loan contracts was almost $160m.

9   See, for example, Sumitomo Kinzoku Kogyo Kabushiki Kaisha (Sumitomo Metal Industries), *Sumitomo Kinzoku Saikin Junenshi (Recent Decade of Sumitomo Metal Industries)* (1967), p.83.

10   Nihon Kaihatsu Ginkou (Japan Development Bank), *Nihon Kaihatsu Ginkou Junenshi (Ten Years History of JDB)* (1963), p.367.

11   See C.Hidaka, 'Tekko-gyo no Setsubi Toushi to Segin Shakkan' ('Capital Investment of the Steel Industries and the World Bank Loans'), *Musashi Daigaku Ronshu*, Vol.44, No.2 (1996).

12   Nihon Tekko Renmei, *Tekko Junenshi – Showa 33nen-42nen (Ten-year History of the Steel Industry: 1958-1967)* (1969), p.495.

13   The International Bank for Reconstruction and Development (IBRD), 91000/018/JA/8, 'Situation, Prospects and Common Problems of the Six Japanese Steel Companies', 20 April 1964.

14   IBRD, 91000/018/JA/8, 'Loans to Six Japanese Steel Companies', 6 April 1964.

15   The International Bank for Reconstruction and Development (IBRD), 91000/018/JA/8, 'Situation, Prospects and Common Problems of the Six Japanese Steel Companies', 20 April 1964.

16   IBRD, 91000/018/JA/8, 'Loans to Six Japanese Steel Companies', 6 April 1964.

17   See C.Hidaka, 'Tekko-gyo no Setsubi Toushi to Segin Shakkan, vol.2', *Musashi Daigaku Ronshu*, Vol.44, No.4, 1997.

18   IBRD, 91000/018/JA/9, 14 Jan 1967.

19   IBRD, 91000/018/JA/9, 'Japan: the Japan Development Bank's Recommendations on Protective Arrangements for the Six Major Steel Companies', 10 Feb 1967.

20   Kawasaki Seitetsu Kabushiki Kaisha (Kawasaki Steel Co.), *Kawasaki Seitetsu Nijugonen-shi (25-Year History of Kawasaki Steel)* (1976) p.564.

21   Okurasho Zaisei-shi-shitsu (Office of Historical Studies, MOF), *Showa Zaisei-*

shishowa 27-48nendo (*History of Fiscal and Monetary Policies in Japan, 1952-1973*), Vol.9 (1991), p.260.

22   For more details, see Okurasho Ginkou-kyoku (Banking Bureau of MOF), *Dai 14-kai Ginkou-kyoku Kinyu-Nenpou, Showa 40 nen-ban* (*The 14th Annual Report on Banking: 1965*) (1965), pp.58-59.

23   Okurasho Ginkou-kyoku, *Dai 14-kai Ginkou-kyoku Kinyu-Nenpou*, pp.59-63.

24   Annual Reports.

25   Annual Reports.

26   Annual Reports.

27   J.Teranishi, 'Main Bank System', in T.Okazaki and M.Okuno (eds.), *Gendai Nihon Keizai System no Genryu* (*The Origin of the Modern Japanese Economic System*) (1993), p.87. See, also, Hidaka, 'A Re-examination of Japan's Post-war Financing System'.

28   Okazaki, 'Nihon ni okeru Corporate Governance no Hatten'.

29   On the development of the petrochemical industry in Japan, see T.Kikkawa, 'Enterprise Groups, Industry Associations, and Government: The Case of Petrochemical Industry in Japan', *Business History*, vol.37 (1995).

30   Sekiyu Kagaku Kogyo Kyokai, *Sekiyu Kagaku Kogyo Sanjunen no Ayumi* (*Thirty-Year History of the Petrochemical Industry*) (1989), p.49.

31   Nippon Sekiyu Kagaku Kogyo Kabushiki Kaisha, *Nippon Sekiyu Kagaku Kogyo Sanjunennshi* (*Thirty-Year History of Nippon Petrochemical*) (1987), pp.99-100; Mitsui Sekiyu Kagaku Kogyo Kabushiki Kaisha, *Mitsui Sekiyu Kagaku Kogyo Sanjunenshi* (*Thirty-Year History of Mitsui Petrochemical*) (1988), pp.73-74; Tonen Sekiyu Kagaku Kogyo Kabushiki Kaisha, *Tonen Sekiyu Kagaku Jugonen* (*Fifteen Years of Tonen Petrochemical*) (1977), pp.238-240; Sumitomo Kagaku Kogyo Kabushiki Kaisha, *Sumitomo Kagaku Kogyo Kabushiki Kaisha*, (*History of Sumitomo Chemical*) (1981), pp.560-563; Mitsubishi Kasei Kogyo Kabushiki Kaisha, *Mitsubishi Kasei Shashi* (*History of Mitsubishi Kasei*) (1981), pp.324-328; Sekiyu Kagaku Kogyo Kyokai, *Sekiyu Kagaku Kogyo Nijunenshi* (*Twenty-Year History of the Petrochemical Industry*) (1981), pp.186-187.

32   Mitsui Toatsu Kagaku Kogyo Kabushiki Kaisha, *Mitsui Toatsu Kagaku Shashi* (*History of Mitsui Toatsu Chemical*) (1994), pp.521-522.

33   *Sekiyu Kagaku Kogyo Sanjunen no Ayumi*, p.50.

34   *Sekiyu Kagaku Kogyo Sanjunen no Ayumi*, p.51.

35   Kabushiki Kaisha Fuji Ginkou, *Fuji Ginkou no Hyakunen* (*One Hundred Years of the Fuji Bank*) (1980), p.400.

36   Kabushiki Kaisha Fuji Ginkou, *Fuji Ginkou no Hyakunen*, pp.400-401.

37   *Sekiyu Kagaku Kogyo Sanjunen no Ayumi*, p.106.

38   *Sekiyu Kagaku Kogyo Nijunenshi*, pp.280-291.

39   In order to end friction within the same company group, Mitsubishi Chemical was formed by the merger of Mitsubishi Kasei and Mitsubishi Petrochemical in 1994, and Mitsui Chemical was established by the merger of Mitsui Petrochemical and Mitsui Toatsu in 1997.

40   Annual Reports.

Chapter 8

Corporate Governance, Management and British Venture Capital since 1945

Richard Coopey

Introduction

In recent years, there has been an increasing focus on corporate governance. This has been driven by a number of factors ranging from functional analysis and the measurement of efficiency to the general recognition that successful firms need to be aware of the wider environment in which managements operate - both internal and external to the firm. In particular, the concept of stakeholder interest in an enterprise has fuelled concern for governance and control. Stakeholders can be seen to embrace formal elements of control (owners and managers), informal elements within the firm (all employees), and a wider community extending to customers or members of society affected by the firm's activities.[1] Issues embraced by this process can be wide-ranging, depending on the particular firm. They may involve straightforward profit maximisation, or extend to much broader ethical or environmental factors, upon which the enterprise may have an impact. In addition, there has more recently been a growing anxiety over fraud or illegal activity by corporations that has added to the debate over corporate governance.

This chapter will take a specific focus, looking at the changing role of investors in firms - the providers of external capital. What part have these played in corporate governance and control? Interest in this aspect of corporate governance in Britain has risen in line with issues outlined above, but has also received added impetus from fears over the security of investments and the need to ensure transparency for investors. This amounts to 'maintaining public confidence in wealth-creating institutions'.[2] Such concerns emerged strongly in Britain, following uncertainties over the system of regulation and control, and in response to a number of corporate failures in the 1980s, precipitating the Cadbury Committee's report on The Financial Aspects of Corporate Governance. These issues have, however, a very long lineage, surfacing periodically throughout the 20th century.

The paper will examine the role of investment institutions in corporate governance, principally banks, and more latterly venture capital investors in Britain. It will address two basic issues. Firstly, have British banks remained traditionally disconnected from industry, particularly in comparison either to their continental European counterparts or to Japanese banks? Has this disconnection reflected the fundamental form in which investment has taken place? Secondly, has there been a change over time in this relationship, with new forms of investor, in this case venture capital, structuring investments differently, and taking a much closer interest in directing or influencing corporate activity. In view of the central role played by 3i (formerly the Industrial and Commercial Finance Corporation, or ICFC) in shaping and influencing the activities of the venture capital sector in Britain, the paper will pay particular attention to this institution and its operating methods.

Corporate Governance and the British Banking System

A recent report on corporate governance was unequivocal on the part played by the major banks in Britain.[3] 'It is a feature of UK corporate governance that clearing banks limit their role in the companies to which they provide finance. They normally see themselves solely as providers of finance and services.' The alleged failure of British banks to become intimately connected to British industry is now one of the central components of the 'relative decline' debate.[4] This particular facet centres around the provision of finance by British banks and capital markets.[5] These are seen to be overly cautious in terms of security and liquidity, consequently resisting any direct, long-term commitment of funds either in the form of loans, or, more importantly, equity. The clearing banks are especially castigated for perpetuating a supply failure in the face of demand for investment funds from British industry, and not becoming involved in issues of control or corporate governance. Comparison has traditionally been strongest between Britain and Germany, following the work of Gerschenkron.[6] The case is frequently made: German banks (and other national systems where a universal banking function predominates) both lend and invest long-term, and appoint representatives to the boards of investee companies. Bank representatives usually take a place on the supervisory board in the two-tier control required by German corporate law. It should noted that there has recently been considerable reappraisal of the extent and effect of this close bank-industry relationship in German history. Revisionist views have questioned both the frequency and the functioning of this system, and, indeed, whether the British banking system functioned more efficiently than that of Germany.[7] It is by no means clear whether the bank's presence on the supervisory board, for example, fulfilled an active role, or, instead, was based on a more passive, observational role. Nevertheless, the accusation of a 'disconnectedness' between banks and industry in Britain continues to be a commonly-held view. Comparison has more recently been made between the remoteness of banks in Britain and the integrated nature of Japanese banks and industry.

In some ways, the development of distance between banks and industry in Britain can be viewed as a 20th century development, particularly following the period of business concentration around the First World War.[8] Recent work on local and regional banking, following the example of Lamoreaux's work in the USA, has shown a much closer connection between industry and banks in 19th century Britain.[9] The argument runs that before the major banks were merged to form the 'big five', and moved their headquarters to London, local bank managers had regional affinities and knowledge.[10] This knowledge could encompass a wide range of criteria from market and trading conditions to the trustworthiness or business record of individual entrepreneurs or firms. Newton has demonstrated that investment decisions revolved around a mixture of assessments, which involved a significant degree of 'subjective' criteria, including notions of virtue, social standing, and reputation.[11] In short, local connections between banking and business could reduce information asymmetries in the case of providing start-up or on-going investment finance. Pre-20th century banks could be part of a particularly strong local nexus of financial and industrial interests. In some cases, this relationship could be formed into a seamless whole - it was not uncommon for local businessmen to be directors of individual banks, for example.

One or two caveats need to be stated at this point. This system could, of course, be open to abuse in the apportionment of savings, as directors channelled funds to suit their own entrepreneurial efforts. Also, it may be the case, as Carnevali has shown, that the demise of local connectivity and decision-making needs assessing and 'periodizing' more accurately. Her study of regional banks demonstrates that, even after the centralisation of control by the clearing banks, local managers retained a good deal of discretion over investments.[12]

Having noted these points, however, there remains a strong case to be made that the concentration of the clearing banks in London fuelled not only distance and remoteness, but reinforced the North-South divide that developed between industrial and financial capital in Britain. The clearers joined the already-remote merchant banks and capital market in London. They may not have shared the latter's preference for overseas investments, but they certainly developed an affinity for government-backed and relatively risk-free projects. The critique is fuelled by the added assertion that the big banks formed themselves into an uncompetitive, informal cartel, overseen by the benign and discrete actions of the governor of the Bank of England and the Committee of London Clearing Bankers. This situation persisted in cosy and docile seclusion until the intrusion of foreign banks in the 1960s. An added dimension to this argument is that the state in Britain was comparatively weak in controlling or directing the banking sector. While acquiescence seemed to dominate policy in Britain, rival economies have been seen to operate a more pro-active series of policies designed to regulate or control financial systems.[13]

In summary, British banks, certainly in the 20th century, are seen by many to be at least partly responsible for relative industrial decline. Their increasing distance from industry, both spatially and commercially, denied investment funds for all the most dynamic sectors of industry. Established sectors of industry could get funding, but only on the basis of near liquid security. In this environment, the question of corporate governance becomes moot. Banks progressively shied away from intimate involvement with firms. Where there was a connection, it was more likely to be of a reactive nature. Overdraft finance or working capital may have been monitored, and immediate market fluctuations discussed, but this bore no relationship to pro-active decision making over longer-term manufacturing, product or marketing strategies.

It must be pointed out that this picture of the relationship between banks and industry in Britain has been vigorously disputed. It is clearly the case that evidence is fragmentary and inadequate. Indeed, in many ways, the assertion of failure invites a counter-factual - the attempt to measure those firms not provided with funds is fraught with assumptions, and not based in empirical analysis. In defence of the banks, scholars such as Capie and Collins have pointed to the stability inherent in the British system. There was no general banking collapse in the depression years of the 1930s, for example, when other national banking systems were dragged down with their investees, as trade and industry collapsed. If there was a distance between banks and British industry - if investment funds were denied - then it must simply have been a failure of demand rather than supply. British industry, for reasons that must be found elsewhere, simply did not offer enough good investment opportunities for the banking sector.[14]

Alternatively, defenders of the banks have pointed out that there was greater involvement by the British banks than has generally been acknowledged.[15] Rebutting accusations of short-termism, several historians have pointed to the ways in which overdraft finance - the provision of working rather than fixed capital - typified the way in which banks lent to British industry. These overdrafts were in fact rolled over as a matter of course. In this way, the provision of short-term funding becomes indistinguishable from longer-term finance.[16] This method of financing could also bring closer relationships. Collins, for example, indicates numerous cases where companies were facilitated with extended overdrafts through periods of prolonged difficulty, involving frequent site visits by bank officials.[17] Ross argues that the roll-over overdraft form of financing reflected a more permissive rather than passive form of investment, and this may indeed involve a close bank-industry relationship.[18] However, such cases involve defensive intimacy, and do not equate with corporate involvement in a pro-active way. It seems clear that, if British banks did resist long-term involvement with firms, then there was a disconnection in terms of corporate influence or governance. At best, rolled-over overdraft funding gave a sporadic level of control, only emerging during periods of crisis. By the clearing banks' own admission, they were deeply distrustful of 'continental' banking, which involved more long-term, pro-active relationships.[19]

Another criticism levelled at British banking, in terms of lack of connectedness, concerns their relationship to small or medium-sized firms. The importance of the small firm in the firmament of a developing or developed economy is a topic that is debated with cyclical frequency. The argument is usually put, following Schumpeter, that small or medium-sized enterprises (SMEs) are more likely to be entrepreneurially-driven, innovative and adaptable. There have been increasing frequency to the cycles of this debate since the assertion that big is beautiful in the 1960s. In a more recent derivative, in the 1980s, SMEs were trumpeted as the most likely sector to boost employment levels in a recessionary economy.

The source of finance for small firms, certainly before the 20th century, was inherently local. Funding was provided through business partnerships and connections, through family networks, or by local banks or stock exchanges. As noted above, the increasing concentration of clearing banking in Britain, eventually into the big five of

Barclays, Lloyds, National Provincial, Westminster and Midland, led to the breakdown of local branch autonomy. Local managers could be expected to form close relationships with industry, and provision of funding might be expected to reflect intimate knowledge of both company history and local market knowledge. Thus, local banks, in an informal sense perhaps, but nevertheless in an important way, could exert a strong influence on a firm's activities. Moreover, local managers could be conversant with and have time for the needs of SMEs. With the concentration of banking, and a parallel concentration of capital markets, the possibility of a local nexus between banks and SMEs was lost, as the Macmillan Committee report of 1931 pointed out.[20] The lasting impression that came out of the report, though not its main conclusion, was that there was a market failure in Britain in terms of finance for SMEs. This may not have been the authors' intention during drafting, but it probably resonated with a widespread business intuition in Britain that something was amiss in the world of smaller business.

Again, in defence of the banking sector, it should be pointed out that SMEs are inherently risky investments, and, even when successful, they consume a disproportionate amount of effort in assessing and monitoring investments. It can also be strongly stated that banks and other investing institutions, in seeking higher or more secure levels of profit elsewhere, were acting perfectly rationally, and had no broader social or economic responsibility to this particular sector. Difficulties in delineating the extent of the problem, or, indeed, where responsibility might lie, remain unresolved. Recently, Ross has revisited the debate on the location and extent of what Keynes identified as a 'fringe of unsatisfied borrowers', though sparse data and the counter-factual nature of the question limit the extent to which an accurate picture can ever be constructed.[21]

Another key feature of the British banking and finance system is its dual nature, divided between banks and capital markets. This paper is restricted to banking finance generally, but it should be borne in mind that the provision of funds through the stock market and its functioning as an independent set of institutions are largely disconnected from the banking sector. This has profound ramifications for corporate control. Problems range from market failure in terms of investment funding for SMEs to the dominance of the stock market by an increasingly-concentrated set of large institutions. The former problem is held to be exacerbated by the demise of the regional stock exchanges and the concentration of trading in London. Accusations have centred on the small nexus of fund managers, which hold large portfolios of shares, and have very little time to take an interest in or a formal role in corporate governance. These fund managers are held to have relied, instead, on short-term indicators of profitability, rapidly switching investments rather than taking an extended interest in individual companies. As we shall see below, the advent of the venture capital investment sector has been seen as bridging this gap.

The failure of the banking and finance sector to form any level of synergy with enterprise in Britain, particularly industrial enterprise, can be viewed as a subset of a bigger 'decline' debate over the identification of an anti-industrial 'culture'. This now very well-trodden path - first negotiated by Weiner - puts forward the case that the

British industrial economy was never fully welcomed by an influential political and economic elite, in the thrall of a vestigial set of aristocratic, rural ideologies. Others, notably Rubinstein, have sought to demonstrate the effect of Britain's external, global financial and commercial economy, which detracted from the primacy of industrial endeavour in Britain. Can bankers be seen as part of this elite by their possessing disdain for domestic industrial enterprise?

The British banking and finance sector, then, has long been the subject of criticism in terms of its relationship to industry. Both the dual structure of the system and the culture operating within the banking sector may have militated against a close connection between banks and industry. In terms of corporate governance, the question becomes one of distance, a lack of connection in a formal or informal sense, with business and banking inhabiting two separate spheres. The balance of this paper will examine the growth of a new group of investment institutions during the post-war period. One of its central features was the development of a closer involvement with investee companies and a direct involvement in corporate governance, so creating a chance to change the mould of British banking-enterprise relationships.

Business Finance and the Role of the ICFC after the War

In 1945, the Finance Corporation for Industry (FCI) was founded to provide capital in larger amounts to facilitate the rationalisation of key sectors of British industry.[22] In contrast, its companion organisation, the Industrial and Commercial Finance Corporation (ICFC), was to provide 'credit' in the form of loans 'or the subscription of loan or share capital or otherwise' in amounts between £5-200,000 to smaller and medium-sized enterprises. FCI was to be supported, principally in the form of debt, to a limit of £125m by a large number of City institutions, mainly insurance funds. ICFC, on the other hand, was to be exclusively funded by the major clearing banks and the Bank of England, which collectively agreed to provide share and loan capital to the value of £45m.

When it was founded in 1945, ICFC was heralded as a belated response to the 'Macmillan Gap', the growing failure of the financial markets and banking system in Britain to provide long-term investment funds to smaller and medium sized companies.[23] However, ICFC and its sister organisation FCI were only established following a great deal of debate among government officials and bankers about the need for any new institutional initiative, as well as its size and scope.

The nature of their announcement, and the circumstances surrounding the establishment of these two new institutions in 1945, meant that they were widely understood to be a government-funded and owned initiative, an impression which has persisted in some circles to the present day. This is perhaps not surprising, given that 1945 was a key moment in terms of state intervention in the economy. While ICFC and FCI were the result of pressures from the Treasury and the Board of Trade, they were also shaped by the Bank of England and the clearing banks, both interested in varying degrees in keeping government out of the financial system. In addition, although they emerged as reconstruction initiatives, they also owe their origins to the problems of the 1930s, which were widely expected to re-emerge at the end of the war.

The Bank of England, in particular, was instrumental in shaping ICFC. It had played a central role in most of the initiatives undertaken in the 1930s, which were aimed at offsetting criticism of the banks, so setting up a more direct relationship between the banking system and industry. These included its own Securities Management Trust and the Bankers Industrial Development Corporation, for example. Opinion remains divided on both the level of involvement of the banks in industrial finance, and whether or not the relationship changed significantly during the 1930s.[24] Nevertheless, it seems clear that the Bank of England's attempts to restructure this relationship were based on the idea of doing just enough to avoid government intervention on any significant scale.[25]

The Bank of England entered the reconstruction process, which began in earnest from 1943 onwards, against this background of limited interventionist initiatives in the 1930s. Other actors in the finance aspect of the reconstruction process included the Treasury, the Board of Trade, and the clearing banks. This list might also include the Labour Party, since, as noted, ICFC was a 'child' of 1945. The corporation opened for business on the same day it became clear that Labour had won the general election. Although the Labour Party had made noises in the 1930s about controlling finance and taking on the City, possibly through a National Investment Bank, by the end of the war these ideas had faded. As Tomlinson has indicated, the party had opted instead for macro-economic intervention, rather than trying to control investment levels by direct institutional means.[26]

By 1943, the clearing banks, aware of mounting criticism, had begun their own deliberations on possible initiatives for post-war finance, especially for small and medium-sized firms. Some emerging suggestions were fairly elaborate. A paper was circulated at the Midland, for example, advocating a 'special advances' corporation to pool risks involved in small to medium long-term lending. Each bank was to pass on high-risk proposals to this institution, which would also be funded by the Bank of England and the Treasury.[27] Some clearing bank staff recognised that wartime had created unique problems of adjustment, as the experience of government intervention and control had significantly changed the ideological argument for supporting industry. These were minority voices, however. There were vociferous detractors among the ranks of chairmen and general managers, who sought a return to business as usual, without the added burden of trying to operate outside the realm of 'traditional' business. This meant sticking to 'self-liquidating advances' and 'readily realisable securities'. Government-sponsored schemes would have them lending to 'the incompetent, the thriftless and the indolent...who are sadly apt to lose other people's money as well as their own'.[28] That the banks should provide capital for an independent company to lend money in this sector was clearly beyond the pale. The proposed scheme from the Bank of England was 'simply an attempt to placate political critics', to which the banks' response should be a firm negative, even if this meant 'some embarrassment on account of misunderstandings in political and other quarters'.[29]

There were some sections of opinion among the clearers that began to take a more pragmatic line, however. By early 1944, following reports in the press that an initiative was definitely in the offing, voices were heard counselling some form of bank participation, 'in order to satisfy public opinion and keep out non-banking advances from our balance sheet'.[30] The bankers did eventually concede that some initiative was necessary, and agreed to set up a committee of general managers to draft a blueprint for what was to become ICFC.[31] Debate continued over the shape of the new corporation and the role to be played by the Bank of England. It was eventually agreed that the Bank should provide a small percentage of capital. This did not reflect the scope of the Bank's continuing paternal influence, however, signalled at this stage by the right to appoint the corporation's chairman.[32] ICFC was incorporated on 20th July 1945.

The first chairman, William Piercy, was faced with two parallel problems. He was the head of a corporation whose own shareholders, on whom he had to rely for capital, were at best luke-warm about supporting him. He also had to fashion a modus operandi for ICFC to enable it to generate profits by investing in the 'Macmillan Gap'. This meant identifying worthwhile enterprises and structuring financial packages accordingly, in addition to devising a system to monitor investments and provide follow-up support. Throughout the 1940s and 1950s, ICFC developed a range of methods which enabled it to do this, and which marked it off from the mainstream of British banking.

Assessment of potential investments was carried out on several levels. Balance sheets were examined and credit references sought in the normal way, but ICFC also established an Industrial Department, staffed by people with experience in industry, to assess the technical merits of an investment. Extensive reports were then submitted, and included not only financial information but appraisals of products, markets, and, importantly, managerial capabilities. Many of these reports place great stress on the latter, and the decision to invest often depended on the personality of the entrepreneur seeking finance. Prospective investments went before a Cases Committee, where they would be subject to a roundtable examination before a decision was reached. Local contacts and market intelligence were deemed important, and ICFC set up a nationwide branch network from the early 1950s onwards.

Investments were also structured differently to those of the banks. In order to offset the risk inherent in investing in smaller, often unproven, businesses the corporation began to seek equity wherever possible, usually as part of a loan-equity package. This often proved difficult, given the reluctance of many owners to part with a share of their company, and it meant that significant proportions of ICFC's balance sheet were illiquid, there being a limited market for unquoted shares. Nevertheless, this strategy meant that larger returns could eventually be made from successful investments, and, in the long run, this proved to be a success. An early investment of this type was George Godfrey and Partners, an aircraft engineering firm, in which ICFC gradually built up a 40 per cent stake. When the company was floated in 1956, ICFC made a profit of over £1.25m. This presaged later, even more spectacular successes, such as British Caledonian.[33]

Once investments had been allocated, a series of monitoring procedures were put in place. It is here that we find the most radical departure in investment practice, and one that had a most direct effect on corporate governance. It was the corporation's policy from the outset not to nominate ICFC staff as directors of client companies, so avoiding the problems of dual loyalties.[34] ICFC did, however, take an active role in corporate governance. The Corporation did often insist on a range of conditions affecting the boards of companies, including reduced or fixed directors' fees, agreed distribution of profits, long-dated service agreements for key directors, and, in some cases, life insurance on individual directors considered to be key figures in the running of a business.[35] The corporation also nominated people not employed by ICFC to directorships in investee firms, although this procedure was itself not without problems, as in the case of Pest Control in 1949, when the finance director whom ICFC had nominated went completely 'native' in supporting the firm against ICFC.[36] However, ICFC's role in direct control or the monitoring of corporate activity amongst its investee companies should not be overestimated. As Piercy was to note later, the corporation was continually faced with the difficulty of 'improving the efficiency of management while declining entrepreneurial functions ourselves'.[37]

The problem was indirectly reduced by a system of 'after-care', which was to become an important feature of ICFC's organisation. This function was coveted for a while by both technical and accounting staff, and involved the monitoring of monthly reports on sales, purchases, credit, and so on, with the object of reporting any disturbing trends to the after-care committee. In this way, ICFC investments forced firms to adopt good accounting practices, so keeping accurate cost and budget records.[38] We can see, in this process, the way in which ICFC's method of operation added value, and brought an extra benefit to the investment relationship. In many cases, firms chose to borrow from ICFC precisely because this system was in place and was judged to be of material help.[39]

By the early 1960s, the corporation's balance sheet was sufficiently strong and the opposition of the clearers had dissipated to such an extent that ICFC was able to persuade its shareholders to allow it to raise funds in the market. Somewhat ironically, the fact that the clearers were the majority owners of ICFC meant that the corporation was able to attract funding at good rates, and expand its activities significantly. In 1973, ICFC merged with its sister organisation FCI to form Finance for Industry (FFI). This gave the new group the formal ability to fund investments beyond the Macmillan Gap, although a significant proportion of its portfolio remained in the small and medium-sized firm sector, reflecting the accumulated expertise of the organisation. In the 1980s, the group - renamed 3I, or Investors in Industry - went on from this base to become the central player in the growth of the British venture capital industry, and it pioneered new forms of investment, most notably the Management Buy-Out (or MBO).

Although 3i Group is considerably larger and more diverse than the original ICFC was ever intended to be, the core of its operations - its methods and culture - remain rooted in the organisation forged in the 1940s and 1950s. Two factors are important in understanding the shaping of ICFC and 3i. Firstly, the competing ideas of those influencing the establishment of ICFC led to the formation of a corporation in the private sector, as the Bank of England wished, yet it was indirectly connected to national investment goals. The hostility of its owners, the clearing banks, ensured that it received the protection of the Bank, and a degree of autonomy in operating methods enabled it to survive. Secondly, there was the method developed by ICFC to invest successfully in the SME sector. Assessment, loan-equity structuring, and the monitoring of investments all evolved in the early years of the corporation, and were refined as the group expanded. It is these methods which marked ICFC off from investment banking generally in Britain, especially in the role of corporate governance related relationships. 3i was later to have a formative role in shaping another radical sector of British investment finance, namely venture capital.

Business Finance in the 1970s and 1980s

3i emerged into the 1980s as the largest investment bank in Britain, with a broad portfolio of investments, many of which involved equity funding. During the late 1970s, it had successfully pioneered one particular form of investment that was to become an important feature of the British economy - the Management Buy-Out (MBO). Another related feature of the 1980s in Britain was the emergence of a wider venture capital investment sector. The nature and origins of the venture capital industry are difficult to delineate with any precision. As early as 1971, the Bolton Committee report, for example, referred to the 'emergence of a number of venture capital companies specialising in small firms'.[40] Many accounts see venture capital as an import from the USA, where, from the 1950s onwards, specialist investors in selected high growth industries, most notably computers and electronics, had achieved spectacular returns when companies such as Apple and DEC became public companies.[41] There are a number of definitions of venture capital, but most encompass some element of permanent or long-term capital provision, usually in the form of equity, for unquoted or smaller quoted companies, often start-ups, and concentrated in what are generally referred to as 'high technology' or high growth fields. It can be differentiated from other forms of investment in terms of reward. The greater risk inherent in equity finance is offset by the possibility of an eventual capital gain, rather than interest income or dividend yield. Venture capitalists, by virtue of the inherently higher risks involved in equity participation, are themselves seen to be a new entrepreneurial class of investor. The key feature often quoted to differentiate the venture capitalist organisations from other types of investor is the claim that these new institutions add value to investments by a more hands-on approach, enhancing managerial, product and market efficiencies. Venture capital investors, in contrast to the traditional model of British banking, are seen as taking an active participatory role, often at boardroom level.

The new institutions deemed to conform to the above, rather general, parameters emerged in Britain from a number of different sources in the 1980s, and, in fact, operated in a variety of ways. An initial distinction between the various institutions collectively defined as venture capitalists lies in their ownership and source of funds to invest. A principal divide emerges here between the 'captives' - subsidiaries of other institutions such as banks and pension or insurance funds - and 'independents'. Among the venture capital institutions expanded or formed in the late 1970s and early 1980s were a set of clearing bank subsidiaries: County Natwest Ventures, Barclays Development Capital, Lloyds Development Capital, and Midland Montagu Ventures. Rival organisations included Prudential Venture Managers, Legal and General Ventures, and CIN Ventures from the insurance and pension fund sector; Merchant Bank subsidiaries such as Schroder Ventures and Morgan Grenfell Development Capital; Stockbroker-backed Phildrew Ventures; and a number of independent funds, including Electra, Candover, Apax, and ECI. At one end of the spectrum, namely the 'captives', clearing bank subsidiaries had access to an internal source of funds, whereas the 'independents' needed to attract funds from a diverse range of external sources, predominantly pension funds, insurance companies, fund management groups, foreign institutions, private individuals and trusts.

Another defining feature of venture capital funds is its role in creating a bridge between the large institutions of the City and a range of investment possibilities. This is done by subsidiary ownership relations, as noted above, or by providing the vehicle whereby large funds can make investments of a large scale, subsequently parcelled out by the venture capitalists. In this way, monitoring and representation by the venture capitalist acts as a proxy for larger financial institutions, which have traditionally avoided involvement as being too time-consuming.

3i is inextricably linked with the venture capital industry in a number of ways, not least because many of the people involved in setting up venture capital funds, or recruited into the expanding institutions in the 1980s, had 3i origins. The rapid expansion of the venture capital sector naturally made for a very volatile labour market. 3i's dominant position in this market, allied to the company's tradition of training, which was without peer in the finance community, made it 'the first place every headhunter would look'.[42] An early concentration on graduate recruitment had been pioneered by ICFC, and carried on throughout the 1970s.[43] This had combined with a commitment to an ongoing training programme at 3i, which few, if any, rival institutions could afford to match.[44] When merged with the experience gained on the job in finding and constructing investments, this had resulted in 3i becoming popularly known as 'the university of venture capital'. In short. 3i had generated 'a new kind of investment banker', and, in its rapid expansion during the early 1980s, the industry was bound to view the company as 'a natural source of talent'.[45]

The amount invested by British venture capital organisations in 1981 was around £200m. By 1989, this had reached an annual peak of over £1.6bn, invested in over 1,500 companies, 86 per cent of which were in the UK.[46] Independent venture capital institutions, excluding 3i and clearing bank subsidiaries, showed spectacular growth in the level of funds attracted for investment, raising £1.7bn in 1989 alone. This growth is even more marked when international comparisons are drawn. Direct comparisons are difficult to make, given variations in classification, but Britain's venture capital industry was, by the end of the 1980s, by far the largest in Europe.[47]

There are a number of contributory factors that explain the growth of the venture capital industry in Britain during the 1980s. Government policy and changes in the financial markets afford a partial explanation. The breaking up of public sector industries provided a few early opportunities, bus companies and shipyards being notable examples. The government also established the Business Start-Up Scheme, later renamed the Business Expansion Scheme (BES), which allowed individuals to obtain tax relief on investments up to £40,000 in unquoted equity for a minimum period of five years. Collective funds were soon set up to manage these investments, which despite government intentions, gravitated towards property investment, particularly in hotels. The government established a small firms loan guarantee scheme in May 1981, initially guaranteeing 70 per cent of loans up to £100,000. Another stimulus to the activity of venture capital firms came when capital market thresholds were significantly reduced with the introduction of the Unlisted Securities Market (USM) in November 1981. Conditions of entry to the USM were considerably less complicated and cheaper than a listing on the stock exchange, and, by 1985, the USM comprised over 330 companies worth a total in excess of £3.5bn.[48] This had the effect of creating a market for shares, which would previously have presented difficulties in liquidity terms, and thus considerably enhanced the opportunities for smaller companies to float successfully. The USM provided venture capital funds with a relatively earlier exit and increased their ability to realise successful investments.

The restructuring of economic activity, particularly of the type witnessed during the early 1980s, established an environment in which venture capital could thrive. Murray has pointed to the contra-cyclical nature of venture capital, seizing investment opportunities during both recessionary and recovery periods.[49] It is perhaps better described as multi-cyclical, since any period favouring corporate restructuring or regeneration presents opportunities for venture capital investment. The recession of the early 1980s, for example, saw a wave of business failures and retrenchment, as many large companies began to hive off difficult or unprofitable subsidiaries. This provided the opportunity for a growing number of management buy-outs (MBOs) and buy-ins from parent companies or the receiver. Later, in the 1980s, corporate acquisition waves and the trend in some industries to revert to core activity provided similar opportunities, as unwanted subsidiaries were hived off. The creation of new industries, where technological barriers of entry were periodically lowered, so favouring smaller, skill-intensive operations, with information technology and biotechnology companies being notable examples, generated the opportunity for a new level of high risk, equity-based investment.

MBOs represent one of the archetypal venture capital investments. The growing publicity afforded to buy-outs, taxation incentives, and changes in the 1981 Companies Act, which 'deskilled' the process of organising MBOs, led to an increasing level of new entrants into this sector, as the 1980s progressed.[50] The overall number of MBOs held steady at around 300 per year from 1982 onwards. Then, as recovery was consolidated in some sectors of the economy, a steady rise began, from 1985 to the peak year of 1990, when over 465 MBOs took place.[51] This period also saw a considerable rise in the number of management buy-ins (MBIs); a process identical to

MBOs, but involving a buy-out by a team of managers from outside the enterprise, often teams which had originally attempted an unsuccessful MBO. In 1989, 147 MBIs totalling £3,599m were completed, compared with only 5 to the value of £11m in 1981.[52] By 1989, MBOs and MBIs, 65 per cent of which were in the manufacturing sector, accounted for over 22 per cent by value of the total transfers of business in Britain.[53]

A notable trend in the buy-out market from the mid-decade onwards was the increasing size of transactions. A list of all the buy-outs worth in excess of £150m - 27 in all - includes only one pre-1985 entry, all the rest taking place between 1985-90.[54] This includes some very large deals, including Reedpack, MFI-Hygena, Magnet, and the Lawson Mardon Group, all of which exceeded £500m at 1992 prices. This rise in values was partly the result of increasing competition, including that from trade buyers, one effect of which was that gearing levels began to rise significantly. Though not reaching the scale involved in some of the more notorious leveraged buy-outs in the USA, deals in the UK involving ratios of 5:1 debt to equity were not uncommon by 1989. Some were higher, sometimes involving no equity at all. The larger deal size was facilitated by increasing resort to syndication among investors. The process of setting up a larger buy-out would typically involve an initial approach to various venture capital firms, perhaps through an intermediary, such as one of the major accounting firms. Tenders submitted - a 'beauty parade' - would result in the choice of a lead investor, who would subsequently look for syndicate partners, frequently investors involved in the initial tendering process.[55]

The MBO and MBI were, as noted above, very much symbolic of the venture capital industry in general and the meteoric rise in activity during the late 1980s. The subsequent decline in the early 1990s has led to many reappraisals by both practitioners and commentators. The trend towards increasingly large deals also led to accusations that one of venture capital's positive benefits, the provision of start-up and growth capital to smaller companies, was being forgotten. The Financial Times, for example, commented at the end of 1985 that the 'venture capital industry is being drawn increasingly into an area which has more to do with corporate finance than with fostering the development of small businesses'.[56]

Problems came to a head in the early 1990s, when some of the more ambitious large-scale buy-outs began to run into trouble, either collapsing completely or calling for large levels of refinancing. This was due to a combination of over-gearing, rising interest rates, and the onset of recession, which together limited growth in trading profits, and prevented the early asset realisation necessary for a reduction in debt burdens. Troublesome buy-outs like Lowndes Queensway and the MBI at Isosceles, which had been very highly geared at 11:1, led to a fall off in the number of larger deals. There was a simultaneous restriction of gearing levels, which, typically, fell back to a ratio of 1:1 by 1992, as the banks in particular placed more conservative limits on the level of finance they were prepared to provide.

Expected realisation values had to be revised as the capital markets began to take a less favourable view of larger flotations. Despite early optimism that the USM would provide early realisation opportunities for venture capital investments, it was proving less attractive than expected. With the exception of a brief revival in 1988, the number of companies joining declined steadily, and a report by the Stock Exchange in 1992 recommended the closure of what was now 'widely regarded as a dying market'.[57]

Problems subsequently emerged both with the supply and demand for venture capital funds. The very large amounts raised in 1989 failed to be replicated in following years, as institutional suppliers of funds to the independent sector of the venture capital industry began to question the level of return that could be expected.[58] The capacity of the British economy to supply enough companies with sufficient growth potential to justify investment came into question.[59] Many venture capital institutions continued to hold high levels of uninvested funds, particularly after 1989, the peak year of fund raising. In general, doubts began to be expressed over whether or not the industry had generally oversold itself in the mid-1980s, particularly to institutional investors.[60]

Captive funds in their turn, which did not view venture capital as their core activity, began to withdraw from the market. The banks had been drawn into the venture capital sector during the early 1980s by the promise of large returns. While this seemed to be the case, particularly while MBOs were relatively cheap and risk-free, they were able to tolerate the non-traditional, unorthodox operating methods by their venture capital subsidiaries - notably the involvement at boardroom level of bank staff, and the practice of carried interest. However, when the investments began to yield less spectacular returns, banks quickly retrenched, and cut back their funding in this sector.

Conclusion

In summary the venture capital model of investment seemed to promise a radical change in the relationship between investors and enterprises, bringing a range of direct and indirect controls into effect. In doing so, the sector stood in marked contrast to the traditional model of banking in Britain. In following this pattern, venture capital, in its British form, was strongly influenced by the example of ICFC/3i's methods, and, importantly, by 3i's influence on the labour market in investment banking. However, an increasing concentration on management buy-out investments has led many observers to criticise venture capital, seen as moving away from advanced technology, start-ups, or long-term investments generally.

While this is true, there still remain many fundamental differences between venture capital and traditional banking practices. Venture capitalists, by virtue of equity involvement, are drawn towards increasingly direct control of their investments; drawn, therefore, towards some role in corporate governance. Traditional bank-lending need only monitor performance to ensure repayment security. Venture capitalists with an equity stake have an interest in adding value through direct involvement, or, at least, monitoring progress very closely, since they will gain in proportion to the firm's success. In terms of corporate governance, this may not mean intervention in an executive form, but will certainly involve strong advice on firm strategy.[61] Despite general criticisms, MBOs do bring with them a strong element of intervention by investors. Venture capitalists, by virtue of their proportionately large equity involvement, will frequently appoint two board members to monitor each MBO investment, for example. In the later 1990s, British venture capital saw a resurgence, attracting increasing levels of institutional investment funds. A large proportion of these funds is being directed towards investments, particularly MBOs, in continental Europe. It remains to be seen whether or not this investment sector will genuinely change the face of British banking.

Notes

1   See, for example, RSA, *Tomorrow's Company Project* (1997).
2   International Capital Markets Group, *International Corporate Governance* (1995).
3   International Capital Markets Group, *International Corporate Governance: Who Holds the Reins?: An Overview of Corporate Governance Practice in Japan, Germany, France, USA, Canada and the UK* (1995).
4   F.Capie and M.Collins, *Have the Banks Failed British Industry?* (1992); M.H.Best and J.Humphries, 'The City and Industrial Decline', in B.Elbaum and W.Lazonick, *The Decline of the British Economy* (1987); J.J.Van Helten and Y.Cassis, *Capitalism in a Mature Economy: Financial Institutions, Capital Exports and British Industry* (1990).
5   A discussion of the capital market sector of British industrial finance lies beyond the scope of this paper. There are similar arguments that may be applied, however, particularly in terms of centralization in the City, and the prevalence of short term investment criteria, which have allegedly affected the levels and direction of finance into British industry.
6   F.Capie and M.Collins, *Have the Banks Failed British Industry?*, pp. 26-27.
7   C.Frohlin, 'Bank Securities Holdings and Industrial Finance before World War I: Britain and Germany Compared', *Business and Economic History* (1997), vol.26; J.Edwards and S.Ogilvie, 'Universal Banks and German Industrialisation: A Reappraisal', *Economic History Review*, (1996), vol.xlix; D. M.Ross, 'Commercial Banking in a Market Oriented System: Britain Between the Wars', *Economic History Review* (1996), vol.xlix.
8   W.A.Thomas, *The Finance of British Industry, 1918 - 1976* (1978), pp.55-7.
9   N.R.Lamoreaux, '"No Arbitrary Discretion": Specialisation in Short-Term Commercial Lending by Banks in Late Nineteenth-Century New England', in G.Jones (ed), *Banks and Money: International and Comparative Finance in History* (1991), pp. 93-118.
10 E.Nevin and E.W.Davies, *The London Clearing Banks* (1970), pp.33-56; L.S.Pressnell, *Country Banking in the Industrial Revolution* (1956).
11 L.Newton, 'Trust and Virtue in English Banking: the Assessment of Borrowers by Bank Managements at the Turn of the Ninteenth Century', *Financial History Review* (2000), vol.7. See also J.Wale, 'What Help Have the Banks Given British Industry? Some Evidence on Bank Lending in the Midlands in the Late Nineteenth Century', *Accounting, Business and Financial History* (1994), vol.4.
12 F.Carnevali, 'Finance in the Regions: the Case of England after 1945', in Y.Cassis, G.Feldman, and U.Olsson (eds), *The Evolution of Financial Institutions* (1995).
13 T.M.Rybczynski, 'Industrial Finance Systems in Europe, the US and Japan', *Journal of Economic Behaviour and Organisation* (1984), vol.5.
14 Capie and Collins, *Have the Banks Failed British Industry?*
15 M.Collins, *Banks and Industrial Finance in Britain* (1991), pp.25-6; M.Collins, 'English Bank Development Within a European Context, 1870 -1939', *Economic History Review* (1998), vol.li.

16 D.Ross, 'The Clearing Banks and Industry: New Perspectives on the Inter-War Years', in J.J.Van Helten and Y.Cassis (eds), *Capitalism in a Mature Economy: Financial Institutions, Capital Exports and British Industry* (1990).
17 Collins, 'English Bank Development'.
18 Ross, 'The Clearing Banks and Industry'.
19 R.Coopey and D. Clarke, *3i: Fifty Years Investing in Industry* (1996).
20 Report of the Committee on Finance and Industry (1931), c.3897. For a discussion of the subsequent development of SME finance, see J.Stanworth and C.Gray, *Bolton 20 Years On: The Small Firm in the 1990s* (1991).
21 Ross, 'Commercial Banking in a Market-Oriented Financial System', pp.229-330.
22 It is not proposed here to examine the structure and functioning of FCI in any great depth. For a fuller account of its funding and investment, and its eventual absorption into 3i, see Coopey and Clarke, *3i: 50 Years Investing in Industry.*
23 The public memorandum of the Committee of London Clearing Banks (CLCB), which outlined the form ICFC should take, specifically detailed the findings of the Macmillan Committee, and subsequent accounts usually follow the same pattern. The Bolton Committee report of 1970 into small firms, for example, describes ICFC as 'a new institution specifically designed to fill the Macmillan gap'. See Report of the Committee of Inquiry on Small Firms (1970), c.4811, p.154. A more recent account by Heim takes the same line, seeing ICFC as 'designed to close the Macmillan gap'. See C.E.Heim, 'Limits to Intervention: The Bank of England and Industrial Diversification in the Depressed Areas', *Economic History Review* (1984), vol.xxxvii, p.534.
24 D.Ross, 'The Clearing Banks and Industry: New Perspectives on the Inter-War Years', in J.J.Van Helten and Y.Cassis (eds), *Capitalism in a Mature Economy; W.A.Thomas, The Finance of British Industry 1918-76* (1978), pp.74-78.
25 See Coopey and Clarke, *3i: 50 Years Investing in Industry.*
26 J.Tomlinson, 'Attlee's Inheritance and the Financial System: Whatever Happened to the National Investment Board?', *Financial History Review* (1994), vol.1.
27 Midland Bank Archive (hereafter Midland), W.F.Crick to C.T.A.Sadd, 'Special Advances', 2 Nov 1943, 200/10.
28 Midland, Unsigned Memo., 29 Dec 1943, NLS 8699/1.
29 Midland, Unsigned Memo., 29 Dec 1943, NLS 8699/1.
30 Barclays Bank (hereafter Barclays), 'Finance for Industry After the War', Fisher Memo., 31 Jan 1944, NLS 8699/1.
31 Barclays, C.Campbell, Chairman of CLCB, Memo., 15 Mar 1944, NLS 8699/1.
32 Barclays, Memo. of a Meeting between Colin Campbell and Lord Catto, 1 August 1944; Catto to Campbell, 2 August 1944, NLS 8699/1.
33 When British Caledonian was sold to British Airways, 3i received over £100m for an initial investment of £4.5m.
34 ICFC, Board Minutes, 5 March 1946.
35 ICFC Board Minutes, 30 July 1946; 24 September 1946; 7 January 1947; 4 March 1947; SA(47)10, 3i.
36 ICFC, SA(47)5, 3I; Kinross, *ICFC*, pp.290-1.
37 ICFC, Piercy to Cripps, 31 Dec 1947, Piercy 9/180.
38 Kinross, *ICFC*, pp.122-3.
39 ICFC, SA(47)13, East Anglia Chemical Company, 3i.
40 Bolton Report, p.155.
41 W.D.Bygrave and J.A.Timmons, *Venture Capital at the Crossroads* (1992), pp.1-30.
42 J.Foulds, interviewed by R. Coopey, 1 Dec 1992.
43 In 1976, for example, staff at ICFC included 92 graduates, 20 with MBAs, representing 27 per cent of the total number of employees. See ICFC, Annual Report, 1977.
44 Robert Smith, interviewed by R. Coopey, 24 June 1993.
45 A.Butt-Philip, interviewed by R.Coopey, 6 December 1991: 3i, Annual Report, 1983, p.6.

46 Figures from 3i; BVCA reports. The figure for 1989 is inclusive of 3i investment.
47 EVCA, *Venture Capital in Europe: Its Role and Development* (1993).
48 *Financial Times*, 3 Dec 1985. The USM was followed by similar initiatives in Europe, including the Deuxieme Marche formed by the Paris Bourse in 1983, and the Dutch Parallelmarkt in 1984.
49 G.Murray, *Change and Maturity in the UK Venture Capital Industry* (1991), p.17.
50 Until then, the transfer of ownership involved in MBOs required a rather complex and labyrinthine procedure, only practised with any success by the development capitalist, 3i.
51 Nottingham Centre for Management Buy-Out Research, *Annual Review 1990*.
52 Nottingham Centre for Management Buy-Out Research, *Annual Review 1990*.
53 G.Bannock, *The Economic Impact of Management Buy-Outs* (1990), p.6.
54 Figures at constant 1992 prices. See NCMBOR, *Annual Review 1992*, p.15.
55 'Capitalists and Their Ventures', *Accountancy*, October 1992, p.51.
56 *Financial Times*, 3 Dec 1985.
57 *Daily Telegraph*, 22 Dec 1992
58 'Investors are Calling the Tune', Investors Chronicle, 9 October 1992; 'Competition Intensifies in Venture Capital', *Investors Chronicle*, 4 Oct 1991.
59 'Growth Companies - Are There Enough to go Round?', *UK Venture Capital Journal*, September 1992, pp.22-7.
60 Murray, *Change and Maturity*, pp.ii,52.
61 Interview with Roger Lawson, 3i Director, spokesman on corporate governance.

Chapter 9

Authority and Direction in British Manufacturing Companies, 1945-2000: Models, Realities and Consequences

Nick Tiratsoo

What matters is that the board should consider and take decisions in an informed way on what counts: that the executive should be competent to drive the business forward, and that the board should be strong enough to say 'No' when it feels it must. (J.Charkham, *Keeping Good Company* (1994), p.268.)

Everything is arranged and agreed before I even get there…He presents us with deals and figures, wants us to nod like fools and then leaves. (Lonhro director, reflecting on life with the tycoon 'Tiny' Rowland, quoted in Tom Bower, *Fayed. The Unauthorized Biography* (1998), p.56.)

We are very aware that there are very serious shortcomings in British boardrooms. (T.Melville-Ross, Director-General of the Institute of Directors, quoted in *Financial Times*, 16 July 1998.)

Introduction

The recent resurgence of interest in corporate governance in Britain has largely focused on the issue of stakeholding and director's remuneration.[1] By contrast, debate about authority and decision-making within companies remains far less developed. This chapter aims to redress the balance somewhat by examining how intra-firm governance operated in British manufacturing companies during the second half of the 20th century. It seeks to describe how senior managers interacted, together and with subordinates, and understand the rules and conventions that governed these relationships. The argument advanced is that while a textbook model of best practice circulated throughout this period, relatively few actually followed its prescriptions, and this had damaging consequences for overall corporate performance.

Good Governance: the Axioms

Debate about intra-firm governance has a long history in Britain, but there is no doubt that events during and after the Second World War gave the subject an enhanced salience. The experience of total mobilisation, together with the subsequent advent of a nationalising Labour government, provoked much anxious reflection about business's responsibilities and ultimate purpose, while the launch of the American technical assistance programme in 1948 provided a further source of fresh ideas. The new thinking was codified in a stream of books and articles: E. F. L. Brech's encyclopaedic 752 page edited work on 'the principles and practices of management'; the popular Pitman series, particularly F. C. Hooper's *Management Survey*, a volume that was successful enough to be later published in paperback by Penguin; the pamphlets produced by the Institute of Directors (IoD); and numerous US publications, including the sizeable output of the American Management Association, a raft of articles in *Time* and *Fortune*, and several accessible introductory overviews, such as Herrymon Maurer's *Great Enterprise*.[2] What such work contained was no less than the blueprints that could be used to rebuild the private enterprise system in line with the values of a changing age.

Most of the emerging literature was based upon the observation that an era of rationality was dawning. The age of the bucaneering entrepreneur was over, and the future belonged to the corporation. In practical terms, this meant that governance systems needed to be re-cast, jettisoning the idiosyncrasies of the past. Four axioms of good practice were proposed. First, it was widely agreed that directors must in future play a much more central role in corporate life. The board was to stand fully independent from senior management and adopt a watching brief. Its tasks were to make sure that company policy was carried out effectively, and at the same time generate longer-term strategy. Turning to the question of internal organisation, there was much discussion about the efficacy of different spans of control and lines of authority. But the general consensus was that, while organisational forms might vary according to circumstance, each must aim to encourage certain kinds of interaction. Second, therefore, it was vital to recognise that, though managers would inevitably come from different backgrounds, they were above all part of a team, a co-operative effort. Modern manufacturing required inputs from a number of different specialists, with the chain of operational relationships stretching all the way from the design department via purchasing and the shopfloor to marketing and the sales office. Each function was indispensable, and a firm would only prosper if it was both integrated and co-ordinated, organised so as to guarantee that 'proper relationships' were 'established and maintained among the different work units'.[3] Third, it was essential to ensure that all decision-making processes were based upon transparent and strictly logical reasoning. There was no room in executive thinking for emotion, bias or sloppiness. Cool appraisal of the relevant data was to be followed by clear-cut and appropriate judgement. As Brech emphasised, 'true management' began with 'an examination and assessment of the relevant facts', and only then moved to the formulation of policy.[4] Finally, the pundits agreed that much greater emphasis must be placed on the question of management development. The age of nepotism was past. The modern corporation demanded a new breed of rational manager. As a consequence, it was argued, selection and training procedures needed to be expanded, systematised, and closely geared towards recognising and rewarding talent. Managers of all grades required careful nurturing, using the most modern techniques, for example insights provided by the emerging discipline of psychology.

During the next 20 or 30 years, much of this thinking gradually attained the status of common sense, and was repeated again and again by both management and organisational theorists. However, its impact on firms was rather less pronounced, with many clinging to very different traditions and practices. This point can be illustrated by looking at each of the four axioms already referred to in turn.

The Board: Master or Servant?

The textbook model of board behaviour and functioning was certainly only ever partially observed. To begin with, it is clear that many boards clearly failed to maintain any real distance from senior management. One important indicator of the elision of roles was the fact that, for much of the period, the chief executive officer was also chair of the board in probably as many as half of big companies.[5] Indeed, the overbearing managing director was something of a cliché in contemporary accounts. Reporting on their research into the electronics industry, Burns and Stalker commented:

> The one constant element of all the studies…was the extraordinary importance ascribed to the personal qualities of the managing director…In many firms, almost every interview would contain reference to the 'outstanding personality', 'the flair', the 'wisdom', the 'tremendous personal courage', even the 'genius' of the managing director, and the all-important part he had played in the success of the firm.[6]

Ken Rogers made much the same point in his well-known study of the household products sector.[7] The pages of the business and management press featured many further striking examples. Leading industrialists seemed happy to vie with each other as to who was the biggest personality or most imposing leader. Fairly typically, the much admired boss of Marks and Spencers in the 1980s and 1990s, Sir Richard Greenbury, made sure that visiting journalists always saw a cushion in his office which was inscribed 'I have many faults, but being wrong is not one of them', a motto that the *Economist* remarked was 'a joke perhaps, but close to the bone all the same'.[8]

One further telling sign of this syndrome was the fact that checks and balances on the concentration of power rarely seem to have worked effectively. For example, while reformers consistently advocated that every board should feature a proportion of non-executive directors (NEDs), who could keep a detached eye on the business, such admonitions frequently fell on deaf ears. In the 1950s, the ratio of part-time to full-time directors in Britain was said to be relatively low compared to the US.[9] Moreover, the appointment of NEDs was usually seen as a chance to reward friends or gain influence, rather than as a way of promoting critical scrutiny. A columnist in the business journal *Scope* commented:

> We pick one up here, to keep potentially troublesome shareholders quiet; one there, because he was a distinguished general or ambassador and 'lends weight' to our Public Relations; or one elsewhere, because of his useful 'business contacts'. But do we choose these outside directors because of *their* knowledge of *our* business? Do we 'go for' the know-how they will contribute at, and in between, board meetings? We do not.[10]

In later decades, the situation improved, but problems were still in evidence.[11] One of the few detailed studies of NEDs found that they perceived themselves as passive rather than active players in boardroom affairs.[12] Many companies were loath to appoint outside a charmed circle of known contacts, preferring if at all possible to stick with 'serial directors' – a relatively small group who held many portfolios each. In 2002, a National Association of Pension Fund spokesman commented: 'The pool of NEDs is neither wide enough nor deep enough. If they are choosing their own people all the time there's little diversity'.[13] Significantly, after a string of well-publicised corporate scandals at the turn of the 21st century, involving such erstwhile blue-chip firms as Equitable Life and Marconi, the government felt it prudent to launch an inquiry into the whole NED issue, and, in particular, the question of whether they were playing a robust enough role in preventing abuse.[14]

Given these various trends and pressures, it is unsurprising to find that many boards mirrored their chief executive's preoccupation with immediate issues, and relatively few focused on longer-term strategy.[15] In fact, the research that specifically tried to measure boardroom knowledge of strategic goals usually uncovered an extraordinary degree of imprecision, even straightforward ignorance. Norburn and Grinyer studied directors' attitudes in 21 companies at the beginning of the 1970s, and found that 'lack of agreement' about corporate direction was 'extremely high'. The median number of primary company objectives stated to exist within each company of the research sample was six. Yet, when a simple majority test of consensus was applied, the figure slumped to one. The authors were shown a list of 17 primary objectives posted on the boardroom wall in one company, yet when they later asked the directors to talk about these, the majority could only agree on three. 'The entire picture of objective setting within the 21 companies', they concluded, was 'one of confusion'.[16] At about the same time, Hewkin and Kempner studied the narrower question of corporate planning in a 24 firm sample, and came to equally damning conclusions. They reported:

> Long-term objectives are not always clearly stated. There is little exploration and evaluation of alternative courses of action on a wide front in order to establish the best means of achieving broad objectives. Decisions often seem to result more from management's forced reaction to current circumstances. The detailed examination of possible strategy is usually linked to specific situations, and much planning tends to be product or project-based.[17]

This was certainly a long way from the much discussed ideal of a far-sighted board providing clear and considered guidance on the strategy that was necessary to secure the firm's long-term prosperity.

Teams or Hierarchies?

The exhortation that those running firms should work together as teams was little more respected. Indeed, many managements were divided into strict hierarchies, with each grade maintaining its own customs, norms and prejudices about those above and below. The most obvious classification was based on seniority, and made manifest by a complex web of enhancements and perks. Writing in 1958, the journalists Roy Lewis and Rosemary Stewart noted 'the variety of the status symbols which in some companies are used to distinguish each tier in the organisation'.[18] The badges of rank encompassed everything from dining facilities and lavatories to diaries, Christmas gifts, and carpets, even the colour of filing cabinets and the positioning of desks. One managing director had a series of waiting rooms named after prime ministers; the most important guests would always be shown into the Winston Churchill suite, the next most important into the Eden suite, and so on down the social scale.[19] Inevitably, during the following decades, such ostentatious displays of superiority gradually came to be frowned upon, but they certainly did not disappear. A survey of 550 workplaces by the Manufacturing Science and Finance union in 1997 revealed 'wide gaps' between constituents of the management hierarchy, with those at the top, for example, often enjoying separate dining facilities and lavatories, better private health care, and longer holidays.[20]

    In addition to seniority, managers also increasingly categorised and judged themselves on the basis of function. In the immediate aftermath of the Second World War, the most potent division was between generalists and specialists, with the latter regarded as second class citizens, to be kept 'on tap but not on top', in the President of The Federation of British Industries' memorable phrase.[21] But, by the 1960s, there is no doubt that a more elaborate and complicated classificatory system was in play, based upon pay, inevitably, but also less tangible variables like the cleanliness or not of the working environment. So-called 'gin and tonic' professions such as marketing and accounting were judged to be on the rise. On the other hand, production's star was very definitely waning.[22] Thus, Ray Wild, an ex-engineer who taught at Bradford University's business school, ended a 1972 textbook by regretting: 'Production occupies a fairy-tale position in...industry...but unfortunately the role played is that of Cinderella rather than Prince Charming'.[23]

The dominant view of production management was made evident in several very concrete ways.[24] For example, while management training of all kinds was expanding during these years, there is no doubt that production managers always found it difficult to access a fair share of the provision. A survey of Institute of Production Engineering members in 1965 found that the most popular way into the profession was 'to leave school at 16, to take an apprenticeship and HNC and to rise steadily through the industrial ranks, taking evening classes in the first few years'.[25] When Prabhu and Russell investigated 280 manufacturing firms fifteen years later, they found that some change had occurred, but also noted that production managers were still far more likely to be offered straightforward on-the-job training than the more challenging external courses often enjoyed by their peers.[26] Relative pay was another revealing indicator. Production specialists began the period near the top of the ladder – recognition of their important role during the war - but gradually fell to the bottom.[27] Tellingly, students in the rapidly expanding business studies field quickly adjusted their preferences to the changing economic realities. In 1975, one widely experienced university academic summed up the undergraduate view as 'Accountancy – yes, Marketing – yes, Personnel – yes, Production – NO!'.[28]

Rational Decision-Making?

In public, most business people throughout this period cultivated the impression that, as the textbooks recommended, their thinking was based on logical reasoning, an analytical methodology cleansed of sentiment and emotion. Some outside observers agreed that a new age of rationality had dawned. Writing in the current affairs monthly, the *Twentieth Century*, during 1958, one commentator described how big companies now absolutely insisted on a calm and measured approach:

> The men at the top...speak to-day with soft voices...Nobody wants to be caught barking out orders. The executive's job is to persuade in order to get agreement. In meetings a soft voice is a valuable weapon. Less exalted colleagues sit on the edge of their chairs lest some important inference should escape them. The atmosphere is not unlike that of a college tutorial. Disagreements do not end in slanging matches but in agreements to differ'.[29]

Yet, in reality, much of corporate life actually continued to run on very much less cerebral lines. Decisions were often imposed rather than discussed; while there were also various filters in operation that privileged certain voices over others. Rationality might be an aspiration, but everyday management remained a messy business, as much shaped by the illogicalities of power and prejudice as anything else.

To begin with, it is important to underline that British managers remained deeply influenced by military codes and customs. Many senior and junior grades had either fought in one of the world wars, or been drafted for national service (a compulsory stint in one of the armed forces).[30] Management journals often held up military leaders – particularly recent heroes like Montgomery – as role models. Indeed, the head of the IoD went so far as to claim that 'Generals are often the best kind of men to run business'.[31] At a deeper level, business had adopted military terminology and concepts more completely than virtually any other part of the civilian sphere. Looking at prevalent discourses, two psychologists observed: 'In much of managers thinking about management, war has dominated the scene...Most of the language of business policy has been borrowed from the armed forces'.[32]

One consequence of this was that many managers were prone to ape the military way of interacting with colleagues and making decisions. They would issue orders, and expect them to be carried out, promptly and with the minimum of fuss. Discussion was eschewed, and questioning viewed as insubordination. The tone could be peremptorily and aggressive, even unforgiving. The managing director of GEC from 1963 to 1999, Arnold Weinstock, often dubbed Britain's premier industrialist, apparently believed that 'it was necessary for his managers to be put through the fire, that they would become better managers for it', and so he would regularly and publicly humiliate his senior executives for their failings.[33] His style was widely admired and copied, by managers in small firms as well as large. Of course, Weinstock and his ilk had their critics, too, and there were periodic attempts throughout these years to promote more respect for the individual, and encourage the proliferation of less regimented ways of thinking. But it is significant that such initiatives usually floundered on the rocks of the dominant authoritarianism. Thus, for example, though 'empowerment' became a popular buzzword during the early 1990s, research showed that it was much more talked about than actually implemented because many managers found it difficult to surrender even a degree of authority to their subordinates.[34] The growing awareness of bullying in the workplace, as the century drew to a close, and the research finding that it was most prevalent *amongst* management grades were testament to how little things had in fact changed.[35]

At the same time, company decision-making was also marked – and circumscribed – by the status hierarchy amongst specialists. This meant in practice that some kinds of professional found it easy to have their opinions listened to, while others did not. Norburn and Grinyer reported that British boardrooms continued to be highly receptive to accountants, and the apparently 'hard' data that they provided. Their observation was that 'the mystique of financial statements, and of the accountant as the clinical magician, seems to continue'.[36] On the other hand, production management's declining status was reflected in the fact that, as survey after survey showed, it was frequently all but ignored. In 1964, Isabelle Blain of the National Institute of Industrial Psychology examined the relative power of different managers in 38 large and small firms, and reported: 'Management in the *production services* group...less often [than others] found their chiefs readily available when discussion seemed necessary'.[37] Prabhu and Russell painted a very similar picture. Production managers, they discovered, were rarely if ever consulted about strategy, even though this impacted directly on their jobs.[38]

Management Development: Meritocratic or Oligarchic?

Finally, what of the admonition to make management development more methodical and meritocratic? At first sight, this seems to have been taken quite seriously. Thus, for example, by the 1990s, most companies recruited reasonably systematically, and also operated a range of executive training programmes. Yet a closer look at the evidence reveals that the situation was, in fact, rather less satisfactory than it appeared. Professionalisation had occurred, but only slowly and unevenly.

Table 9.1 Percentage of Firms Using Specific Techniques, North West of England Sample, 1957

Technique	% of Firms Using Technique
Job Specifications for Managerial Posts	25
Systematic Interviewing	37
Periodic Progress Reviews	42
Use of Instruction Manual	13
Job Rotation	13
Encouragement of Membership of Professional Bodies	55

Source: British Institute of Management and the Manchester College of Technology (1957), Figure 5.

The promotion of 'human relations' techniques grew considerably in the early post-war period, with innovations like personality testing receiving a good deal of publicity in the business press. However, while some firms assiduously overhauled their procedures, many did not. A survey of 112 companies in the north west of England during 1957 found that a substantial number operated with only the most rudimentary notions of management development (see Table 9.1), and barely one-third had schemes that could be called comprehensive.[39] Family contacts continued to be important. Assessing the extent of nepotism at the end of the 1950s, Lewis and Stewart observed: 'In some companies it plays an important part and it exists in all'.[40] When the net had to be cast wider, the emphasis was usually on 'upbringing'. Lyndall Urwick, the pioneer management consultant and theorist, advised that candidates for management jobs should be quizzed about parents, school, army career, and club, on the basis that 'We don't buy a horse or a dog without looking at its breeding'.[41] If few industrialists were quite so candid, most tacitly agreed. Thus, when a Liverpool University team looked in detail at management life in the late 1950s, it concluded that 'social background' was 'an implied criterion in many selection procedures', as expressed in phrases like 'It is important to get a man who will fit'; 'He must of course be the right type'; and 'I always ask myself if he would make a decent son-in-law'.[42]

By the early 1960s, the balance had finally begun to shift decisively in favour of a more professional approach. The majority of large companies now took management development more seriously, and participated in a variety of forums designed to spread knowledge of the latest best practice.[43] Some outsiders concluded that a new meritocratic age was dawning. Yet, as a substantial body of research revealed, change was still by no means universal. The National Economic Development Council surveyed 102 firms in detail during 1965, and found that about a third were without satisfactory provision.[44] A Political and Economic Planning investigation of the same year reached similar conclusions. It reported bluntly that 'many' managing directors appeared to be unaware of the full meaning of management development.[45] Significantly, rather similar observations continued to be made in each of the following decades. An inquiry in 1986 suggested that more than 50 per cent of UK companies provided no executive training at all. Moreover, it was increasingly recognised that, even where appropriate schemes had been introduced, their impact had not been as great as was sometimes claimed. The scale of activity was often disappointing. Half of the managers in an exhaustive 1992 study judged that they had received either 'too little' or 'far too little' training, while one in eight reported that they had received none at all. To make matters worse, many schemes were run without adequate monitoring and evaluation. In the Institute of Management's view, the perseverance with training was frequently based upon little more than a 'considerable act of faith'.[46]

Tellingly, the drive to professionalisation was probably least well established in the boardroom. Appointment procedures remained opaque, but there was suspicion even in 2002 that some directors owed their elevation simply to the fact that they were considered – in the tycoon Tiny Rowland's caustic phrase – 'Christmas Tree decorations'.[47] Once on the board, few received any training.[48] According to the Industrial Society in 1996, four-fifth of firms did not even give directors written guidance on their roles.[49] Indeed, by the end of the period under review, the IoD had become concerned enough about the paucity of provision to offer courses of its own – a diploma in 1992 and then a chartered qualification (C.Dir.) in 1999.[50] Yet the idea that being a director came naturally still retained its potency. In 1998, 35 per cent of respondents to an IoD survey reported that they had not prepared in any way for their boardroom role.[51]

Given these propensities and procedures, it was inevitable that the leadership of British companies would be drawn from the same, rather narrow kinds of background. Men dominated almost totally. Indeed, only 5 per cent of directors in the top 100 companies at the end of the 1990s were women.[52] Moreover, it was clearly an advantage to have attended a private school. In the mid-1950s, Copeman found that 58 per cent of directors had been so educated.[53] Forty years later, the *Sunday Telegraph* discovered that little had changed. More than half of the chairmen, chief executives and finance directors of Britain's leading companies were ex-private schoolboys, an astonishing figure given that 93 per cent of secondary school pupils were now state educated.[54] On the other hand, no great value was placed on a degree. When the IoD surveyed its members in the late 1950s, it concluded: 'The striking feature is the relatively small proportion with a University Degree and the high number who think that experience alone qualifies them for directorship'. Some 64 per cent were said to fall into the latter category.[55] Even in the 1990s, such prejudices persisted. For example, as many a third of the *Sunday Telegraph*'s sample were without higher education qualifications of any kind.[56] The hoped-for establishment of a meritocracy at the top of business had not, therefore, been fully realised.

Assessing the British Way

How much difference did any of this make? Most importantly, what impact did British business's determination to follow its own idiosyncratic principles of governance have on corporate performance? There can be little doubt that the chosen methods brought some advantages. Centralised authority structures aided decisive decision-making, clear-cut judgement made without prevarication. Hierarchies encouraged ambition. The promise of a better company car or the key to the executive lavatories could be a spur to industry and invention. If accountants were more influential than other professionals, this was partly because they frequently made good managers, and performed a function that was obviously vital to a firm's survival.[57] Recruiting from a restricted social circle helped cohesion, while the emphasis on experience no doubt did the same for continuity. Yet, when a fully comprehensive balance sheet is drawn up, there can be no doubt that the British system imposed more costs than benefits. The following sections look at three of the main disadvantages in a little more detail.

Consequences: Short-Termism

First, the boardroom aversion to strategy, combined with the priority – even reverence – granted to financial measures, inevitably encouraged a degree of short-termism. When challenged by changing circumstances, firms would examine cost data and react accordingly, regardless of what this meant for future operations. As several observers noted, corporate behaviour was often reduced to a matter of reflex. A stimuli – declining market share, or lower profits – would be met by an automatic response, cost-cutting. Conditioned in this way, firms found themselves forever reacting to circumstances, much more rarely setting their own agenda.[58] With time, and the growing strength and reach of the stock market, such behaviour became self-reinforcing. If new management tools or approaches emerged, they were quite often bent to fit the dominant model. A good example occurred in the early 1990s over re-engineering. When this idea was first aired, it was proposed as a method of streamlining or removing bureaucratic procedures, making work systems more efficient, and thus improving profits. However, in the burst of publicity that followed, many ordinary managers apparently heard a very different message – that what re-engineering really meant was cutting costs by firing workers. In the end, the originators were forced to issue a stream of more and more forthright clarifications, explaining that their insights had been widely misunderstood, even perverted.[59]

Of course, short-termism always had its critics, and, by the mid-1990s, these were becoming more vocal. Indeed, the tide seemed to be finally turning for good when the so-called 'guru of downsizing', Morgan Stanley chief economist, Stephen Roach, publicly recanted, and declared that 'slash and burn' tactics were simply a recipe for industrial extinction.[60] However, because corporate mentalities were so embedded, the subsequent degree of change was unspectacular. In 2002, a large-scale PricewaterhouseCoopers survey of chief financial officers found that British respondents were still notably more wedded than others to quick-fix solutions. Almost all agreed in principle that aggressive job cutting strongly damaged morale, and that investment should continue in a downturn. But when questioned about their strategies in the recent recession, two-thirds reported that they had fired staff, and just under half that they had drastically reduced their capital budgets.[61]

Consequences: 'Bad Production'

Second, it is clear that the pervasive lack of focus on production directly caused inefficiencies on the shopfloor, especially regarding machine set-ups and work processing. Since firms were not spending enough time and care over the planning of the manufacturing stages, hold-ups and delays were endemic. Raw materials and semi-finished products would enter the system, and then progress spasmodically, leaving machines and personnel underemployed. Detailed enquiries into specific industries underlined the scale of typical difficulties. A government-sponsored study of 17 printing firms in the mid-1950s found that, due to poor planning and sequencing, machines were running on average about 40 per cent of the available time.[62] Twenty years later, the academic N. A. Dudley examined more than 80 companies in the Midlands metal sectors, and again uncovered large but entirely avoidable problems relating to machine utilisation. His findings were startling:

> In medium sized batch production factories (200-300 employees) no more than 20% of the time taken to progress materials through a factory is spent productively. After allowing for time actually spent in transporting materials between machines and workstations, and in waiting for completion of the batch of work, at least 70% of materials throughput time is wholly non-productive.[63]

With greater attention to factors like flow, Dudley argued, firms could increase their output by up to 100 per cent. What industry urgently required, he believed, was educational courses which would 'bring practising managers up to date on planning, organising and control procedures', the staples of production engineering.[64]

These were fairly average cases, but sometimes firms became embroiled in even more serious difficulties. On occasion, production descended into total chaos. Alistair Nicholson, professor of production management at the London Business School, encountered one such example in the mid-1970s. He found the 16 members of one factory's control department shuffling half a million job tickets. They had no authority for scheduling work, and so virtually every job was late. The works manager told him: 'There was so much work on hand...we couldn't get anything out of the door'.[65] In the 1980s, Houlden and Woodcock investigated ten plants and found that as many as four were 'out of control', with two of these needing major remedial action to prevent long-term failure. Their overall assessment included a familiar refrain: 'At present many companies view production control only in terms of engineering...Real control, however, depends additionally on production managers playing their full part...in deciding corporate strategy'.[66]

A second consequence of downplaying production was that firms were slow to adopt new manufacturing techniques. As production managers were relatively powerless in their organisations, their pleas to innovate were likely to be ignored. Typically, no action would be taken at board level to sanction expenditure on processes and machinery until absolutely unavoidable. The inadequacy of this kind of decision-making was regularly noticed in the literature. The Institute of Works Managers claimed that 'the gulf between the leaders and the shop floor' was 'an important factor' in explaining why companies were slow to adopt improved production systems'.[67] Dudley reached equally forthright conclusions. There was a clear relationship between 'a lack of adequately trained personnel at middle management level, particularly of executives concerned with engineering production', and 'a lack of awareness of the benefits that could accrue from the employment of modern methods'.[68] The same kinds of observations were still being made in the 1980s. When Oakland investigated the introduction of quality control procedures in 1986, he found that 'the most frequently occurring barriers' were either 'lack of knowledge' or 'lack of support' from senior management.[69] Some sections of British industry gained an unenviable reputation for technical backwardness. The journal *Management Today* observed that 'the large mass of British companies' were 'halting uncomprehending and limp' in their take-up of innovations, and similar points were made in many more systematic enquiries.[70] For example, when Wild and Swann examined 50 small and medium-sized companies in West Yorkshire at the beginning of the 1970s, they were particularly struck by the 'low utilisation of accepted and well-proven techniques'.[71]

The cumulative impact of these various weaknesses could be observed, at the end of the manufacturing process, in the relationship with customers. For poor production meant that clients' specifications and deadlines were rarely met on anything like a consistent basis. There were, for example, persistent difficulties over quality standards during this period.[72] Performance in meeting delivery dates, too, was frequently lamentable. A National Economic Development Office report on the mechanical engineering industry in 1969 observed: 'There is a serious lack of appreciation throughout the country of the importance of good delivery. In the case of capital goods it is often more important competitively than price and may even outweigh the intrinsic functional or design aspects'.[73] Seven years later, C. C. New surveyed 186 factories, and found that the overall position remained deeply unsatisfactory: 'On a 90% "on time performance" criterion only one in five plants achieve satisfactory performance. One in four plants delivers more orders late than they do on time!'.[74] Similar complaints were made with depressing regularity during the following decades. The subordination of production management, therefore, had direct and damaging consequences.

Consequences: Disaffection and Disengagement

Finally, the prevalent system of governance also had a detrimental impact on intra-firm morale. Some managers simply resented the rather arbitrary mode of decision-making that predominated, and the fact that they were always expected to follow orders. Many more accepted their place in the hierarchy more or less unquestioningly, but still believed that not enough time was ever spent on explaining why particular policies were being pursued. Indeed, a large-scale Institute of Management/University of Manchester Institute of Science and Technology survey of 1997 reported that as many as 60 per cent of junior and middle managerial grades saw themselves as 'in the dark about future strategies in their organisations'.[75] Given such lack of care, it was hardly surprising that cynicism about those at the top was often endemic. The continuing popularity of satires on corporate life – from *Parkinson's Law* and *Up The Organization* to *The Dilbert Principle* and *The Little Book of Management Bollocks* - told its own story.[76]

Similar pathologies were evident in managerial dealings with the shopfloor. Managers schooled in the conventional mores inevitably believed that the best method of ensuring workforce commitment was through leadership and discipline. Their stance could be dictatorial.[77] In the mid-1950s, the experienced social psychiatrist J. A. C. Brown argued that the regime in an average factory was less 'tolerant, broad-minded, progressive and fair' than was the case in the British army.[78] Nearly 50 years later, Richard Scase, the professor of organisational behaviour at the University of Kent, observed that managers still operated 'with the assumption that they know best'.[79] Yet, as the evidence increasingly showed, such an approach in fact often did more harm than good. Managers who relied on 'command and control' methods tended to remain aloof, and thus unaware of the everyday practical problems of working life.[80] In addition, they were shown to be largely indifferent to the whole question of providing adequate information about strategies and goals. In 1999, a Siegel and Galle survey, based upon more than 1,000 interviews, found that communication systems were so poor that only a third of employees felt that they knew enough about their companies to do their jobs well, while less than a fifth understood their employer's long-term aims.[81] Finally, there was also no doubt that 'wielding the big stick' could easily provoke workforce resentment and even anger. This was particularly the case from the 1960s and 1970s onwards because social attitudes in general were becoming more liberal. By the end of the 20th century, the situation here had degenerated enough for it to be widely recognised as a critical problem. New production methods demanded flexible attitudes and concentrated minds. But workers in Britain seemed more demoralised and less committed than was the case in virtually every other leading European country – a fact reflected in soaring absenteeism, turnover and sickness rates.[82] The BBC TV series 'Back to the Floor' in 2001-2, which followed various leading executives doing a week's work alongside their employees, highlighted the prevailing misunderstandings. In one episode, the new head of Wedgewood's Stoke factory, Brian Patterson, was filmed helping an experienced decorator, Yvonne Morrall. Their conversation began with some innocuous banter, but soon deteriorated sharply:

Yvonne: When people have been here two, three and five years and they don't even know what you look like, then they're only going to get one impression of you aren't they? People on the shop floor feel that people like yourself are all about profits – less people, more machines, more profits.

Brian: And that's it? Nothing else?

Yvonne: They just feel as though they're not worth anything anymore. Why bother...It feels as though you drive off in your BMWs and that's it...

Brian: We don't care?

Yvonne: You don't care.

Brian: Listen...I've had enough. I've had enough [walks away].[83]

This was eloquent testimony, indeed, to the fact that, as Scase put it, 'disengagement' remained at the very heart of the corporate culture.[84]

Conclusion

One way of classifying firms is to divide them into the centripetal and the centrifugal. The former are united in pursuit of agreed goals - in today's terms, 'focused'. The latter are marked by internal strife, with different constituent elements pulling against each other, often with damaging consequences. Looked at from this perspective, the importance of intra-firm governance is obvious: if the system is right, it can provide cohesion and purpose, and thus help create or reinforce centripetal tendencies. The problem in Britain during the period under review was that too few companies were willing to scrutinise themselves in these terms. Commentators and pundits urged action and provided blueprints, but the impetus to change was blunted by apathy and inertia. Many British companies remained centrifugal, and in the end paid for it dearly.

Notes

1   J.Kay and A.Silberston, 'Corporate Governance', *National Institute Economic Review* (1995), no.153, pp.84-96; J.Charkam and A.Simpson, *Fair Shares: the Future of Shareholder Power and Responsibility* (1999); R.H.Carlsson, *Ownership and Value Creation: Strategic Corporate Governance in the New Economy* (2001); A.Nicholson, 'The British Production Cinderella. 1. - Causes', *Management Today* (1976), June, pp.66-71.
2   H.Maurer, *Great Enterprise: Growth and Behavior of the Big Corporation* (1955); Institute of Directors, *Standard Boardroom Practice* (1961); F.C.Hooper, *Management Survey* (1960); E.F.L.Brech, (ed.), *The Principles and Practice of Management* (1953); F.C.Hooper, *Management Survey* (1948). See N.Tiratsoo, 'The American Quality Gospel in Britain and Japan, 1950-1970', in K.Sahlin-Andersson and L.Engwall (eds.), *The Expansion of Management Knowledge: Carriers, Flows and Sources* (2002).
3   E.Dale, *Planning and Developing the Company Organization Structure* (1952).
4   Brech, *Principles and Practice of Management*.
5   H.Parker, 'The Basic Role and Functions of Boards', in H.Parker, M.Bower, E.E.Smith, and J.R.Morrison (eds), *Effective Boardroom Management* (1971), pp.9-27; R.Heller and G.Foster, 'Managers at the Top', *Management Today* (1968), January, pp.81-5; R.Heller, 'Britain's Boardroom Anatomy', *Management Today* (1970), September, pp.83-5.
6   T.Burns and G.M.Stalker, *The Management of Innovation* (1961), p.211.
7   K.Rogers, *Managers – Personality and Performance* (1963).
8   Greenbury was much admired, and was several times voted 'the bosses' boss'. See, for example, the *Independent on Sunday*, 18 July 1993; *Economist*, 19 November 1998.
9   I.McGivering, D.Matthews, and W.H.Scott, *Management in Britain: a General Characterisation* (1960).
10 Anon., 'What's wrong with the Board', *Scope* (1958), September, p.51.
11 D.Hobson, *The National Wealth: Who Gets What in Britain* (1999).

12 A.C.Spencer, *On the Edge of the Organisation – the Role of the Outside Director* (1983).
13 *Observer*, 17 March 2002.
14 *Independent*, 30 April, 2002.
15 R.I.Tricker, *Corporate Governance: Practices, Procedures and Powers in British Companies and their Boards of Directors* (1984).
16 D.Norburn and P.Grinyer, 'Directors without Direction', *Journal of General Management* (1973-74), vol.1, pp.37-48.
17 J.Hewkin and T.Kempner, 'The Way Companies Plan', *Management Today* (1968), October, pp.110-13.
18 R.Lewis and R.Stewart, 'Men at the Top', *Encounter* (1958), vol.11, pp.44-54.
19 *Daily Herald*, 5 February 1955; A.Rubner, *Fringe Benefits: the Golden Chains* (1962); V.Mortensen, 'Are Status Symbols Inevitable?', *Industrial Welfare* (1962), vol. 64, pp.151-4.
20 *Independent*, 14 July 1997.
21 N.Tiratsoo, 'Standard Motors 1945-55 and the Post-war Malaise of British Management', in Youssef Cassis, Francois Crouzet and Terry Gourvish (eds.), *Management and Business in Britain and France: the Age of the Corporate Economy* (1995), pp.88-108.
22 P.Lawrence, *Management in Action* (1984).
23 R.Wild, *Management and Production* (1972).
24 N.Tiratsoo, '"Cinderellas at the Ball": Production Managers in British Manufacturing, 1945-80', *Contemporary British History* (1999), vol.13, pp.105-20.
25 E.N.Corlett, 'Production Engineers: their Education and their Work', *Production Engineer* (1965), vol.44, pp.79-91.
26 V.Prabhu, and J.Russell, 'The Man with his Head on the Block', *Production Engineer* (1979), vol.58, pp.27-30.
27 R.W.T.Gill and K.G.Lockyer, *The Career Development of the Production Manager in British Industry* (1979).
28 K.G.Lockyer, *Production Management: the Unaccepted Challenge* (1975).
29 S.J.Cox, 'The Priesthood of Industry', *Twentieth Century* (1958), vol.163, pp.356-7.
30 M.Roper, *Masculinity and the British Organization Man since 1945* (1994).
31 A.Sampson, *Anatomy of Britain* (1962).
32 J.Morris and J.Burgoyne, *Developing Resourceful Managers* (1973).
33 A.Brummer and R.Cowe, *Weinstock. The Life and Times of Britain's Premier Industrialist* (1998).
34 *Independent*, 12 May 1993; A Comax study of 1997 found that, while three quarters of company directors agreed in principle that empowering the workforce was a good thing, fewer than one in ten listed their employees as a business priority. See *Financial Times*, 10 December 1997.
35 *Financial Times*, 28 November 1996; London Chamber of Commerce, *Fact Sheet: Bullying and Harassment in the Workplace* (2000).
36 Nicholson, 'The British Production Cinderella'.
37 I.Blain, *Structure in Management: a Study of Different Forms and their Effectiveness* (1964).
38 Prabhu and Russell, 'The Man with his Head on the Block'.
39 British Institute of Management and the Manchester College of Technology, *Company Executive Development Schemes* (1957).
40 R.Lewis and R.Stewart, *The Boss: the Life and Times of the British Business Man* (1958).
41 *Daily Herald*, 20 January 1958.
42 McGivering, Mathews and Scott, *Management in Britain*.

43 Anon., 'Developing Executives: How Big Companies Go About It', *Manager* (1966), March, pp.19-27.
44 National Economic Development Council, *Management Recruitment and Development* (1965).
45 D.Insull, 'Two Kinds of Company: the Thrusters and the Sleepers', *Manager* (1965), February, pp.21-8.
46 *Observer*, 13 July 1997; N.Tiratsoo, 'Management Education in Postwar Britain', in L.Engwall and V.Zamagni (eds), *Management Education in Historical Perspective* (1998), pp.111-25.
47 *Independent*, 30 April 2002.
48 W.Puckey, *The Board Room: a guide to the role and function of directors* (1969); J.Charkham, *Keeping Good Company* (1994).
49 *Observer*, 30 June 1996.
50 *Observer*, 6 & 30 June 1996.
51 *Financial Times*, 16 July 1998. It should be noted, too, that the definition of 'prepare' that was used here was pretty loose, and could embrace anything from the attainment of a formal qualification to 'some kind of coaching or course'.
52 *Observer*, 12 December 1999; *Independent*, 8 November 2000.
53 G.H.Copeman, *Leaders of British Industry* (1955).
54 *Sunday Telegraph*, 4 September, 1994.
55 Anon., 'The Life and Times of a Director', *Director* (1959), vol.12, pp.300-1; Institute of Directors, *Who's on the Board* (1961).
56 *Sunday Telegraph*, 4 September 1994.
57 D.Matthews, M.Anderson, and J.R.Edwards, *The Priesthood of Industry: the Rise of the Professional Accountant in British Management* (1998).
58 C.Halley, T.Kennerley, and E.Brech, *Management Performance and the Board* (1983).
59 E.Mumford and R.Hendricks, 'Business Process Re-engineering RIP', *People Management* (1996), May, pp.22-9.
60 *Independent on Sunday*, 12 May 1996; S.S.Roach, 'The Hollow Ring of the Productivity Revival', *Harvard Business Review* (1996), November-December, pp.81-9.
61 *Independent*, 9 April 2002.
62 Department of Scientific and Industrial Research, *Productivity in Letterpress Printing* (1961).
63 N.A.Dudley, 'Industrial Productivity - Scope for Improvement', *Midlands Tomorrow* (1975), no.8, p.2.
64 Dudley, 'Industrial Productivity'.
65 Nicholson, 'The British Production Cinderella'.
66 B.Houlden and D.Woodcock, 'Production under Stress', *Management Today* (1988), October, pp.155-6.
67 *New Society*, 31 January 1963.
68 N.A.Dudley, 'Comparative Productivity Analysis-Study in the United Kingdom West Midlands Engineering and Metalworking Industries', *International Journal of Production Research* (1970), vol.8, pp.397-402.
69 J.S.Oakland, 'Research into Quality Control in British Manufacturing Industry', *Business Graduate Journal* (1986), vol.6, pp.30-4.
70 Anon., *Management Today* (1971), April, p.9.
71 R.Wild and K.Swann, 'The Small Company: Profitability, Management Resources and Management Techniques', *Journal of Business Policy* (1972), vol.3, pp.10-21.
72 Tiratsoo, 'The American Quality Gospel in Britain and Japan, 1950-1970'.
73 National Economic Development Office, *Better Delivery* (1969).
74 C.C.New, *Managing Manufacturing Operations* (1976).
75 *Financial Times*, 16 October 1997.

76 R.Townsend, *Up The Organisation* (1970); C.N.Parkinson, *Parkinson's Law* (1958); S.Adams, *The Dilbert Principle* (1996); A.Beaton, *The Little Book of Management Bollocks* (2001).

77 T.Nichols and H.Beynon, *Living with Capitalism: Class Relations and the Modern Factory* (1977).

78 J.A.C.Brown, 'Surveying the British Scene', in F.A.Heller (ed.), *New Developments in Industrial Leadership* (1955), pp.10-28.

79 *Observer*, 26 August 2001.

80 Elliston Research Associates, *What the Girls Think!* (1973).

81 *Financial Times*, 7 April 1999.

82 *Financial Times*, 14 May 1997; *Independent*, 8 April 2002.

83 This is an edited version of the transcript, taken from the BBC's website.

84 *Observer*, 26 August 2001.

Chapter 10

Corporate Governance and Management Structure: the Nationalised Railway Industry in Britain

Terry Gourvish

Introduction

What is corporate governance? How effectively may the concept be applied to the state-owned enterprise sector? Charkham has noted that 'there is some doubt about what "corporate governance" means'. For some, it is merely a phrase to convey the idea that professional managers should be accountable to the owners, namely the shareholders of the companies they manage. For others, the definition is much broader. According to Keasey and Wright, 'corporate governance concerns the structures and processes associated with production, decision-making, control and so on within an organisation'.[1] Tricker defined it as 'the processes by which companies are governed', while the Cadbury Committee on Financial Aspects of Corporate Governance of 1992 defined it as 'the system by which companies are directed and controlled'.[2] According to Kay and Silberston, the importance lies in the 'relationship between the structure of rules, laws and conventional practices within which the companies operate and their style of management and the decisions which they make'.[3] As Hart puts it, corporate governance arises where 'there is an agency problem or conflict of interest, involving members of the organisation' - whether owners, managers, workers or consumers - and where 'transaction costs are such that this agency problem cannot be dealt with through a contract'.[4] Thus, a governance system, according to Zingales, is 'a complex set of constraints that shape *ex post* bargaining over the quasi rents generated in the course of a relationship'.[5] The literature has burgeoned over the last five years, notably in the fields of political science, public policy, management, and accounting, and extends to issues such as mergers, takeovers and the struggle for corporate control; the relationship between finance and business; the significance of ownership paradigms; incentives and rewards for owners and managers; and effective legal, regulatory and monitoring structures.[6] The topic has a high contemporary resonance. For example, the collapse of Enron and Railtrack, and the issue of senior executives' bonuses, for example at Prudential and Vodafone, provide instructive case studies. Whatever the emphasis, there is no doubt that the concept *can* be applied to the public sector, though, in any evaluation of 'direction' and 'control', the relationship between managers and the several layers of government is clearly crucial.

In the growing attention to corporate governance, interest has generally focussed on the rights of shareholders or stakeholders. Commentators have argued that there is a pressing need, in the Anglo-Saxon countries in particular, to protect shareholders' interests and their share in the corporation's long-run profits from certain actions by salaried managers, and, specifically, frauds, excessive salaries, and unduly favourable share option schemes, which run counter to that interest.[7] In the public sector, where the nation is both shareholder and stakeholder, this interest is filtered through the elected government of the day, then further filtered by the devolution of authority to the relevant Minister of State, and the department over which he or she presides. It will be argued here that the main difficulty which has confronted public sector enterprises, such as Britain's railways, is the fact that there is too much 'governance', in the sense of control by the government on behalf of the stakeholder. A situation of what may be termed 'reverse governance' has existed, in which the professional managers have sought more freedom to act, and lobbied for the modification or removal of statutory obligations and restraints imposed in the public interest. Later on, of course, the privatisation of most of Britain's public sector in the 1980s and 1990s raised the more familiar issues of 'corporate governance' in the newly-privatised utilities.[8]

This chapter examines some of the governance issues affecting the British railway industry during the period of nationalisation from 1947 to 1994. The railways were a regulated private sector industry from their inception in the early 1820s. Private Acts of Parliament imposed numerous obligations, including clauses affecting services and pricing, in return for limited liability status and powers of compulsory purchase. Public Acts, beginning in 1840 - and gathering pace with landmark statutes in 1844, 1868, 1873, 1883, 1888 and 1894 - imposed a succession of general regulations dealing with service provision, safety, freight rates and passenger fares, and maximum hours of work and disclosure, which, by the end of the century, amounted to a very substantial regulatory regime indeed. Not only were charges effectively frozen after 1899, but statutory disclosure under an Act of 1873 provided for the publication of all rates in force, together with a statement of their component parts when requested. Furthermore, from 1923, the government, having rejected the alternative of nationalisation, imposed a new corporate structure on the industry. The 123 private companies were statutorily merged into four regional giants, the 'Big Four'. Even tighter control of prices and services naturally followed on from the assumption that four regional monopolies had been created.[9] Nationalisation was in some ways the inevitable outcome of the failure of this strategy, first because road competition intensified, and second because of the depredations of war-time use and under-maintenance of the assets during the Second World War, although the owners were fully compensated for their shares.[10] The process of privatisation began in the early 1980s with the disposal of the British Railways Board's subsidiary companies, the hotels, shipping, hovercraft, engineering workshops, and catering establishments, together with large tracts of non-operational property.[11] The disposal of the rail network itself began in 1994, with the creation of a private track-owning authority called Railtrack, followed by rolling stock companies, and the franchising of rail services to operating companies.[12]

Salaries and Appointments

Under the Morrisonian, 'arms-length' model of nationalised industry in Britain, appointments to the boards of the public corporations and the salaries of board members were a matter for the sponsoring departments of state, subject to the endorsement of Cabinet and Parliament. In terms of 'governance', the main concern here was to find vigorous and competent people at the low levels of remuneration fixed from the late 1940s. It is clear that the pay-scales introduced by Labour in 1946-8 and maintained by successive governments thereafter encouraged the appointment of retired businessmen and bureaucrats with full pensions. When the British Transport Commission was established in 1947, the chairman, Sir Cyril [later Lord] Hurcomb, former Permanent-Secretary at the Ministry of Transport, was paid £8,500 a year. However, the Treasury did little to endear itself to those who felt that public sector pay in the large mega-corporations of coal, railways, and electricity should match conditions in the private sector by immediately reducing it to £7,000 on account of his civil service pension. The other full-time members were paid a basic rate of £5,000, while part-time members received sums up to a maximum of £1,000. The BTC team was regarded by a senior civil servant as 'elderly and safe'; they were scarcely dynamic. Furthermore, little was done in the 1950s to alter this pattern. Hurcomb was succeeded in 1953 by a retired general, Sir Brian Robertson, whose generous army pension made the level of remuneration a less pressing issue.[13]

The salary question only became a matter of more public concern in 1961, when the Conservative Government sought to replace Robertson with a leading manager from the private sector, Richard Beeching, a 47-year old director of ICI. The object was to give impetus to its drive to restructure and rationalise the loss-making and heavily subsidised railways. The Minister of Transport, Ernest Marples, had promised Beeching that he would match his ICI salary of £24,000, more than twice the amount (£10,000) then paid to Robertson, along with the chairmen of the coal and electricity corporations, and nearly five times Marples's salary (£5,000) as Minister. Beeching certainly earned his salary. The BTC was replaced by a slimmed-down British Railways Board, and a major period of rationalisation ensued. The furore over Beeching's salary was merely a highly visible example of the patent fact that, over the 1950s, managerial pay in the private sector had greatly outstripped that for comparable jobs in the public sector.[14] There was an additional problem. Low salaries for board members acted as a 'glass ceiling' on pay for executives lower down, many of whom could double or treble their salaries by deserting the public sector for the private. This issue came to the fore in 1967, when Barbara Castle, then Labour Minister of Transport, removed Beeching's successor, Stanley Raymond, as chairman of the British Railways Board (salary only £12,500), and tried to replace him with Peter Parker, a left-leaning executive and director of Booker McConnell. Parker refused an offer of the post at Raymond's salary, citing the glass ceiling as a major factor. As he put it, he was keen to see that the salary matched 'the competitive realities of management'. By this time, morale inside British Rail management had been devastated by Beeching's decision to bring in nearly forty men from the private sector at much higher salaries than those paid to career railwaymen. However, Parker's demand for £17,500 a year was blown away in Cabinet by the devaluation crisis, and, in the end, an internal (railway) appointment was made.[15]

Not only was little done to redress the position in the 1970s, but periods of major financial crisis in Britain, which provoked policies of pay restraint, sometimes statutory, sometimes informal in nature, made the disparity between rewards in the private and public sectors much worse. At the same time, recourse to younger (and therefore cheaper) recruits was inhibited by the limitations imposed by the government's insistence on fixed-term appointments, usually for five years. In 1974, when the railways' sponsoring ministry, the Department of the Environment, undertook an internal inquiry into the procedures for public appointments, the British Railways Board pointed out that the recruitment of younger managers was inhibited by the insecurity of employment, coupled with the absence of a pension scheme for board members.[16] The difficulties became clear when the DOE pressed British Rail to strengthen its representation, by appointing specialists in finance and marketing. Richard Marsh, then chairman with a salary of £23,100 a year, later recalled his abortive search for a private sector finance man. The standard salary for board members of nationalised industries, originally £5,000, had been raised to £7,500 in 1957, £8,000-9,500 in the late 1960s, and stood at £13,500 in the mid-1970s. It was difficult to recruit, he was reported in *The Times* as saying, 'because the rate being offered would not buy the fifth man in an average London firm of accountants'.[17] The Board then turned to an internal candidate, Derek Fowler, a Beeching appointee, who had been Controller of Corporate Finance since 1972. A relatively young man - he was 46 - he not unnaturally had some qualms about accepting the standard five-year appointment with no guarantee of reappointment by the Ministry, or of re-employment by the Board. It required the most protracted negotiations with the DOE over pension contributions before he could be induced to join the Board in 1975. However, the episode was useful in that it established a valuable precedent for the future. When Peter Parker agreed to be British Rail chairman in 1976, he quickly set about restructuring the Board on a functional, executive director basis. Having decided to promote four younger railwaymen - Campbell, Reid, Rose and Urquhart - to the Board in 1977, he was able to convince the Ministry that an undertaking to reappoint, together with appropriate pension safeguards, were essential accompaniments.[18]

Ironically, in view of his stance in 1967, Parker's own experience of public sector pay was a gloomy one. He had succeeded Marsh at a salary of £23,300. This was more than the £20,000 paid to James Callaghan as Prime Minister, but was only a third of Parker's previous salary (£65,000) as chairman of the Rockware Group, the glass and plastic container company.[19] However, absolute levels of pay were one thing; increases to reflect career progression, performance, and protection of the real value of pay were important too, and here public sector managers were often at a disadvantage compared with their colleagues in the private sector. In the mid-late 1970s, when inflation was running at extraordinarily high levels, it was the government's policy of pay freeze, strictly applied in the public if not the private sector, which was the major irritant. Reporting in 1974, the Boyle Committee on Top Salaries noted that there had been no major review since 1969, and had recommended substantial - 30 per cent - increases for the higher judiciary, senior officers in the armed forces, senior civil servants, and public sector board members.[20] The government failed to enhance the pay of the latter group, however, and token increases in 1977 - a £4 a week rise agreed in May in line with pay restraint, and Prime Minister Callaghan's announcement of a five per cent increase in December - merely served to heighten the sense of frustration.[21] This imposed restraint at the very top of the public corporations' managerial hierarchies caused enterprises such as British Rail to complain formally about the problem of 'pay relativities'. Its submission to the Boyle Committee in October 1977 argued that the failure to advance board members' salaries had created an impossible situation with regard to *executive* salaries, and, from 1975, it had been forced to hold down its senior executive scale. The alternative, rejected by British Rail but taken up by British Steel and Cable & Wireless, for example, was to pay executives more than board members.[22] There was no real move to advance board members' salaries until after the Boyle Committee's Report of June 1978 had conceded that these were 'seriously out of date', and the government pledged to implement its recommendations in three stages ending in April 1980.[23] Even so, the situation remained bleak. Increases agreed in June and August 1978 and April 1979 took the chairman's pay from £23,539 to £32,948, and that of the average board member from about £15,000 to £19,000, but clearly failed to correct pay levels for the ravages of high inflation. The chairman's pay of £23,100 in 1974, and the £13,600 paid to ordinary board members were equivalent to £49,386 and £29,063 respectively in 1978 prices. These senior managers were thus earning in real terms only two-thirds of the salaries they had enjoyed four years earlier.[24]

The position of non-executive or part-time members was also a matter of debate. The effective deployment and monitoring functions of these directors were a key element in the corporate governance debate of the 1990s, where attention was focussed mainly on the private sector.[25] In the public sector, it could be argued, the role of independent experts as part-timers was equally important, but the derisory salaries offered by the government since nationalisation certainly limited the field to the committed or the disengaged. Lord Taylor of Gryfe, whose experience derived from retailing and the Co-operative movement, was a part-time member of the British Railways Board from 1968 to 1980. In 1971, he had led a review of the Board's McKinsey-style organisation, and used the opportunity to complain about the impotence of part-timers in the McKinsey-style, planning-oriented board of 1970-6. It was also clear that the low level of remuneration - £1,000, a sum fixed in 1946 - served to restrict the field to those who felt some commitment to the railways, but were able to offer only limited amounts of time. British Rail was able to circumvent the problem by paying additional sums for special responsibilities. Lord Taylor himself had been paid £3,000 since 1970, and Sir David Serpell, a civil servant who joined the Board in 1974, received the same in 1978. The Boyle Committee recommended that *all* part-timers' pay should be based *pro rata* on the full-time salary according to the time given, with a minimum of £1,500 (1974), then £2,000 (1978). However, all they received before the change of government was a share in the 10 per cent increase applied in August 1978, which took the basic rate to £1,100. This was the sum offered to Lord Caldecote, chairman of Delta Metal and Legal & General, when he joined the Board in March 1979.[26] It was left to the Conservatives to make further adjustments to public sector pay after the Election in May,[27] though, as late as 1992-93, part-timers were paid only £7,267, and the evident disparities remained a matter for debate until privatisation dominated public policy.[28] One conclusion, which is somewhat ironic in view of the reactions of the Greenbury Committee of 1995 to excessive rewards in the private sector, is that nationalised industries, such as the railways, were handicapped by *low* pay, which not only restricted choice when recruiting, but brought with it a relatively low esteem in managerial circles.

As the public sector was progressively privatised in the 1980s, the corporate governance debate naturally focussed on the operations of the private sector. With the disposal of British Petroleum (1979-87), British Telecom (1984-93), British Gas (1986-89), British Steel (1988), the water companies (1989) and electricity (1991), there were few substantial businesses left in state hands in the late 1980s and early 1990s. The exceptions were, of course, British Coal, sold in 1994, and British Rail, privatised in 1993-97. These enterprises were the subject of governance issues while they were being 'prepared' for privatisation.

The first change we should note was the introduction of bonus payments for full-time members of the British Railways Board. In a 'spirit of governance', where the intention was to link pay to performance, British Rail asked the Treasury and Department of Transport in 1986 to endorse a bonus scheme, to be paid only if specific management objectives were met. In British Rail, the initiative seems to have originated among the part-time members of the Board, and notably Oscar de Ville, chairman of the Remuneration Committee, a man with a wide experience of industry.[29] Initial thinking was that bonuses should amount to about 12-25 per cent of the basic salary. At the time, the Board's performance was impressive. It was well on the way to achieving the three-year objective set it by the Department in October 1983, namely to reduce the size of the public subsidy paid to railways (the Public Service Obligation or PSO) to £635m in 1983 prices by 1986, a reduction of about 25 per cent in real terms.[30] In February 1986, British Rail chairman Sir Bob Reid wrote to Nicholas Ridley, the Secretary of State for Transport, with suggestions for a possible bonus scheme. Drawing on the experience of the British Airports Authority, he suggested that a bonus should be calculated on the basis of five factors, including an individual component. The four corporate factors were: the financial results of the passenger business; the financial results of the freight and other businesses (parcels, freightliner); the performance of passenger train operation (punctuality); and a quality performance factor (based on train cancellations).[31]

Negotiations with the Department and with the Treasury proved somewhat frustrating. The Department felt the scheme was over-complex, and Ridley much preferred to have the bonus linked specifically to the three-year objectives for the PSO. The Treasury was happy to endorse a trial, based on a multi-factor scheme, for the financial year 1986-87, but it created disappointment by reducing the size of the bonus to the range 7-15 per cent.[32] De Ville expressed some incredulity at the response of Whitehall:

> To someone from the private sector it is incomprehensible that a proposal of this kind, drawn up with care by experienced, worldly-wise, Government-appointed part-time Members as a matter of urgency and intended to provide bite, incentive and motivation for executive management, in good time for the BR financial year, should be:
> - subject, so far, to six months interminable and remote debate and delay;
> - repeatedly amended;
> - well-nigh emasculated;
> all presumably with the intention of making us tired and ready to settle for any positive response.'[33]

In July, the scheme was amended further to embrace four, instead of five, factors, together with a sliding-scale of rewards where managers improved on the planned targets, but it was not until October 1986 that the scheme was approved, and by Ridley's successor, John Moore. Even then, the new Secretary of State raised further questions about the calculation of the bonus for individual performance.[34] It was left to a third Secretary of State, Paul Channon, to receive the results of the trial scheme of 1986-87. It produced a bonus of 3 per cent for the passenger business, nil for the commercial (freight and so on) businesses, and 2 per cent for passenger service performance. With individual payments of 2.5-3.5 per cent, the total for the five managers amounted to 7.5-8.5 per cent of the basic salary, producing payments of between £3,788 and £6,200.[35]

From this rather tentative start, the bonus scheme became progressively sophisticated, embracing specific targets relating to the disposal of businesses, as the railway privatisation programme gathered pace from 1993. There were lean years in the prolonged depression after 1989. In 1989-90 and 1990-91, for example, there were no bonuses for financial performance, and the total bonus amounted to only 4-5 per cent of the basic salary.[36] However, the size of the bonuses increased with the intense demands of privatisation. In the year 1992/3, they amounted to 23 per cent, ranging from £15,845 to £48,960, and, in the following year, 35 per cent, ranging from £25,085 to £77,300.[37] Of course, the payments were not large in comparison with those routinely paid to chief executives in private companies. However, the scheme certainly had something to teach the private sector in the care and sophistication with which it was constructed and monitored.

The salary issue appears to have died down in the 1980s and 1990s. Corrective measures were certainly taken. When Robert Paul Reid (Sir Bob Reid II) left Shell to become chairman in 1990, he was paid £200,000, for example, and his senior executives on the Board £65-£100,000.[38] Here, there was certainly a contrast with the experience of Sir Bob's predecessor, also called Bob Reid. Sir Bob Reid I, somewhat cruelly dubbed 'half-price Reid', to distinguish him from his 'full-price' successor, had been paid only £90,950, after seven years as chairman. Unsurprisingly, there had been a difficulty in attracting leading managers from the private sector to succeed him. The same was true of the posts of finance director and engineering specialist, where the overall scale of reward was not large, given the size and responsibility of the management task. Nevertheless, such was the low level of pay in the public sector that the initial salaries paid to James Jerram and Dr Peter Watson, respectively £85,000 and £100,000 in 1991, were 10 and 30 per cent more than the highest paid railwayman on the Board, the chief executive, John Welsby (£77,000), and 30-53 per cent more than the pay of other railwaymen.[39] Occasionally, disputes arose which reminded everyone about how wide the continuing disparity between the two sectors was. The decision of John Welsby to resign from the Board but to remain as chief executive raised all the issues that had been evident in the discussions involving Parker, Fowler and others much earlier. When his five-year Board appointment expired in October 1992, Welsby, who had served as Chief Executive since 1990, was offered and refused re-appointment for a further three years. It can be revealed that the salary offered (£82,000) was substantially lower than comparable rewards in the private sector, and out of line with the pay received by key personnel both inside and outside the Board (for example, Robert Horton's salary as deputy chairman, and chairman designate of Railtrack, was £120,000 in January 1993). The Treasury refused to increase the salary, however, and Welsby invoked his right to re-employment following board service, becoming chief executive without board membership, at a salary of £140,000. His role and responsibilities remained unchanged. He was regarded as having 'the status and authority' of a board member, and was counted as a board member for quorum purposes. Needless to say this manoeuvre irritated both the Department of Transport and the Treasury, but it served to demonstrate the point that quality in management was not being matched by rewards, and, therefore, it was becoming increasingly difficult to obtain the level of commitment, especially in an industry which was effectively killing itself.[40]

Management Structure

There were variations in management structures in the nationalised industries, affecting degrees of centralisation and decentralisation, the number of management tiers, and the preference for either a planning or an executive board. However, the central issue in the context of governance is that the organisational forms adopted by the railways, and the rest of the public sector for that matter, were subject to government approval, as indeed were all appointments at board level. Although it is difficult to be precise about the origins of the several organisational initiatives, it is clear that the influence of civil servants and their advisers in the relevant ministries was pervasive. The initial structure adopted for the nationalised transport industries in 1947 was drawn up inside the Ministry of Transport. It established the BTC as a planning board, a quasi-holding company, presiding over executive boards for each of the transport modes, including railways. This controversial structure, which was intended to execute Labour's aspirations for transport co-ordination, and to break 'the railway domination [sic] of inland transport',[41] was resented in professional railway management circles. The members of the Railway Executive, like the members of the BTC appointed by the Minister of Transport, openly resisted the BTC's efforts to share in strategic and operational management decision-making, while the regional railway managers, with a secure framework based on past capabilities, resisted their own Executive's attempts to impose control. Unsurprisingly, then, the organisation was a conspicuous failure.[42]

In 1953, in order to satisfy the competitive and decentralising philosophies of the Conservative administration, the Ministry tried again. The Railway Executive was abolished, and six Area Boards were established, these being responsible to the BTC. This new structure, introduced in 1955, was equally disastrous. Part of the difficulty came with parliament's ambivalence about full decentralisation in drafting the 1953 Transport Act, and with Robertson's determination as chairman of the BTC to 'manage' rather than 'preside'. Furthermore, the 1955 organisation, with its several tiers - the army-style 'General Staff' at headquarters, committees, sub-commissions, divisions, and the area boards - was altogether too cumbersome and alien for much of railway management. It, too, was soon replaced.[43] In 1963, the BTC was abolished, and separate boards were created for railways - called the British Railways Board, which adopted a functional, executive form under Beeching - London Transport, the docks, and the waterways. The pendulum was to swing back and forth again over the period 1963-82. In 1970, a McKinsey-type planning board was established, with a railway management group below it led by a chief executive, who was not a board member. However, this also failed to work properly. There were tensions between the 'corporate' and 'planning' functions, on the one hand, and the 'railway' and 'operating' functions, on the other. In short, the Board had too much of the former, and too little of the latter. Detached from the realities of railway management, planning became in many ways an artificial exercise, starved of information from railway-based departments, and more concerned with outputs than inputs, or the consequences arising from decisions taken by engineers and operators. The financial function was, also, largely a response to operating requirements rather than a genuine control mechanism. This situation was reinforced by the 1974 Railways Act, which required the Board to maintain passenger services at the existing level. Seven years later, Parker returned to an executive board with the chief executive *on* the board, though below it a long-standing three-tier structure - region, division and area - was retained, having resisted McKinsey's proposals to flatten it. In the difficult circumstances of the late 1970s, with the industry required to maintain operations but short of investment, it made good sense to seek to return to the railways' essential core competencies and a clearer line management.[44] Unfortunately, the move carried with it a danger of retreating into old habits best described as 'engineers and operators know best'. Furthermore, the problems of containing the pressures on the Chief Executive (Railways) and of controlling senior and middle managers in the regions were not resolved by a rather odd structure at the top, which, in addition to the chief executive, found room for a full-time chairman, full-time deputy-chairman, a part-time vice-chairman, and a full-time 'vice-chairman (rail)'.[45] Thus, in 1982, there was yet another change, this time a substantial shift to decentralised management, with the appointment of sector directors responsible for defined parts of the railway business (Inter-City, London & South East, Provincial, Freight and Parcels), together with a determined effort to give these new managers for the first time a 'bottom-line' responsibility for profitability and performance.[46] This organisation proved more satisfactory, after initial teething troubles, but, by the late 1980s, it was caught up in the drive to privatisation.

At each point, the influence of government was evident. All too often, its response to the railways' market weakness, mounting financial deficits, and industrial relations problems was to intervene in organisational terms. For example, the 1963 organisation emerged from a full-scale examination of the BTC's difficulties by a quasi-governmental advisory group led by Sir Ivan Stedeford of Tube Investments. The Transport Act of 1968 gave the Ministry of Transport a statutory responsibility for agreeing major organisational changes, and the McKinsey planning board emerged, *inter alia*, from the detailed, and sometimes heated deliberations of a joint Ministry-British Rail steering group in 1966-67.[47] The move to sector management was consonant with the steps taken by the government from 1976 to impose a firmer financial control of nationalised industries, and to monitor performance against agreed targets. This can be seen in the adoption of cash limits in 1976, and, in 1978, the publication of a third white paper (the others were in 1961 and 1967) clarifying the relationship between government and the public sector.[48] That is not to suggest that railway managers had no say in organisational choices. Parker was an enthusiast for an executive board at a time when the public debate, notably about 'industrial democracy' and consumer representation, plus an enthusiasm for two-tier boards on the German model, led in another direction.[49] However, the more important factors were, from the public sector manager's perspective, the pervasiveness and capriciousness of government intervention, which frequently disconcerted them. On the other side were the concerns of ministers and civil servants about the difficulties they faced in controlling the corporations' investment flows, costs, and current account deficits, in the face of inadequate information.

The major element of dissatisfaction came in the period 1990-93. The considerable effort put in by British Rail to transform sector management into 'Organising for Quality' (OfQ) - a fully-accountable business-led system in which the sectors, or businesses, were given control not only of traffic assets but of infrastructure as well - was rendered superfluous, when the government decided to privatise by separating the infrastructure from the other assets. This is not the place to tell the story in full. It has been fully documented elsewhere. However, the refusal of ministers and government departments to heed the warnings of professional railwaymen about the potential chaos they were causing with their elegant formulae and chalkboard diagrams has contributed substantially to the industry's current difficulties.[50]

Disclosure

Disclosure was a key issue for public sector governance, just as it has been for the private sector. Like private companies, public corporations were required to produce reports and accounts, but their documentation had to be presented to and could be debated by Parliament. From the 1950s, most of the supervisory functions of Parliament were delegated to a Select Committee on the Nationalised Industries, which undertook a series of searching reviews, in the case of the railways in 1960, 1968, 1973 and 1977. In addition, there was a penetrating investigation of railway finances by a committee set up by the Department of Transport, and chaired by Sir David Serpell. After its report, in 1983, the government proceeded to fix stiffer financial targets for the railway businesses, and to initiate the privatisation of British Rail's engineering activities. At times, as Parker observed, British Rail was subject to such an 'intense period of public accountability' that it is difficult to envisage senior managers having much time left over to actually run the business. There were no fewer than sixteen different enquiries, audits and policy reviews in the years 1976-78, in effect a state of 'perpetual audit'.[51] Yet, for all that, it was the quality and the candour of the information supplied that was critical. This was clear throughout the period of nationalised railways, but some examples may be instructive. An earlier white paper dealing with the nationalised industries of 1967 had stipulated that public sector investment projects had to be presented in discounted cash-flow form, and were to satisfy defined rates of return. However, department officials were clearly frustrated by the quality of the information they were fed. As a British Rail manager noted in 1969: 'it is not necessary for us to give to the Ministry any information other than that strictly necessary to prove the project ... The Ministry have never been happy with this arrangement, as ... they regard the investment provisions in the [1968] Act as 'the only door' through which they can see the board at work and influence its policies and decisions'.[52] The Ministry's enthusiasm for 'corporate planning' in the 1970s was clearly a way to obtain more information in a management accounting sense. During Marsh's chairmanship, the 1974 Railways Act strengthened the Ministry's control of the railways' corporate planning activity, and firmed up the existing requirement (under the 1962 Transport Act) on disclosure of information, by adding a clause to the effect that the annual report was to 'include such information as the Secretary of State may from time to time specify'.[53] The new rules did little to improve the railways' relations with the DOE, however. On one side, there was a suspicion about the withholding of information, on the other resentment at interference in the management of the business. While affairs did not deteriorate to the extent that they did in the steel industry, where Select Committee reports of 1977 castigated both the steel corporation and its sponsoring ministry for misinformation in the annual reports, there was much ground for the more emollient Parker and the reconstituted Ministry of Transport (hived off from the DOE) to make up after 1976.[54]

The extent of information disclosure became more critical with the post-1974 funding regime, where the government paid British Rail an annual subsidy - the public service obligation - to support the passenger service network as a whole. This left freight and parcels to operate commercially, something they patently failed to do in 1975-77 and 1979. Railway managers argued that most track and signalling costs should be charged to the subsidised passenger business, whose capacity, speed and safety requirements were critical. Ministry officials were more sceptical, nursing the idea that the 'avoidable costs', including infrastructure costs, attributed to the freight and parcels businesses were being underestimated. The extent of British Rail's disclosure, seen in ever more forthcoming annual reports, was also a response to the government's determination to obtain more detailed breakdowns of the PSO support, and to work towards specific financial objectives for components or sectors of the passenger business, in line with the general thinking in the 1978 white paper. The presentation of convincing and transparent methods of costing was a major and long-running issue that exercised both the Board and the Ministry over the next decade. This formed part of the wider debate about the need for improved information to facilitate government monitoring of nationalised industry performance - with required rates of return for investment, financial objectives, and operating performance indicators. All this was to have a profound effect on the way in which profitability was calculated and the railway businesses were financed and controlled in the future.[55]

Disclosure became more evident as the government issued ever more refined three-year targets for the railway industry in 1983, 1986, and 1989, and as the industry itself led the way in publishing performance indicators and quality benchmarks. Arguably, these more detailed and transparent mechanisms helped the industry's managers to meet the increasingly exacting financial and quality-based targets they were set during the Thatcher governments, between 1979-90. The disappointment lay in the fact that many of these mechanisms were obscured, and subverted by the privatisation process after 1993.

Conclusion

Governance is a complex issue in both the private and public sectors; in the latter, it is a shorthand term for the complexity of the government's relationship with its several industrial corporations; the difficulty of objective-setting and monitoring; and the consequences which the pay and management structures of the public sector had for managerial status, morale, and ultimately performance. In this paper, we have advanced the hypothesis that over the period from the late 1940s to the late 1970s nationalised industry would have benefited from less governance than it received, and from more precise, consistent and long-term objectives than it was given. Managerial quality was undoubtedly affected by government-imposed pay and conditions. The evolution of appropriate management structures was also hindered by the frequency of government intervention, though we should be wary of arguing that the private sector has always got it right. Disclosure was clearly above average for British industry as a whole, though the emphasis here should be on the *quality* of the information revealed, and its usefulness to the monitoring process. It is also evident that the government's search for more satisfactory controls began a process in which it was easier for the privatisation alternative to take root. The debate gave encouragement to those who argued that the *real* issue in terms of disclosure was to discover how exactly the nationalised industries redistributed income from one group to another. By implying that this redistributive element was both inequitable and unaudited, right-wing economists were able to assert that the important issue in terms of management structure was to make nationalised industries more responsive to the disciplines of the market.[56] Of course, questions of corporate goals, accountability, rewards, and customer representation have remained to haunt the managers of the newly privatised enterprises.

Notes

I am grateful to Nick Tiratsoo for his help with this paper.

1   K.Keasey and M.Wright, 'Issues in Corporate Accountability and Governance: An Editorial', *Accounting and Business Research* (1993), 23, p.291.
2   R.I.Tricker, *Corporate Governance: Practices, Procedures and Powers in British Companies and their Boards of Directors* (1984), p.6; J.Charkham, *Keeping Good Company: A Study of Corporate Governance in Five Countries* (1994), pp.4,248; K.J.Hopt, et al. (eds.), *Comparative Corporate Governance* (1998).
3   J.Kay and A.Silberston, 'Corporate Governance', *National Institute of Economic Research* (1995), no.153, p.85.
4   O.Hart, 'Corporate Governance: Some Theory and Implications', *Economic Journal* (1995), 105, p.678.
5   L.Zingales, *Corporate Governance* (1997), quoted in K.Gugler (ed.), *Corporate Governance and Economic Performance* (2001), p.3.
6   See X.Vives (ed.), *Corporate Governance* (2000); J.Schwalbach (ed.), *Corporate Governance* (2000); S.Sheikh and W.Rees (eds), *Corporate Governance and Corporate Control* (2000); W.Lazonick and M.O'Sullivan (eds), *Corporate Governance and Sustainable Prosperity* (2001).
7   See S.Vitols, et al., *Corporate Governance in Large British and German Companies: Comparative Institutional Advantage, or Competing for Best Practice* (1997), pp.1-2.
8   See K.Keasey, et al. (eds.), *Corporate Governance: Economic and Financial Issues* (1997).
9   T.R.Gourvish, 'The Regulation of Britain's Railways', in J.McConville (ed.), *Transport Regulation Matters* (1997), pp.3-10.
10 T.R.Gourvish, *British Railways, 1948-73: A Business History* (1986), pp.1-28; G.Crompton, '"A Very Poor Bag of Physical Assets": The Railway Compensation Issue, 1921-47', *Accounting, Business and Financial History* (1996), pp.73-91.
11 T.R.Gourvish, 'British Rail's "Business-Led" Organization, 1977-90: Government-Industry Relations in Britain's Public Sector', *Business History Review* (1990), 64, pp.135-47.
12 T.Gourvish, *British Rail 1974-97: From Integration to Privatisation* (2002), chs.7,12-13.
13 Gourvish, *British Railways*, pp.31-3,142-4.
14 Gourvish, *British Railways*, pp.322-4; P.Parker, *For Starters: The Business of Life* (1989), pp.124-5.
15 Henry Johnson, at £12,500 p.a. See Parker, *For Starters*, pp.132-40; B.Castle, *The Castle Diaries, 1964-70* (1984), pp.322-7,330,333-4; Gourvish, *British Railways*, pp.360-1.
16 Gourvish, *British Rail 1974-97*, pp.24,523.
17 Marsh, comment in the *Times*, 11 October 1977, cited in Gourvish, *British Railways*, p.573.
18 Gourvish, *British Rail 1974-97*, pp.25,28 -30,525.
19 *Punch*, 3 November 1976.
20 Review Body on Top Salaries, *Report No.6: Report on Top Salaries* (December 1974),

P.P.1974-5, xxxii, c.5846; NBPI, *Report No.107 on Top Salaries in the Private Sector and Nationalised Industries* (March 1969), P.P.1968-9, xlii, c.3970.

21 The May 1977 increase was back-dated to 1 Jan 1977. The December increase of 5 per cent applied from 1 Jan 1978; up to 10 per cent could be paid to board members earning under £13,000. The government conceded the full 10 per cent in Aug 1978, as part of its staged acceptance of Report No.10.

22 BRB Memo. 18 Oct 1977, cited in Gourvish, *British Rail 1974-97*, pp.46,530; NEDO, Report, 1976, p.35.

23 Review Body on Top Salaries, *Report No.10: Second Report on Top Salaries* (June 1978), P.P.1977-8, xlviii, c.7253; Gourvish, *British Railways*, p.573; Prime Minister's Written Answer, 4 July 1978, *Parl. Deb. (Commons), 1977-8*, vol.953. The Committee suggested a salary of £40,000 for the Chairman of BR, £21-26,000 for BRB members.

24 Parker, correspondence with Peter Lazarus (Ministry of Transport), 1978-9, cited in Gourvish, *British Rail 1974-97*, p.530. Salaries were adjusted using the GDP deflator.

25 *Report of the Committee on the Financial Aspects of Corporate Governance (Cadbury Committee)*, 1 Dec 1992, pp.20-4. See criticisms by Hart, 'Corporate Governance', p.682.

26 Review Body, *Report No.10*, para.88; Parker-Lazarus correspondence, 1978-9, cited in Gourvish, *British Rail 1974-97*, pp.34,46,530.

27 An award in August 1979, back-dated to April, took Parker's salary to £36,950 and the average board member to £21,500. See British Railways Board, *Report and Accounts 1979*, p.44; Gourvish, *British Rail 1974-97*, p.531.

28 Gourvish, *British Rail 1974-97*, p.395.

29 A part-time member of BRB between 1985-91, he had experience of timber (Meyer Int.), the motor industry (Ford) and engineering (BICC, Balfour Beatty). See *Who's Who 1986*.

30 Gourvish, *British Rail 1974-97*, pp.108,147.

31 Robert Reid (Chairman, BRB) to Nicholas Ridley (Secretary of State for Transport), 18 Feb 1986, BRB archives.

32 Ridley to Reid, 7 March 1986; John Batley (Secretary, BRB) to Oscar de Ville (BRB), 23 April 1986; BRB, 'Proposed Bonus Payments to Full-time Board Members', 1 May 1986; Batley to Jim Coates (Dept of Transport), 30 July 1986, BRB archives.

33 De Ville-Batley, 30 July 1986, enclosed in Batley to Coates.

34 BRB, 'Proposed Bonus Payments to Full-time Board Members', 30 July 1986; De Ville to John Moore (Secretary of State for Transport), 10 Nov 1986, BRB archives.

35 De Ville to Paul Channon (Secretary of State for Transport), 19 May 1987, BRB archives.

36 See Coates to David Rayner (BRB), 12 June 1990, et seq., BRB archives.

37 Gourvish, *British Rail 1974-97*, p.396; Department of Transport-BRB correspondence, Oct 1994, BRB archives.

38 Gourvish, *British Rail 1974-97*, p.261.

39 Gourvish, *British Rail 1974-97*, pp.138,260-1,559,609.

40 Gourvish, *British Rail 1974-97*, pp.397-8,660-1. Welsby returned as chairman and chief executive, April 1995, at £180,000. See Gourvish, *British Rail 1974-97*, pp.437-8 (T. 13.1).

41 S.S.Wilson to Sir Cyril Hurcomb, 28 November 1945, MT74/1, Public Record Office.

42 Gourvish, *British Railways*, pp.24-5,33-67.

43 Gourvish, *British Railways*, pp.137-72.

44 See R.R.Nelson and S.G.Winter, *An Evolutionary Theory of Economic Change* (1982); G.Hamel and C.K.Prahalad, *Competing for the Future* (1996).

45 BRB, *Annual Report and Accounts, 1978*, p.2.

46 Gourvish, 'British Rail's Organization', pp.114-17.

47 Gourvish, *British Railways*, pp.307-22,352-74.

48 Treasury, *The Nationalised Industries*, March 1978, c.7131.

49 NEDO, *A Study of UK Nationalised Industries: their Role in the Economy and Control in*

the Future (1976); National Consumer Council, *Consumers and the Nationalised Industries* (August, 1976); *Report of the Committee of Inquiry on Industrial Democracy,* January 1977, c.6706; Charkham, *Keeping Good Company*, pp.6-58,363-4. The Bullock Committee argued that it would be difficult to introduce the German system into British company law.

50 See R.Freeman and I.Shaw (eds.), *All Change: British Railway Privatisation* (2000); C.Wolmar, *Broken Rails* (2001); and Gourvish, *British Rail 1974-97*, chs.11-13.

51 BRB, *Annual Report & Accounts 1976*, p.5; Parker, Dimbleby Lecture 1983. The audit comprised 9 white papers, a consultation document, a select committee report and the government's response, plus 4 independent reports.

52 Treasury, *Nationalised Industries: A Review of Economic and Financial Objectives,* November 1967, c.3437; Gomersall, quoted in Gourvish, *British Railways*, pp.522-3.

53 Railways Act, 1974, s.4.2, 4.3 and 4.5a.

54 *Reports of S.C. on Nationalised Industries: The British Steel Corporation*, 1977, HC26-I, HC127-I.

55 HC, *Seventh Report from the Committee of Public Accounts, 1983-4*, HC139; H.R.Wilkinson (Chief Management Accountant), Memo. to BRB Railway Executive on 'Profit Planning & Cost Centre Analysis; Sector Avoidable Costs Study', 1979; Gourvish, *British Railways*, p.395, and 'British Rail's "Business-Led" Organization', pp.118,124; BRB, *Measuring Cost and Profitability in British Rail* (1978).

56 See S.C.Littlechild, 'Controlling the Nationalised Industries: Quis custodiet ipsos custodes?' (1979).

Chapter 11

Recent Changes in Inter-Firm Relations in Japan: the Six Largest Corporate Complexes

Masahiro Shimotani

Introduction

After enjoying a long period of prosperity, the Japanese economy plunged into a serious slump in the 1990s. What is interesting is the irony: its traditional strong factors turned out to be its weaknesses. Among those old factors that lifted the Japanese economy to become one of the economic superpowers, this paper places a particular emphasis on the changes in inter-firm relations, which have generally been called *keiretsu*. Though there are all sorts of *keiretsu*, ranging from long-term transactions to stable links in equity and personnel among member firms, the most typical *keiretsu* should be considered the so-called Six Largest Corporate Complexes. Sometimes called the 6CCs or CCs, they have been composed of leading large enterprises in various fields, and characterized by presidential meetings, cross shareholdings, and preferential transactions. Many people agree with the fact that they contributed to the high economic growth that followed the Second World War. In recent years, however, both the sequential mega-mergers among the major banks, which have long played significant roles within the respective CCs, and the on-going dissolution of cross shareholdings among the member companies have resulted in drastic changes in traditional structures. This paper will trace their historical backgrounds, more recent changes, and analyze their latest reorganization.

Recent Changes in Inter-Firm Relations

Stockholder Structure

The Japanese economy has been in a long and serious slump since the collapse of the Bubble economy in the early 1990s, especially since the financial crisis in 1997. For example, the average stock price fell to almost one fourth of the highest level attained at the peak of the Bubble boom in 1989. It seems noteworthy that the drastic fall in share price has caused significant changes in stockholder structure, which has traditionally been composed of roughly 65-70 per cent corporate stockholders, including financial institutions, 25-30 per cent individuals, and 5 per cent or so foreign investors. Furthermore, quite a number of the shares possessed by the corporate stockholders have been interlocked between large firms, often called 'cross shareholdings'. The possessing of other firms' stocks has long formed the hidden assets of Japanese firms, due to highly rising stock prices, and this Japan-specific practice has been found far and wide as a means of stabilizing shareholders and cementing friendly relations in transactions between firms. In particular, stockholdings by major banks has created the famous 'main bank system'. Such traditional Japanese stockholder structures, however, began weaken due to the recent fall in stock prices.

Table 11.1 Stockholding Structure in Japan, 1985-2000 (per cent)

	(A)	(B)	(C)	(D)	(E)	(F)	(G)	(H)
1985	42.2	21.6	2.6	13.5	4.5	24.1	25.2	5.7
1990	43.5	16.4	9.8	13.2	4.1	25.2	23.1	4.2
1995	40.3	15.4	10.1	11.2	3.6	23.6	23.6	9.4
1996	40.2	15.1	10.8	10.9	3.4	23.8	23.6	9.8
1997	39.2	14.6	11.1	10.2	3.3	24.1	24.6	9.8
1998	38.3	14.0	11.7	9.4	3.2	24.1	25.4	10.0
1999	34.9	12.8	10.9	8.3	2.9	23.7	26.4	12.4
2000	36.2	11.5	14.3	7.6	2.8	22.3	26.3	13.2

Notes: (A) Financial Institutions in Total   (B+C+D+E); (B) Banks; (C) Trust Banks; (D) Life Insurance Companies; (E) Non-Life Insurance Companies; (F) Corporations; (G) Individuals; (H) Foreign Investors.

Changes in Stockholder Structure

As is mentioned above, the average stock price fell in the recession to almost one fourth of that reached in the Bubble period, specifically from 38,915 yen in December 1989 to 9,504 yen in September 2001. Furthermore, banks that had struggled with enormous amounts of bad loans sold stocks, and dissolved cross shareholdings in order to balance their losses, in turn forcing down stock prices. Though Japan's financial institutions, including banks, have played the major role of stable stockholders, the recent downward fluctuation of stock prices became an unstable factor for the banks. So, new regulations urge them to reduce their stockholdings to a level equal to their own equity capital by September 2004. But the stockholdings of the major 15 banks are now estimated at 33 trillion yen, which exceeds their own equity capital by 10 trillion. Since sales on this scale must push stock prices down, the government is now trying to found an organization outside the market that can take responsibility for these purchases.

The steep decline in stock prices naturally reduced the hidden assets, which have long underpinned the powerful influence of Japanese banks and companies. For example, though the unrealized profits of the major 15 banks were estimated to be as much as 17.8 trillion yen in 1992, they have fallen to below zero, meaning they have finally turned into unrealized losses. Since the market-value accounting system was newly introduced to Japan in 1991, banks were forced to deduct as much as 60 per cent of unrealized losses from their accumulated equity capital. While banks rush to unload stocks, industrial firms in turn sell off the banks' stocks, bringing not only a further fall of prices, but also an unwinding of mutual shareholding arrangements. Changes in the stockholder structure in Japan follow.

Table 1 shows the recent trends. Roughly speaking, up to the mid-1990s, while around 40 per cent of stock have been shared by financial institutions, more than 20 per cent has been in the possession of corporations and individuals respectively, and less than 10 per cent by foreign investors. We can observe, however, recent drastic changes in structure, namely the fall in the shares of financial institutions, and the high-growing ratio of foreign investors. Among financial institutions, whose total percentage went down from 46.0 at the peak in 1989 to 36.2 in 2000, the latest ratios of banks and life insurance companies is striking. The percentages of these two institutions declined to almost half previous levels by 1985. As is said later, since these two have long played significant roles within the 6CCs to stabilize shareholding, their decline directly affects the stakeholder structure.

Mergers amongst the Major Banks

Another feature of the recent Japanese economy is the sequential mega-mergers amongst the major banks. As is seen later, the 6CCs have been composed around each of their six core banks. Among these six major banks, Fuji Bank and Daiichi-Kangyo Bank or DKB were merged in September 2000, with the involvement of the Industrial Bank of Japan, to create the new financial holding company, Mizuho Holdings. This was followed by the merger between Sumitomo Bank and the former Mitsui Bank, Sakura, in April 2001, establishing Sumitomo-Mitsui Bank. Another two financial holding companies were formed in April 2001 by Tokyo-Mitsubishi Bank and Sanwa Bank, respectively Mitsubishi-Tokyo Financial Group and UFJ, so integrating other banks and trust banks together. In short, Japan's six largest banks converged into four financial groups, which are often called the 'Big Four'. As a result of these mergers, Mizuho emerged as one of the largest mega-banks in the world with assets of 151 trillion yen, followed by Sumitomo-Mitsui Bank with 107 trillion yen, Mitsubishi-Tokyo FG with 100 trillion yen, and UFJ with 90 trillion yen. Such mega-mergers are often said to create the scale necessary for international competitiveness, but the main purpose has been the clearance of bad loans by restructuring, cost cutting, and integration.

Keywords for the Japanese economy during the 1990s were 'deregulation' and 'financial Big Bang'. Actually, the deregulation of holding companies was finally enacted in 1997, after long debate, in order to assist restructuring, so ending a fifty-year long history in which 'pure holding companies' had been prohibited under the Antitrust Law, as implemented by the US occupying forces. How have recent changes in stockholder structure and the emergence of the Big Four affected the 6CCs?

Table 11.2 Firm Membership of the 6CCs, 1999

	Mitsui Nimokukai	*Sumitomo Hakusuikai*	*Mitsubishi Kinyokai*	*Fuyo Fuyokai*	*DKB Sankinkai*	*Sanwa Sansuikai*
Bank	Sakura	Sumitomo	Tokyo-Mitsubishi	Fuji	Daiichi-Kangyo	Sanwa
Insurance	Mitsui Trust	Sumitomo Trust	Mitsubishi Trust	Yasuda Trust		Toyo Trust
	Mitsui Life	Sumitomo Life	Meiji Life	Yasuda Life	Asahi Life	Nippon Life
	Mitsui Marine	Sumitomo Marine	Tokyo Marine	Yasuda Marine	Fukoku Marine	
				Nissan Marine		
				Taisei Marine		
Sogo-Shosha	Mitsui	Sumitomo	Mitsubishi	Marubeni	Itochu Kanematsu Ind.	Nichimen Iwatani
				Itoki		
				Nissho Iwai	Nissho Iwai	
Mining	1	1	-	-	-	-
Construction	2	2	1	1	1	4
Food	1	-	1	3	-	2
Textiles	1	-	1	2	-	2
Pulp Paper	2	-	1	1	1	-
Chemical	2	2	3	3	8	7
Petroleum	-	-	1	1	1	1
Rubber	-	-	-	-	1	1
Cement/Glass	1	2	1	1	1	-
Steel		1	1	1	3	4
Metals	1	3	4	-	3	1
Machinery	1	1	1	2	2	1
Elec. Machinery	1	1	1	3	5	5
Autos, Shipbdg	3	-	2	1	3	3
Optics	-	-	1	1	1	1

	Mitsui Nimokukai	Sumitomo Hakusuikai	Mitsubishi Kinyokai	Fuyo Fuyokai	DKB Sankinkai	Sanwa Sansuikai
Dept. Stores	1	-	-	-	1	1
Financing	-	-	-	-	3	1
Real Estate	1	1	1	1	-	-
Transportation	2	2	1	2	3	3
Others	-	1	-	1	1	-

Table 11.3   Subsidiaries and Affiliates of Top Twenty Firms, 1995

	Subsidiaries	Affiliates	Total
1. Tokyo Elect. Power	30	18	48
2. NTT	146	74	220
3. Toyota	196	139	335
4. Hitachi	858	198	1,056
5. Mitsubishi Co.	546	411	957
6. Matsushita	n/a	n/a	670
7. Mitsui & Co	473	269	742
8. Nissan	550	150	700
9. Marubeni	514	236	750
10. JR East	144	39	183
11. Itochu Co.	726	335	1,061
12. Kansai Elect. Power	31	17	48
13. Chubu Elect. Power	24	14	38
14. Toshiba	535	154	689
15. Sumitomo Co.	349	234	583
16. Nissho Iwai Co.	336	160	496
17. Orix	105	47	152
18. Nippon Steel	248	191	439
19. Sony	901	49	950
20. NEC	n/a	n/a	320

The Six Largest Corporate Complexes

Structure

There are now about 2.9 million corporations in Japan, and half of them are joint-stock companies. Of course, though almost all these firms are small in size, around 2,500 larger companies are listed on the stock exchanges. And among them, 181 large enterprises belong to the 6CCs. Table 11.2 shows the arrangements of member firms within the 6CCs in the late 1990s. They are horizontally composed of large corporations in various fields. One will observe that all the 6CCs are almost similar in that they all include large banks, insurance companies, a *sogo-shosha* or general trading companies, and various manufacturing and service businesses. Sometimes this is referred to as the 'one-set structure'. The distinguishing features of the 6CCs are considered to be their presidential meetings and cross shareholding. Membership in a CC involves participation in the presidential meeting. Participants vary in number from 20 for Sumitomo's *Hakusuikai* to 48 for DKB's *Sankinkai*, and the total for all of the 6CCs is 181 members.

These 181 represent 7.4 percent of the 2,430 firms listed on the stock exchanges, and a mere 0.007 percent of Japan's corporations, but their financial clout is disproportionate to their numbers. A recent survey found that, excluding the financial sector, these 181 companies control 15.3 percent of the capital stocks, 12.5 percent of the total assets, and 13.8 percent of total sales. These figures, however, underestimate the reality, because the survey counts only figures related to 'parent companies', and we should not forget that the parent companies have many and sometimes hundreds of their own, related firms, or *keiretsu*, that form their own, pyramid-like corporate groups. Table 11.3 shows the number of subsidiaries and affiliates of the twenty largest enterprises. The member firms of the 6CCs thus have enormous importance in the Japanese economy.

History

Three of the 6CCs - Mitsui, Mitsubishi and Sumitomo - emerged in the 1950s. They are direct descendants of the three largest pre-war *zaibatsu*, which were broken up by the occupation forces after the Second World War. In other words, three of the old *zaibatsu* conglomerates were stripped of their family holding companies, reemerged in changed guise, and flourished. When dismantled, the *zaibatsu* family and their old leaders were banished. Furthermore, the *zaibatsu*'s headquarters, which had served as holding companies, were banned, since the Antitrust Law prohibited their existence in order to prevent the revival of the *zaibatsu*'s pyramid structure once and for all. As a result, the groups adopted a horizontal structure, mainly on the basis of cross shareholdings. In the midst of the post-war chaos, the old member firms of the three forerunners took holdings in each other's stock shares, becoming 'stable shareholders' for each other. They were reborn in the new form of Corporate Complexes.

In the 1950s, it seemed to have been the banks and *sogo-shosha* that played the important role in reassembling the old *zaibatsu* members into the new CCs, simply because banks had the money and *sogo-shosha* had the information required to meet the circumstances prevalent the war. Subsequently, three newcomer CCs emerged during and after the period of rapid economic growth in the 1960s: Fuyo, Sanwa and DKB. The smaller pre-war *zaibatsu* such as Yasuda, Furukawa, Asano, and so on, and some of other *new konzerns* that emerged in the 1930s could not approach the scale of the three forerunners, and so banded together. In the case of newcomer CCs, it was also the banks that took the initiative, trying to create the same one-set structure as the forerunners. In this way, they were able eventually to put together new CCs to rank alongside the forerunners.

Functions

Corporate members of the 6CCs have engaged in shared investments and conducted preferential transactions among member firms. However, the primary pivots holding these member firms together as a coherent CC is the cross shareholding and the presidential meeting. In general, it is obviously irrational for companies to hold each other's stocks from the viewpoint of capital efficiency. One of the main purposes of mutual stockholding is said to be the stabilization of shareholdings to prevent takeover bids and demonstrate intimate business relations. Of course, we would note that mutual stockholding is not just confined to the 6CCs; rather, it is a common phenomenon that is widely practised in Japan. A grid-shaped pattern of shareholding among member companies in the 6CCs can be observed. Currently, the degree of cross shareholding is the highest at Mitsubishi's *Kinyokai* at 27.3 percent, followed by Sumitomo's *Hakusuikai* at 22.2 percent.

It is commonly stressed that the phenomenon of interlocking shareholding among member firms has been a key distinguishing feature of all the 6CCs. We should note, however, that, while mutual shareholding is certainly a marked characteristic of the three forerunners, it is much less evident in the three newcomers. For example, the ratio of mutual shareholding is only about 15 percent for Fuyo and Sanwa, and as little as 11 percent for DKB. Furthermore, in the case of the three newcomers, the inter-corporate shareholding tends to be confined to the financial institutions, making a star pattern network rather than an interlocking matrix. We should be careful not to overstate the significance of interlocking shareholding as a common characteristic of all the 6CCs. Moreover, the ratios of mutual shareholding and also intra-group transactions have been on a downward trend in this long recession and in the climate of financial instability.

The present-day presidential meetings, meanwhile, have little authority, and serve primarily as a kind of forum for coordinating group-affiliated activities and exchanging information. They no longer have the role of their pre-war predecessors as a control-tower exercising authority on behalf of the *zaibatsu*'s main business. In short, the presidential meetings, including a variety of lower liaison activities, no longer actively intervene in the important decisions of individual member firms, or determine strategy for the CC as a whole. From the opposite perspective, this means that member firms have enjoyed total and unfettered decision-making authority to run their respective businesses as they see fit. Details of the presidential meetings show that their main purposes are 'communication, exchange of information, and mutual understanding' among the member firms.

The 6CCs of today are a much looser kind of confederation composed of largely autonomous and self-directed companies. This represents a decisive difference with the old pre-war *zaibatsu*, in which the *zaibatsu* main firm did exercise real control over its members. As was mentioned earlier, the three forerunner CCs are directly descended from three of the most powerful *zaibatsu*. Therefore, these three CCs are said to exhibit a somewhat higher degree of cohesiveness than the three newcomers, but, in fact, there is little difference. Indeed, one view holds that, aside from the initial phase, when these three forerunners were first launched, they can no longer be considered business *keiretsu*. So, regarding them just as a group of descendants with a common ancestor would be closer to the mark.

The Impact of Recent Changes in the 6CCs

Diminishing Coherence

As was seen earlier, the CC is a loose confederation, mainly composed of large banks and *sogo-shosha* as primary members, together with other large companies from various industrial fields. They are linked by cross shareholdings and the presidential meetings, forming the distinguishing features of the post-war Japanese economy. Table 11.4 shows the shift in the ratios of cross shareholdings in the 6CCs. We can see that the ratios have gradually fallen, though the latest figures are not available because of the drastic extent of changes in these years. We can easily guess, however, the trend from current news. For instance, Sumitomo Bank has continued to reduce its stockholding ratios among eleven of the eighteen *Hakusui-kai* firms. Cross shareholding ratios of all listed firms, 2,472 in March 2000, fell to 10.5 percent, having been stable at around 17 percent in the first half of the 1990s. In addition, recent changes in the economy such as mega-mergers amongst the major banks suggest a fundamental impact on the traditional framework.

Table 11.4   Ratios of Cross Shareholdings, 1990-2000 (per cent)

	Mitsui	Sumitomo	Mitsubishi	Fuyo	DKB	Sanwa
1990	26.2	32.5	27.3	25.9	21.5	21.1
1995	24.2	30.1	26.1	23.4	20.3	19.6
1996	24.9	27.6	26.8	20.5	19.0	18.5
1997	24.2	27.3	27.0	18.4	19.0	17.9
1998	20.8	26.5	24.9	19.7	17.1	17.4
1999	23.1	23.1	23.1	16.2	16.5	14.3
2000	18.8	19.1	19.4	14.9	17.3	11.8

One day in September 1999, directly after the announcement to form Mizuho Holdings from Fuji Bank, DKB, and IBJ, it was reported that Fuji Bank quit serving as organizer of the regular presidential meeting, *Fuyo-kai*. It did not seem suitable any longer for the bank to be present when it had merged with other major banks, and the meeting decided to select three member companies - Marubeni,

Yasuda Life Insurance, and Yasuda Marine Insurance - as the new organizers. The same decisions were reported informally in the case of Sakura Bank at Mitsui's *Nimoku-kai*, after announcing its merger in Spring 2001 with Sumitomo Bank. Since presidential meetings are informal, and recent changes have been swift and far-reaching, precise material is not available. But it is obvious they are no longer the apparatus for strategy formation across the CC as a whole. Meanwhile, one interesting dimension is that several firms have been members of two or three presidential meetings. We can find four such firms as early as the late 1970s, one of which is Hitachi. While these cases were confined to the newcomer CCs at the beginning, the number of such firms grew to six in 1991, affecting even the forerunner CCs as a result of mergers. In 1995, the number was 9, and then ten in 1999. Though these cases are exceptional, their existence means that the presidential meetings do not act as the semi-secret apparatus for 'communication, exchange of information, and mutual understanding' only. Recent mega-mergers among major banks bring a much more complicated phase for the 6CCs and the possibility of fusion.

Integration amongst Former Rival Firms

In general, it has been said that there exist too many competitors in each business field within Japan, their scale, therefore, remaining much smaller compared to counterparts in the global market. Theoretically speaking, more than six firms have been able to survive in each field, supported by the CC framework, and guarded by their main banks. In fact, they have long continued excessive competition for market share. In short, a coherent framework has made it difficult for rival firms to integrate outside the borders of the CCs. Cases have been very rare, with exceptions in declining field such as cement and pulp, despite constant pressures from global competition for merger and scale. Furthermore, the financial sector has been protected by the infamous 'convoy system', a tacit guarantee of the continuation of major financial institutions. So, even with the financial crisis of 1995, the three long term banks, seven trust banks, 11 city banks, 64 local banks, 65 minor local banks, and more than 4,000 smaller banking institutions survive. In the insurance sector, as many as 29 life and 26 non-life institutions continue. Thanks to the protection of convoy system, no major bank or insurance company went bankrupt before the collapse of Hokkaido Takushoku Bank and Nissan Life Insurance in 1997. In the same year, Yamaichi Securities, one of the four largest securities companies in Japan, ended its hundred-year history.

The position is changing due to de-regulation and the financial Big Bang. It was in 1993 that financial institutions - banks, insurance, and securities companies - were allowed to enter each others' fields of business, so bringing sharp competition. In fact, at least five large banks and seven insurance companies have since disappeared. In addition, the emergence of the new framework, the so-called 'big four regime', is having an impact. It is now much easier than before for former rival firms to merge outside the old 6CCs framework. In the case of the Sumitomo-

Mitsui *keiretsu*, for example, two non-life insurance companies, Sumitomo Marine and Mitsui Marine, merged into Sumitomo-Mitsui Marine in October 2001. It will be followed by the formation of a holding company between Sumitomo Chemical and Mitsui Chemical in October 2003. Two large *sogo-shosha*, the Sumitomo Co. and Mitsui & Co., are also cooperating in various fields. In the case of Mizuho, its three non-life insurance companies - Yasuda, Nissan, and Taisei Fire - merged into Sompo Japan in April 2002. Kawasaki Steel and NKK, which both have large steel firms affiliated to DKB and Fuyo respectively, announced a merger through a holding company in October 2002. DKB's Itochu Co. and Fuyo's Marubeni Co. are also forming links.

As was seen in this paper, the emergence of the financial Big Four makes it much easier for former rival firms to integrate, shifting the old framework of the 6CCs into the 4CCs. Of course, however, the situation is complicated, with several tie-ups among firms beyond even the new framework. For example, Mitsubishi's Tokyo Marine, the largest non-life insurance company in Japan, organized a holding company, Millea Holdings, in April 2002, in cooperation with Asahi Life and Nichido Fire Insurance, which were originally affiliated with Mizuho.

Conclusion

The 1990s are often called 'lost decade' for the Japanese economy. But, on the other side, it could be said that, owing to the unprecedented recession, the economy has had a good opportunity to change its entrenched systems, which are obsolete in the period of global competition and the IT revolution. The Japanese economic system that had worked well for almost a half century is changing into a new one. This is being achieved by sequential mega-mergers and drastic reorganization both in the financial and industrial sectors, aiming at reinforcing the international competitiveness in terms of scale and quality. The remaining issue is, following the scaling up attained through mega-mergers among large firms, the extent to which they will contribute to further developments in international competitiveness.

Index

insurance industry 1, 4, 20-8, 60-2, 108,
  120, 128, 134-5, 151, 191-200
Inter-City 185
Isosceles 153
Itochu 195, 200
Iwakuni chemical plant 133
Iwazaki family 4, 48
Iwazaki, H. 64
Iwazaki, K. 64, 68
Izuki, S. 20
Izumi, S. 21, 28

Japan Development Bank 127-35
JR East 195
Japan Steel 5
Jerram, J. 183
Jugo Bank 61

kakushin kanryo 112
Kamagai, T. 12
Kamata, S. 13
Kameoka, T. 23-4
Kanakin Cotton Cloth Company 18-19,
  30
Kanegafuchi Spinning 49, 61
Kansai Electric Power 195
Kansai Petroleum 136
Kasei Mizushima 133
Kashima chemical plant 134, 136
Kataoka, N. 20-30, 110
Kawai, T. 22
Kawamura, R. 13
Kawasaki chemical plant 133
Kawasaki Shipbuilding 48, 61
Kawasaki Steamship 48
Kawasaki Steel 126-7, 129, 131, 200
Kay, J. 176
Kay, N. 52-3
Keasey, K. 176
keiretsu 1-10, 109, 191-200
Kent University 166
Keynes, J.M. 145
Kirby. A.R. 79
Kiwa Railroad 24
Kobe Bank 61
Kobe Steel 126, 129
Koezuka, G. 13, 22-3
Komura, K. 17
Konoike, Z. 20-2, 26-7
Konoike Bank 21
konzerne 196

Koshino, K. 22, 28
Koya, G. 21
Kubata, S. 17
Kumagai, T. 20-1
Kusama, S. 20
kyocho yushi 5
Kyodo Trust & Bank 61
Kyosei Life 111
Kyoto 13, 24, 114

Labour Party 147, 159, 178-88
Lamoreux, N.R. 142
Lancashire 45-6
Lancashire Cotton Corporation 47
Later Five 133
Law Life Assurance 76
Law on Temporary Adjustment of
  Interest Rates 1947 132
Lawson Marden Group 153
Law Union 81, 85
Lazonick, W. 2
Legal & General 181
Legal & General Ventures 151
legislation, *see* the state
Lewis, R. 162, 166
Life Assurance Association of Japan 118
Light Nippon Steel 61
linen industry 43-45, 52
Linen Thread Company 43-5, 52
Lithgow 41-2
Lithgow, H. 42
Lithgow, Sir J. 42
Liverpool & London 81, 85
Liverpool University 166
Lloyds Bank 145
Lloyds Development Capital 151
locomotive industry 38-9
London 79, 85, 143, 145-7
London & Lancashire Insurance 81, 85,
  101
London Business School 169
London Guarantee & Accident 74-105
London Stock Exchange 154
Long-Term Credit Bank 128, 134-5
Lowndes Queensway 153

MacMillan Committee 145
MacMillan Gap 146, 148, 149
Magadi Soda 93
Magnet 153
Mainer, H. 159